"A hopeful prescription." —*GQ*

"Plank's empathy and hope are palpable." —Pop Sugar

"[A] compassionate and skillful social analysis. Plank's thoughtful approach and ability to elicit emotional responses from men by engaging them about masculinity as a curious, compassionate outsider yield a well-rounded picture of what contemporary men are facing."
—*Publishers Weekly*

"Liz Plank is leading a vital debate about gender, power, and feminism in a style that opens wider dialogue and reaches beyond the politically converted. She also shows it's entirely possible to have fun while tackling challenges like gender norms and cultural repression. Liz has established herself as a leader and an expert in the field of gender politics—all without conforming to some of the old rules about what it means to be an expert. Whether you find yourself nodding in agreement or laughing in exasperation, you will always learn something when engaging with Liz's ideas, which is why we call on her so often on air."
—Ari Melber, host of *The Beat with Ari Melber* on MSNBC

"Over the last decade or so, I've liked to tell anyone who will listen that the biggest problem facing America is the scourge of testosterone poisoning. The thing is, I'm not really joking. And as Liz Plank demonstrates in her extremely timely new book, *For the Love of Men*, toxic masculinity threatens the well-being not just of the women and children around them, but men themselves. Has it gotten worse? I don't know. Maybe I'm just noticing it a lot more. But what I DO know is that, as Plank puts it, the 'crisis in masculinity is not just about boys, it's about all of us.' We need a new model of maleness. This book is a great place to start."

—Anna Holmes, founder of *Jezebel*

"If there was ever a woman who could write thoughtfully about how to be a man, it's Liz Plank. With sensitivity, insight, and a healthy dose of rage, Liz takes on the subject of systemic toxic masculinity. She is well known as a champion of the disenfranchised, for bringing the issues of the marginalized to the forefront of discussion. This book is no different. By tackling the source of gender inequality, Liz forces us to open our eyes to invisible biases and how we can start to think about them differently. I believe she gives men (and women, really) a path forward to be both different yet equal; a way to raise a new, more evolved breed of man, and gives permission to women to accept nothing less."

—Stacy London, *New York Times* bestselling author of *The Truth About Style*

For the Love of Men

FROM TOXIC TO A MORE MINDFUL MASCULINITY

Liz Plank

ST. MARTIN'S GRIFFIN
NEW YORK

Published in the United States by St. Martin's Griffin, an imprint of
St. Martin's Publishing Group

FOR THE LOVE OF MEN. Copyright © 2019 by Elizabeth Plank. All rights
reserved. Printed in the United States of America. For information, address
St. Martin's Publishing Group, 120 Broadway, New York, NY 10271.

www.stmartins.com

The Library of Congress Cataloging-in-Publication data is available upon
request.

ISBN 978-1-250-19624-8 (hardcover)

ISBN 978-1-250-75720-3 (trade paperback)

ISBN 978-1-250-19625-5 (ebook)

Our books may be purchased in bulk for promotional, educational, or
business use. Please contact your local bookseller or the Macmillan
Corporate and Premium Sales Department at 1-800-221-7945, extension
5442, or by email at MacmillanSpecialMarkets@macmillan.com.

First St. Martin's Griffin Edition: 2021

10 9 8 7 6

*For my dad, who would
have much preferred this
book be about math*

Contents

Author's Note

Between most chapters is a short essay about a man with interwoven identities that captures and reveals the urgency of a conversation about mindful masculinity. Thomas Page McBee, a journalist and author, who understood the challenges of being a "real man" when he transitioned. Victor Pineda, an immigrant with a disability, who challenges the myth of the so-called self-sufficient man. Wade Davis, one of the few openly gay members of the NFL, who grew up believing that being queer and a man were mutually exclusive. Glenn Canning, a father who became an outspoken advocate for men to stop violence against women after his daughter took her own life. Maurice Owens, an advocate for boys of color, who followed an unlikely path to the White House. D'Arcee Charington Neal, a gay black man with a disability, who has a unique understanding of how cookie-cutter masculinity prevents the full expression of men's humanity. And Nicolas Juarez, a Mexican-American with Tzotzil ancestry, who has firsthand experience of how little indigenous men profit from a system built on outdated notions of masculinity that are aligned with white supremacy. This book cannot capture all of the complexities of the male experience, but these amuse-bouches are a start.

Why don't we say "boys will be boys" when a man wins the Nobel Peace Prize?

—MICHAEL KIMMEL

Introduction

Although the news often focuses on the threats of terrorism, natural disasters and nuclear war, there is no greater threat to humankind than our current definitions of masculinity.

It's a bold statement. If you've never thought about it, it may even seem overblown. But before you put this book down, take a moment to put a gender lens on men. In ten years of both academic and media reporting on gender theory, I've long focused on the numerous consequences of the patriarchy for women, because there's no shortage of them. But when I started talking to men about their own gender, I was dumbfounded. It changed my entire outlook on feminism. I started to wonder why the lies that we tell about masculinity aren't on the first page of every newspaper every single day of the year.

Psychologists have sounded the alarm. For the first time in its history, the American Psychological Association (APA) has created a set of explicit guidelines for practitioners treating men and boys. Their report warns therapists about the dangers of what they call "traditional masculinity ideology" negatively impacting men's mental health as well as physical health and well-being. Although the APA has often produced guidelines for therapists dealing with vulnerable populations like women, minorities or LGBTQ people, they've identified that the falsehoods we've all absorbed about men are putting their own health at risk.

And this is not just an American problem. It's an international crisis. In China, recently a new term has emerged, 直男癌, which translated from Mandarin means "straight man cancer."

In Iceland it's *eitruð karlmennska,* which means "toxic" or "poisonous masculinity." Hindi people in India refer to it as *Mardaangi.* In Québec, where I'm from, we call the guy who defines himself through domination of men and women "un macho." His polar opposite, the man who is in touch with his feelings, is referred to pejoratively as *l'homme rose,* which translates to "the pink man."

No matter what continent I visited and conducted interviews with men on, from Scandinavia to North America to Sub-Saharan Africa, I heard the same things over and over again. Toxic masculinity is an epidemic that knows no borders. No society has yet found the cure for it.

It presents itself in subtle ways, such as the way we raise boys differently from girls. It starts when we equate emotion with weakness and direct boys to display strength no matter what. It shows up in the way we expect and encourage girls to show their true emotions while we demand that boys hide them from us. It reveals itself in the way we're more comfortable with the image of a boy playing with a toy gun rather than a boy playing with a toy doll, because we're more comfortable seeing a boy hold something that kills rather than something that cries.

While we've spent a fair amount of time examining the negative effect of princesses and Barbies on the development of girls' perception of themselves, we haven't paused to question the consequences of the video games marketed to boys that have names like "Manhunt," "Thrill Kill" and "Mortal Kombat." We don't blink twice when the NRA releases a free target-shooting video game (one month after the

Newtown massacre, no less) and marks it as suitable for boys ages 4 and up. We indoctrinate boys and it starts early.

As Mr. Rogers said during a Senate hearing on PBS funding in 1969, "feelings are mentionable and manageable." But you wouldn't know that from the kind of programs targeted to boys today. In fact, Rogers was very critical of the violence both verbal and physical so often contained in the most mainstream shows shown to kids. "I think that it's much more dramatic that two men could be working out their feelings of anger—much more dramatic than showing something of gunfire," Mr. Rogers said. But before a boy can even make a choice about who he becomes, a cozy relationship with violence is encouraged, even rewarded, while proximity with tenderness is penalized. The violent images we feed boys have power. Just ask MIT scientists who were successfully able to create the world's first psychopathic robot through one simple act: showing it "the darkest corners of Reddit." They even named it after Norman Bates, the main character in *Psycho*. Violent men aren't born; they're created.

We live in a culture that teaches boys stoicism over authenticity, dominance over empathy, and that if they don't follow their script, someone will take notice and take their "man card" away. Boys are taught not to ask questions because asking for help would suggest a lack of leadership, instead of being an acute sign of it. Their behavior is highly monitored, their gender constantly surveilled for any sign of misstep or mistake. Boys become fluent in emotional self-censorship. They become anesthetized to feelings to avoid getting caught having any. The love is stripped away from them. As bell hooks argues in *The Will to Change*, boys learn that "it is better to be feared than to be loved."

Under the current circumstances we've set as a culture, it's an uphill battle for boys to find and reveal their true selves, and if they do it's perceived and noted as a flaw. Whether it's showing sadness or vulnerability, a core part of the human experience, it's corrected with a simple statement underpinning the poisonous ideology we raise them into: *boys don't cry*. And when they act in horrifying ways, when they hurt, beat or assault others in a way that goes against the human spirit, what do we say? *Boys will be boys*. We are puzzled when boys act terribly, failing to realize that this is precisely the bar we set for them. We have such low expectations of boys that we made up a term for it. What message do these two most commonly used expressions about boys signal to them?

We act as if boys being terrible is inevitable, then act surprised when they fulfill these expectations.

The consequences of this indoctrination have perplexed child psychology experts: while girls go on to become more emotionally mature and literate with age and time, boys become emotionally stunted. Male toddlers emote more than girls, but scientists notice an inexplicable drop in the boys' emotional expressions starting at the ages of 4 to 6 years, while it remains steady for young girls. It turns out that while parents encourage girls to fully express themselves, boys don't receive the same treatment. Much of this is largely unconscious and parents of all genders contribute to this. The phenomenon continues into adulthood, where in every age bracket men suppress their emotions far more than women do. Although very little gets universal consensus among academics, they are effectively unanimous that systemically suppressing one's emotions is one of the most damaging experiences for a human being to endure. What the scientific community has labeled as dangerous and unhealthy is the current model for the way we raise boys. As researchers Tara M. Chaplin and Amelia Aldao, from the Yale School of Medicine and Ohio State University, respectively, put it, "an accumulating body of evidence suggests that when a person is either limited in the range of emotions expressed, or encouraged to express particular emotions to the exclusion of others, there is a greater likelihood of compromised socio-emotional functioning and of risk for developing psychopathology."

Reductive versions of masculinity are instilled in young boys like a computer chip at an early age. Mounting research on the effects of traditional masculinity indicates that it does irreparable damage to boys and men across every socioeconomic and identity group. A rigid adherence to idealized masculinity is directly correlated[1] with lower well-being for men. Research[2] has shown that men who have a fear of showing emotions also happen to display the most violent behavior. Men who identify most strongly with conventional masculinity show greater interpersonal problems[3] in their relationships than men who don't. They're also more likely to sexually harass women.[4]

When half the population gets trained to block emotions, they lose the ability for compassion. This was best explained to me by David Hogg. He became one of the most well-known gun control activists after surviving a school shooting in Parkland, Florida. "A really good way for me to describe it is that I didn't feel empathy until the day of the shooting," he told me when we met in Houston. "I didn't even know what it was like to feel someone else's pain because I didn't know what that felt like. I had constantly throughout my life told myself that it wasn't okay to feel emotion and that I had to go out there and be this 'lone wolf' individual. But when I heard my sister crying after the shooting because she had lost four friends that day, I didn't know why I couldn't stand to be in the house and it was because her crying made me so uncomfortable because I was feeling her pain. But it took a mass shooting for me to realize that. So I can't imagine what it makes so many other men across America."

And because it has been left unchecked and omnipresent, this archaic ideology has been absorbed and encoded into every institution. We have state-sponsored gender roles where policy dictates what men and boys can do, practically erasing the opportunity to know their true tendencies, proclivities or desires. For instance, when President, then candidate, Donald Trump proudly presented a drastic new proposal for family leave, the policy made no mention of fathers. In fact, it excluded men entirely. It guaranteed a measly six weeks of partial pay for new mothers and failed to even mention time off for new fathers (or gay fathers, for that matter). After this drew criticism, they expanded it, but the fact that the policy makers on Trump's team didn't even think of including men in parental leave and that there wasn't a backlash to it shows who we naturally tend to think of as parents: *not men*. It also sends a powerful message to fathers: your place is at work, not in the home. That's limiting for women. It's also limiting for men. The flip side is that when states stop encoding defunct masculinity into their policy making, men naturally start spending more time with their children and working inside the home. We've seen public policy offer men more freedom and flexibility in choosing their role in places like Denmark, Sweden and Quebec, setting off a huge transformation in behaviors.

Toxic definitions of masculinity don't just show up in policy—they reveal themselves in our education system and in the growing disinterest boys and young men have in it. Men are the minority in colleges. The gender gap that once advantaged men has reversed completely. The US Department of Education projects that by 2026, 57 percent of the college population will be female. The majority of bachelor, master's and doctorate degrees across the country are held by women, and since 1982 they've earned more than 10 million more degrees than men.

Although men lagging behind in education often spurs a salacious debate about whether schools are too "feminized" for boys, we fail to see that in that very question rests our own faulty assumptions about what boys need. When we subscribe to innate differences in genders we run the risk of encoding discrimination in the way we teach them, which is exactly what we are seeing across the United States and all over the world. One school in Pittsburgh integrated "stories for girls about princesses and fairies and uses tea parties, wands and tiaras as learning incentives." Boys, however, regardless of their interest in sports, were taught with difficult physical challenges "through a modified basketball game," where they had to match words with phrases "while running relays." We codify gender roles in the way we teach children, with no evidence that doing so has any benefits for them.

This discriminatory sex-specific approach to teaching is a million-dollar business. The Gurian Institute, an organization whose principal mission is to tailor education based on gender, receives thousands of dollars from different school boards all over the country, propagating unsubstantiated claims about the difference between what boys and girls need. According to their website, they've already trained sixty thousand teachers in two thousand schools across the United States.

The founder, Michael Gurian, believes the "pursuit of power is a universal male trait" while the "pursuit of a comfortable environment is a universal female trait." He has advocated giving boys NERF baseball bats to "hit things" to help them learn better. Dr. Leonard Sax, the founder and executive director of the National Association for Single Sex Public Education (NASSPE), peddles similar advice to teachers. He instructs teachers to look girls in the eyes but avoid eye contact with boys and even avoid smiling at them. He also directs educators to abstain from asking boys about the emotions of characters and engage in "strict discipline based on asserting power over them" and justifies corporal punishment like spanking for boys while for girls he instructs teachers to "appeal to their empathy." Gurian recommends that boys who don't like sports should be coerced into them. Although a recent trend (mostly argued by people outside the realm of education) asserted that the gap between girls and boys is due to schools being "too girly" and that all male students need to be approached in more aggressive ways, that hasn't been backed up by any data. In fact, Stephanie Coontz, the co-chair and director of research and public education for the Council on Contemporary Families, strongly urged against it in a 2013 briefing paper on the topic: "Making curriculum, teachers or classrooms more 'masculine' is not the answer [. . .]. In fact, boys do better in school in classrooms that have more girls and that emphasize extra-curricular activities such as music and art as well as holding both girls and boys to high academic standards."

The discrepancy between boys and girls is not due to inherent differences in brain skills. As the authors of the paper, professors of sociology at Columbia University Thomas A. DiPrete and Claudia Buchmann, wrote, "Researchers agree that it is not because girls are smarter. In fact, while boys score slightly higher in math tests and girls score slightly higher in reading tests, overall the cognitive abilities of boys and girls are very similar. The difference in grades lies in effort and engagement. On average, girls are more likely than boys to report that they like school and that good grades are very important to them. Girls also spend more time studying than boys. Our research shows that boys' underperformance in school has more to do with society's norms about masculinity than with anatomy, hormones or brain structure."

Their research shows that while girls have a core understanding of how doing well in school is tied to greater opportunities in the job market, that link is less salient for boys. This may be a persisting relic from a time when future success in the workplace for men was tied to manual labor jobs and physical ability, which made grades feel peripheral for boys. For many of them, the correlation between getting good grades and future professional as well as financial success later in life is not highlighted in the way that it is for girls.

Perpetuating the falsehood that boys' natural rambunctiousness is antithetical with school environments might be a seductive solution that sells books and gets clicks. But if it were true, this gender gap in education would be persistent across all economic groups. It's not. Indeed, the gender gap in education practically vanishes in schools that are blessed with resources. Economists who looked at test scores and suspension rates in Florida found that boys and girls were on equal footing in the best schools. It's in the worst schools that boys started to lag behind the girls. We see the same trend in households. Economic policy reporter Jeff Guo found that the gap between boys and girls is almost nonexistent with well-off families.

"[E]arly-life adversity causes boys to struggle much more than girls," he wrote in *The Washington Post*. "It's not yet clear why girls are so tough, but they seem much better suited to the challenges of modern childhood."

Guo concludes that worsening income inequality could lead to greater contrast between boys' and girls' performances in schools. So the gender education gap is less about recognizing that boys are inherently uninterested. To the contrary, it's about recognizing that boys are more vulnerable than girls in poverty and low-resource environments and that they need more intimate attention, not less.

In other words, when we let our gendered biases about boys dictate conversation about their needs, we fail to see what they *actually* need to succeed. Often our solutions to the problems of men are tainted with our own faulty assumptions about what boys and men are like. Those assumptions may make us feel comfortable and offer quick fixes for big problems, but there is no evidence they lead to sustainable change.

Boys also learn that "real men" don't ask for directions. Any woman who's ever driven with a man knows the agony of driving in circles rather than asking for directions. But the consequences of this lone-wolf masculine ideal have repercussions beyond shouting matches between women and men in the car and being late to brunch.

It means that men are less likely to communicate with their doctor or health professional. It explains why men's skin cancer deaths have increased while women's haven't. Men wear less sunscreen, are less likely[5] to wear a seat belt, visit the doctor less often and receive less preventative care. And when they do visit the hospital, they leave earlier than women. These are not biological differences—how often you think you need to go to the doctor is purely rooted in learned behavior. And men have inferred that asking for advice is not for them. Mix an inability to cope with emotions with a reluctance to seek help and you have the perfect—and lethal—mix for a mental health crisis. The way we raise boys and men is a recipe for disaster. And a disaster it has become.

Not all emotionally stunted men go on to do bad things, but the men who go on to commit crimes often have difficulty coping with emotions and a reluctance to ask for help. After all, it makes sense: men don't have the tools to deal with something they're not supposed to feel in the first place. For instance, men who become perpetrators of domestic violence often exhibit emotional ineptitudes. One study on men who were being treated for domestic violence found that "men who reported experiencing affect that was difficult for them to manage are more likely to abuse their partners and also tend to believe that men should not share their emotions or ask for help."

Leaving the way we are raising boys and men unexamined has created a mental health crisis and female partners have become the first line of defense. As therapist Terry Real puts it, millions of men are living with "covert depression," which he warns is a "silent epidemic in men." Most of the behaviors that we most associate with men like anger issues, alcohol or drug use and abusive behavior are often attempts to escape mental illness. Men feel compelled to hide depression from their partners or their own families because it clashes with expectations of ideal masculinity of self-reliance and strength. "Many men would rather place themselves at risk than acknowledge distress, either physical or emotional," Real writes.

Toxic masculinity turns men into a threat to women. Men's violence against women is a worldwide epidemic. No country, community or society has found a way to stamp it out. For many women across the world, the men in their lives are the biggest threat to them. Male partners are the second leading cause of death for pregnant women in the United States. Every single day three men will end up killing their girlfriend, wife or ex. Nearly half of all women who end up murdered are killed by a current or former romantic partner—98 percent of those partners are male. Homicide, primarily carried out by men, is one of the top leading causes of death for women under 45. In the first nine months of 2018, there were three mass shootings in Texas, all motivated by and targeting a woman who rejected the shooter's advances. One researcher who examined fifteen school shootings between 1995 and 2001 found that romantic rejection was one of the most common features in gun-related incidents. As Michael Kimmel has noted, "righteous retaliation is a deeply held, almost sacred, tenet of masculinity: if you are aggrieved, you are entitled to retribution. American men don't just get mad, we get even."

That aggrieved entitlement stemming from the falsehoods we circulate about masculinity showed up in all its awful colors in the chilling manifesto left behind by Elliot Rodger, a 22-year-old student who killed seven people during a mass-shooting rampage at the University of California, Santa Barbara. The video he posted online a mere few hours before the massacre, where he vows to "slaughter every single spoiled, stuck-up, blonde slut I see," describes his intention to murder women as a form of retribution for his inability to attract them. "I don't know why you girls have never been attracted to me, but I will punish you all for it. It's an injustice, a crime," he said, before erupting into a satanic kind of laughter. "I'll take great pleasure in slaughtering all of you. You will finally see that I am in truth the superior one. The true Alpha Male."

If Rodger were in a movie, his performance would be too on the nose. His motivation for the killing of innocent people is what happens when dangerous definitions of masculinity are left unchallenged. Instead of being castigated, he has been hailed as a hero, glamorized by hundreds of men's rights groups and online forums. One of those devout followers praised Rodger in a Facebook post hours before ramming his van into a crowd of people for over a mile in Toronto, killing ten people and injuring fifteen. He described himself as an "incel," short for involuntary celibate, a term men's rights activists use to describe men whom women don't want to have sex with. Although these are considered fringe men's movements, the beliefs that underpin their ideologies aren't that uncommon among regular men. For instance, a *Glamour* survey found that although 77 percent of men believe consent is always necessary during sex, a whopping 59 percent of them simultaneously believed that husbands are entitled to sex with their wives. After all, it wasn't until the mid-1970s that it became illegal to rape your wife.

Toxic definitions of masculinity show up in the way that mass shootings are a uniquely white male disease. Although we focus on their mental health problems, what ties mass shooters together isn't mental health illness (one study of two hundred shooters found that only half of them had clear evidence of mental health issues prior to the act); it's narcissism, a sense that they've been wronged and a sense that they are the victim of injustice. Ironically, it's not refugees who can't find settlement, LGBTQ people who can't get health insurance or African-Americans whose communities are terrorized by police who feel a sense of injustice so great they feel the need to kill others—almost every single mass shooting in American history was perpetrated by a white man or men. Everyone experiences hardship, but only one demographic has been indoctrinated to medicate with revenge.

Although these shootings become fodder for debates around gun control and bullying, rarely does the conversation turn to why they're almost always done by men. Newscasters might not notice, but gun manufacturers certainly have. Their marketing is often explicitly designed to prey on young men's insecurities. For instance, gun manufacturer Bushmaster put out an ad that equated gun owner- ship with renewing one's "man card" only a few days after Adam Lanza used one of their semiautomatic rifles to shoot his mother in the face and go on to murder twenty innocent young children at Sandy Hook Elementary School. For a period of time, the company's website even contained a feature that allowed men to send each other notices that their man card had been revoked to facilitate peer pressure between men to buy more guns. The suggestion is that your masculinity can be taken away at any time (by other men) and that carrying a violent weapon that kills people is a surefire way to get it back. In a case won by some of the families of the Sandy Hook shooting, their lawyer argued that the gun manufacturer "may have never known Adam Lanza, but they had been courting him for years."

Toxic masculinity also turns men into the greatest threat to them- selves. Men aren't just more likely to carry guns; they're also more likely to die from guns. In every single country around the world, male homicide rates are higher than the female homicide rate, and overall, men make up 79 percent[6] of homicide deaths. When men end up being tragically murdered, they are most often killed by another man. Although politicians spend a lot of time trying to spin the gun control debate around racial lines by speaking about so-called black- on-black violence, the more glaring demographic pattern in homi- cide is male-on-male crime. If we were to tackle the problem of men harming other men, we'd make a dent in crime rates across every continent.

But despite mass shootings and murders capturing more media and national attention, the highest incidence of gun deaths is as a result of suicide—86 percent of the people who kill themselves with a gun are men. American men are quite literally stockpiling guns. They are three times more likely to own guns than women and are six times more likely to kill themselves with it. Wyoming, the state of the iconic masculinized image of the lone cowboy, has one of the highest male suicide rates in the country, and incidentally one of the highest rates of gun ownership. Despite these worrying statistics about men's willingness to take their own lives, we are reluctant to see men as being able to suffer. There's a presupposition that maleness and dominance are undistinguishable, leaving no room for any other narrative of being a man. It's so antithetical to view men as victims that the FBI never even included them in their definition of rape until only very recently. The result is that young men are the demographic the least likely[7] to seek mental health help while also being the group who would benefit the most from intervention, given they are also most likely to die by suicide. Men who subscribe to traditional masculinity ideals tend to have worse health outcomes than the men who don't. Men who believe in macho ideals of masculinity are less inclined to seek mental health help. They're also less likely to use condoms, and view impregnating a woman as a strong marker of a man's masculine capabilities. Young men who don't see themselves as able to fulfill the male economic provider role are the ones who put the biggest emphasis[8] on sexual prowess and toughness. The correlation is clear, and yet we do nothing.

Toxic definitions of masculinity also make it harder for men to develop and maintain simple relationships. If you aren't trained to understand your own emotions, it's fairly predictable that you'll have difficulty understanding the emotions of others. Because men are encouraged to play games that center on competition rather than relationships, emotional intelligence is a muscle that never gets developed. Research from Dr. John M. Gottman, one of the world's foremost experts on relationships, has found that a man being emotionally intelligent is one of the greatest predictors of a successful romantic relationship. Gottman finds that while it's a crucial skill, it's not always taught to boys. One of the biggest ways it shows up in his research is men resisting their wife's influence by not attending to her feelings and desires. When a man resists his partner's influence, Gottman says there's an 81 percent chance the marriage will not survive.

It's not just men's relationships with women that lag behind; it's their relationships with one another, too. Men have fewer friends and less in-depth friendships and become increasingly isolated with age. Loneliness is a disproportionately male problem. In the UK alone, there are 2.5 million men who report having zero close friends. The increase in aging isolated men has become such a crisis that governments in the UK and Denmark have launched emergency task forces to tackle the crisis. Aging men are more likely to be lonely than their female counterparts and less likely to have regular contact with their friends or family. Since men are instructed that intimacy is a sign of weakness, they don't develop strong friendships that can sustain them. Loneliness is one of the main predictors for middle-aged white men, the most at-risk demographic for taking one's life.

Lonely men are ignored while violent men are glamorized. Almost all of the top-ten highest-grossing films of 2017 had a white male protagonist who uses violence as a means of self-expression. *Guardians of the Galaxy Vol. 2, Beauty and the Beast, The Fate of the Furious*—all of these movies have one thing in common. When do you become a hero? When you kill the bad guy. What does that tell us about what we value in men?

In so many of the most popular movies of late, almost all of the main characters who engage in violent behavior are, in fact, "good guys." *Beauty and the Beast* is a perfect example. The Beast kidnaps and terrorizes Belle, his romantic love interest, as a way to build an emotional connection with her. And the story teaches us that this is not only acceptable, but hey, it works! It's hard to think of the plot of a single Disney movie the millennial generation grew up with that doesn't have a seriously questionable subtext normalizing men as predators. We often talk about how the princess trope teaches girls that they need to be docile, unambitious, unidimensional, rescued or controlled by men.

But what did those same movies teach young boys? We act surprised when grown men don't understand consent when the most iconic and popular stories send very mixed messages about it. Whether it's *Sleeping Beauty* or *Snow White*, the takeaway is that you don't need permission. Consent is assumed, not affirmed. In fact, not getting consent doesn't make you the villain; it makes you the hero. The guy who does it doesn't assault the girl; that's how he saves her.

This begs the question: If boys are taught that violence is the path to seduction and even redemption in movies, why are we surprised when they engage in it in real life?

Our culture also glamorizes white male violence in the way it is handled by the media. Although the vast majority of acts of domestic terrorism since 9/11 have been committed by white men, the media's narrative is often one of shock at a troubled person whose life just took a wrong turn. Of course if these men weren't white, their treatment would be different. We grade male violence on a curve—men of color receive far greater punishment, scrutiny and collective attention, while violence perpetrated by white men is far more invisible and still considered unexpected. The violence of white men can even be perceived as justified, especially when it's against people of color. We see it in the case of the white police officer who killed Philando Castile for reaching into his glove compartment, or in George Zimmerman, who shot Trayvon Martin, a black teenager coming back from a convenience store with a bag of Skittles.

We see it in the way genocidal white colonialism is systematically glamorized in school curricula—a romantic version of mass murder of indigenous people encoded in the millions of history books our children read. We see it in the way state-sponsored violence and wars against other countries filled with black and brown people are left unquestioned and that any critique is delegitimized as unpatriotic. We see it in the careful selection of the people we allow or don't allow in our country and in the fact that one of the most powerful men in the world calls these places "shitholes."

There is empathy for the violent white man, a desperate attempt to "understand" him or figure out where he went wrong, as if white men hadn't been responsible for the vast majority of the violence that occurred in the United States, from the slaughtering of entire populations of native peoples, to the enslavement of African-Americans, to segregation, the invasion and occupation of Puerto Rico, to the detainment of Asian-Americans and in new modern-day permutations with white-supremacy groups.

The gap left by the absence of a conversation or identity around positive masculinity has been filled by hate groups who offer men a missing sense of belonging and sense of identity. It's no coincidence that experts have warned about a dangerous new uptick in the proliferation of extremist and white-supremacy groups not just here in the United States but all over the world. These groups have preyed on isolated young men who have been made vulnerable by a culture that indoctrinates them to believe that connection can be achieved through violence. Because it's so hard for us to see men as victims, their vulnerability is often invisible.

The most important question is: Where is the version of a feminist movement, but for men?

If you stop to think about it, you realize how astounding it is that we all innately understand the fact that men are responsible for the vast majority of violent acts across the world as inevitable. But what if we wrote a different script for men? How could we better prevent our world's darkest problems if we addressed the link between men's isolation and their disproportionate radicalization? If we viewed their violent outbursts as a weakness, rather than a strength, perhaps we'd properly pathologize rather than normalize the astronomical amount of male violence across the world.

Our toxic definition of masculinity presents itself in not-so-subtle ways. It presents itself in the election of an alleged sexual abuser to the highest office of the US government. History books will not skip the part where a man who bragged about sexually assaulting women by grabbing their genitals and who was credibly accused of sexual misconduct by nineteen women was elected and became the leader of the free world. It is now a part of American history that a man who has repeatedly made incestuous references about having sex with one daughter, fantasized about the future breasts of his other daughter when she was a newborn and barged into the changing rooms of teenage girls at the pageants he held was elected president by the American people.

Toxic definitions of masculinity even pose a threat to the livelihood of our planet. Scientists have started warning about a recycling gender gap. The data shows that men are less likely to practice behaviors that are eco-friendly, like recycling, than women and are more likely to engage in behaviors that hurt the environment, like littering. In fact, research shows that both men and women associate those eco-conscious behaviors with femininity and a repudiation of masculinity. So in other words, it's not that men don't care about the environment; they're just taught to care about threats to their masculinity more. How different would the world look if men had the freedom to care about their planet as much as women do?

Because it's at the root of so many institutional problems, altering the way we raise men and boys could literally change the world. Although the concept of world peace feels so impossible that it only comes out of the mouths of beauty pageant contestants, researchers who have examined wide and extensive global data sets have found that one factor seems to act as a shield for violence and warfare: gender equality.

Gender equality is often presented as a side effect of world order, but it's rarely presented as the cure to political instability—despite mounting data that it is inversely correlated with it. When we ignore gender, whether it's in the exclusion of women's voices or the way that masculinity constructions can increase conflict, we limit the opportunity for lasting peace. Valerie M. Hudson, Bonnie Ballif-Spanvill, Mary Caprioli and Chad F. Emmett, the authors of *Sex and World Peace,* argue that "neither a meaningful decrease in societal violence nor a sustainable peace amongst nations is possible in human society without an increase in gender equality." The authors, through their research, posit that rates of men's violence against women are a better predictor of peace in a country than the level of sophistication of the country's democratic development.

Even when nations recognize the importance of programs tailored toward gender equality, very few are focused on men. Although programs that focus on positive masculinity are rare, one group in Chicago, Becoming a Man, helps at-risk male youth develop mindful masculinity, challenges gender stereotypes and is focused on boys' emotional development. Amazingly, it has brought down arrests and increased young men's graduation rates. Imagine the dent implementing programs like that could make in the reduction of mental health problems or suicide and divorce. When we offer more freedom to men about who they *really* want to become, the possibilities are endless.

It fascinates me that politicians don't talk about masculinity every single day. Given how intimately toxic definitions of masculinity are connected to the most pressing issues facing our world, it's curious it has never received a mention in a major political speech and that it rarely shows up in the lexicons of government leaders and policy makers. Although State of the Union speeches have mentioned the importance of tearing down gender barriers and norms when it comes to women and girls, men and boys don't get that message.

Many world leaders erroneously assign barbaric characteristics to entire ethnic groups and religions as a result of repeated tragedies such as terrorism. It's worth asking, if we started calling toxic masculinity a religion, would politicians start paying attention to it? If we started seeing idealized masculinity as a public health crisis that could be avoided, how differently would policy makers approach it? After all, it's a disease that doesn't discriminate. It doesn't matter where you're from. It's an illness that doesn't care how much money you make. It affects all ethnic groups and races.

I want to make it clear that talking about masculinity is not a distraction from the problems of women—rather, it's the most effective way to properly address them. The biggest lie is that the fight to address male suffering is separate or at odds with the battle to liberate women. We all experience gender. We are all limited by oppressive gender stereotypes. We must transcend the myth of the gender war. We're all on the same team.

Here's how reclaiming masculinity could serve all of us.

*I love being a man but not what
being a man means.*

—THOMAS PAGE McBEE

AMUSE-BOUCHE:
Thomas's Story

"None of the narratives of being a man worked for me," Thomas Page
McBee said. "Am I a real man? Am I a good man?" Thomas started
asking himself questions about what it meant to be a man because
he was new to it. He's trans and, after injecting testosterone for about
twenty months, quickly became recognized as an expert on masculinity, publishing several articles and two books about it. In his lat-
est book, *Amateur,* he writes about being the first trans man to
perform at Madison Square Garden and having what he called a
"beginner's mind" to masculinity. "Having experienced such rapid
socialization, I am so aware of the most basic mediating qualities
that we have, like gender. These things really affect everything about
how we're treated." He came to terms with what being a man meant
and became rapidly aware it was not exactly sunshine and lollipops.
"I love being a man but not what being a man means," Thomas
said to me. He suddenly was seen as part of a group he didn't always wholeheartedly endorse. "I felt apprehensive about men in our
culture," he explained.

As he started experiencing the new perks of being a man, he
simultaneously questioned them. "One massive change was the
way any time I would speak everyone would be quiet. No one was

interrupting me. It was wonderful and a privilege but also weird," he confessed. He also talked about how much easier it was to negotiate a raise or navigate power dynamics at work as a man. "Until I was a man, I had no idea how good men had it at work," Thomas explained. Armed with this newly found male privilege, Thomas suddenly felt a responsibility to effect change, especially given his managerial position overseeing a team at Quartz, a new media company. Since his team was primarily made up of women, he consulted with a professor to figure out ways to ensure that everyone felt like they had a space to feel seen and heard. The professor told him to start every meeting by giving an opportunity for every person to speak because that would make it more likely for people to more freely express themselves throughout the rest of the meeting. It was a small change, but Thomas noticed a huge difference.

But soon the shiny perks were overshadowed by the downsides of living as a man in our culture. Only one year after transitioning, Thomas tragically lost his mother, and what followed he could have never predicted. He confided there was one thing he didn't know he needed until it was robbed from him: human touch. Going through grief as a man was a jarring and isolating experience. He recounted how people didn't reach out to him physically as much as they used to and that suddenly he became self-conscious of what it would look like to be openly sad. He described feeling the difference between anger and sadness and that while the former was acceptable, the latter wasn't. Suddenly he felt a level of isolation he had never felt before. "I knew what that care was, I had it before. . . . What I learned was that I needed that," Thomas said. Although it was normal to see a woman cry in public from time to time in New York City, he felt acutely aware that he wasn't supposed to. "I got the message, explicitly and implicitly, from culture and from my relationships with the people around me, that men weren't 'supposed to' be sad, or show any emotion really except anger." This despite living in one of the most progressive cities in the United States.

He also talked about the pain that came with people around him subtly "encouraging [him] to be more strong." Instead of letting him mourn, they called on him to perform toughness while grieving. It revealed the specific attributes of male friendship for him. Older men in his family, trying to be helpful, would ask for updates about handling the logistics of the death of his mother, such as her will, rather than ask questions about his emotional state. One friend who had known him before his transition asked him "Are you okay?" and Thomas realized no one else had really asked him that question before, or at least asked him and really wanted the real answer. "I felt pressure to be strong and stoic, despite being a feminist who knew better," Thomas said. "It was unconscious, and generally the people in my life—I think in an attempt to affirm my masculinity—were kind to me, but didn't really push the point if I said I was 'fine.'" Thomas realized that people didn't want to disrespect him; in fact, they were acting this way out of respect for conventional gender norms. That's what happens in a gender system that is so ubiquitous: everyone plays their part without questioning if it's even a role they would have picked in the first place.

One of the other difficult realizations for Thomas was that he was perceived as a predator simply for being male. "Within public spaces, I felt like a threat to women and threatened women just by walking down the street," he said as he recalled noticing women changing sides of the street to avoid him. Dating women was also hard as a man. He kept being told he was too vulnerable by women he was romantically involved with. "That was a way of saying I wasn't masculine enough." He recalled feeling watched and observed for his performance of manhood. "A lot of policing. I felt policed."

Because Thomas was new to masculinity and because these messages were not hammered into him from an early age, he could see them for what they were: a box. "This gave me a real education in masculinity," Thomas said. But how do men realize they are living in a box if that's all they've ever seen? Thomas could see it because he knew what life was like before the walls came up. So I asked him how other men, who may not know how much they perform masculinity, could do this. His answer: "Asking a lot of stupid questions about what being a man means." When I asked him why more men didn't follow that path, he confirmed that the very act of interrogating the expectations of masculinity violated it. "The whole idea of masculinity is not failing at it." He described it as a "shame loop" where the feeling of having failed begets overcompensation rather than deeper questioning.

Thomas talks about his journey as developing an intimate relationship with his gender, something so many men fail to do since they're not taught they have a gender to begin with. "The more you understand where it came from, the more equipped you are to disrupt it. It helps you understand it's cultural, not inherent. You can be free from gender, too."

PART I

The Lies We Tell About Men

I don't like to analyze myself,
because I might not like what I see.

—DONALD TRUMP

I'd go to the end of the world for my husband; of course, if he'd just stop and ask for directions, I wouldn't have to.

—MARTHA BOLTON

THE PROBLEM THAT HAD NO NAME

The average male will drive an unnecessary nine hundred miles over the course of his life. Upon realizing they are lost, only 6 percent of men say they check a map or ask for help. These numbers, seeded from a British insurance company, support something we've all witnessed firsthand: men are entitled to a lot of stuff, but asking questions is not one of them.

Although science doesn't offer a verdict about whether women are more likely to get lost than men, it does show that one gender is less likely to admit to it. In fact, many men don't ask for directions because confessing they are lost is interpreted as an admission of fault. This explains why they will often double down rather than pull over. "I know the way," he will grumble while she is in the passenger seat rolling her eyes into oblivion. According to Tristan Gooley, an expert in navigation, men prefer to stick to a system they know, even if it's faulty, rather than admit it's wrong and be open to alternatives. "I think women have less comfort with and faith in a system," he told BBC Four. "Men like systems, so they stay within the system even if it isn't working all the way." And even when men go outside of their comfort zone, it bites them in the butt. For instance, research shows that male managers get penalized for asking for directions.

They are seen as lesser leaders, probably because we're so used to seeing men exude confidence (sometimes over competence). In other words, even if men want to ask for directions, they are punished when they do.

The more I read about men's relationship to directions and maps, the more it explained the absence of a substantive and open conversation about masculinity. While women are encouraged to ask questions, men are expected to pretend like they know everything even when they don't, even when it comes to large and existential questions about their gender and their lives. As I traveled across the world, from Iceland to Zambia, I asked men the same question over and over again: What's hard about being a man? Every single time I asked that question it was like I had just asked them if unicorns can swim.

It was met with a pause, a smile, and then followed by another long pause followed by the words: "I've never actually thought of that." When I asked women that same question about their gender—in other words, when I asked women what was hard about being a woman—it was like I had asked them to name every single thing they loved about puppies. I got nearly the same response from every woman I spoke to: "How much time do you have?" Judging from the conversations I would strike up with (half-)willing strangers, women had spent a lot of time thinking about how their gender impacts their lives, but men visibly hadn't. While that conversation had been blossoming with women for decades, for men, accepting directions was proof that the system was broken, which goes against the natural impulses of what being a man means: not to admit confusion or ask questions. It had me wondering: If men can't ask for directions to the closest gas station, then how the hell are they supposed to ask for directions about being a man?

The more I thought about how rarely men ask for directions, the more I realized that what I had written off as arrogance could actually be rooted in something much bigger, with much more far-reaching consequences than just getting lost on the highway. It made me reflect on all the other ways that not asking questions revealed an inability to show intellectual vulnerability and how it spilled over into the struggle to demonstrate relational tenderness or emotional flaws. It also made me think about a whole host of myths that we entertain about men that could affect their lives in small or large ways.

As far as I'm concerned, being any gender is a drag.

—PATTI SMITH

AMUSE-BOUCHE:
But First, a Quick Crash Course in Gender

Before I debunk some of the most common lies we believe about men and explore how their persistence in our culture impacts men's lives, let's get on the same page about what exactly gender is and why it matters. I promise it will be fun. Gender is one of the most universal ways that we currently organize as human beings. Its omnipresence and influence over our lives is so intrinsic that it can almost feel invisible, but it's actually enormous. Just think about the first question a person gets when they're pregnant: Is it a boy or girl? Before we're even out of our mother's womb, gender is already dictating the way people relate to us and understand us. Our entire society relies on us falling neatly into being male or female. It's one of the first ways we classify human beings; it's how we divide bathrooms and changing rooms; it's required on our passports and driver's license and we need it to get citizenship and health insurance.

Although sex and gender are often used interchangeably, they're not exactly the same. While sex is determined by our bodies, gender is a social construction. Just like we were assigned a name, we were also assigned a gender at birth and socialized according to what our culture has predetermined is acceptable and appropriate for that gender.

Because we are a social species, most of us intuitively integrate the roles we've been socialized into and this is largely unconscious, especially when we're young. Sociologists Candace West and Don H. Zimmerman call the internalization of gendered norms and roles a routine called "doing gender." Their paper that coined the expression was published in 1987 and it remains one of the most-cited papers about gender of all time. It compares our daily lives to a stage where we are all actors simply reading scripts that we've been assigned. Of course, just because we are socialized a certain way doesn't mean we can't deviate from the roles that we were encouraged to take on, but we're all still part of a system that rewards us for how well we perform these lines and alternatively punishes us for writing our own. The most repeated myth about gender, which has wide-ranging impacts for all of us, is that it's fixed, binary and purely rooted in biology. It's actually not! When someone's gender identity and their sex align, they're cisgender. When gender identity and sex don't connect, that person can identify in a number of ways, one of which is as transgender. They may or may not seek to transition.

Although there's a greater appreciation for gender being a spectrum, that progress is often derailed by people arguing that our gender identities should be simply defined by our sex. Unfortunately for those people, it's becoming clearer and clearer that sex is not binary either. And make no mistake, this view isn't just championed by activists; it's coming from biologists, who are beginning to categorize sex as a spectrum rather than a binary. While there's an assumption that the presence or absence of a penis determines one's sex, when we look at nature the answer isn't always that black and white. To put it simply, science doesn't confirm that there are only two sexes. Although "nature" is often used as a tool in the defense of a binary, the irony is that it validates the theory that sex is a spectrum containing a multitude of categories. For starters, one out of one hundred babies simply doesn't neatly fall into either category. Often referred to as "intersex," these bodies are neither male nor female based on their anatomy, hormone levels or chromosomes. Many may never even notice their hormonal or genetic variances until later in life. One of the most well-known examples is Caster Semenya, the Olympic world champion in the 800-meter race. After she won the gold medal at the 2009 International Association of Athletics Federations (IAAF) World Championships, she became the subject of controversy because her body produces high levels of testosterone. She was forced to undergo invasive sex verification to compete in the 2012 London Olympics, where she won a silver medal, but her right to compete with female athletes, despite her being one, continues to be debated. Her case is just one of the many that exemplify how complicated (and obstrusive) defining sex really is.

Although all of our institutions are organized around the premise that gender and sex are a binary, it's a fallacy. Throughout this book, I refer to men and masculinity as interchangeable, but I strongly believe in a world that goes beyond gender. But we must first name the system if we are to break free from it. In this book I am not advocating or supporting a gender binary but am, rather, interested in assessing the damage that occurs in the process of raising men and boys in a society that imposes it.

1   You're Not Born a Man

After trying to interview several men, I realized that masculinity was something you did, not something you talked about. Although most men would eventually come around and answer my questions truthfully, for many it was the first time they had ever talked about masculinity out loud. They had spent years performing it, but talking about it? Not so much. I noticed that men's voices would often get quieter and they would look around as if they were assessing if it was safe to speak. Although I don't have direct experience to corroborate this, the process of talking about masculinity with a man is what I imagine it would feel like to rob a bank. The prospect of the reward might be exciting, but the entire process sounds way too stressful.

But from my research I knew it was harder for men to share their feelings with other men (data shows men are at least slightly more likely to prefer a female therapist), so I wanted to see if they would confide their thoughts about masculinity to someone who isn't part of the club: a woman. Or two, for that matter. So on a scorching-hot Sunday afternoon I put this theory to the test and designed my own social experiment in Washington Square Park. I armed myself with a table and a sign that read: "Free Advice for Men from a Woman." I brought along my dear friend and renowned relationship expert

Esther Perel to offer men some free, useful and what would otherwise be very expensive advice. We sat there for three hours and at no point were there not men at our table seeking advice on a wide variety of topics and issues. As I expected, a majority of the questions were about women. One man pointed to his nearby girlfriend and simply whispered, "How do I make her happy?"

More than one man inquired about the ways to "impress" a woman (Esther's lightning-round advice: if you're just trying to impress her, then you're more into "look at me" rather than "I see you"). Other men asked why men engaged in so much posturing. One asked about how straight white men could talk about their worries and concerns without seeming like they are taking away from the microphone of marginalized previously silenced voices. Interestingly, though, Esther and I remarked after the experiment that very few men actually really asked questions. Most of them just showed up at the table waiting for us to ask them questions. It's like they aren't used to admitting they have any. But once the men started talking, they didn't stop. It wasn't until we started offering men some direction that it was clear how much they longed for it. It's when I did this social experiment that I realized masculinity is a lot like Fight Club; the first rule is that you don't talk about it.

But when I eventually forced it out of them, I kept hearing two things over and over again.

The first one was that nearly all the men didn't feel like they were really men yet, despite all being, in every sense of the definition, undeniably full-grown adult men. Being a man felt less like an identity and more like a job or a reward you received only after going through excruciating circumstances. The men we spoke to felt an unforgiving pressure to perform their masculinity constantly. Being a man was something you earned. But curiously, although all of them had deliberately or inadvertently engaged in tactics to achieve ideal masculinity, none of them really felt like "real men." And this wasn't just the men I spoke to. This phenomenon is supported by what sociologists call "precarious manhood." What this theory boils down to is that masculinity needs to be constantly proved, while womanhood is more static, or fixed. Women have more permission to drift away from traditional feminine norms; men can't do that with as much flexibility. Women can wear pants, have boy names like Charlie or Riley; they can even wear ties and a tuxedo at a wedding. As long as they adhere to a baseline of traditionally feminine characteristics, they can adopt certain masculine traits and it's perceived as edgy, sexy—it can even give them cachet. Of course, this doesn't apply to all women equally; more on that later.

But masculinity is much more rigid and requires constant self-regulation. Just think about the common expression a "real man." A "real man" doesn't cry. A "real man" doesn't wear makeup. A "real man" doesn't wear skirts. No such expression exists for women. Even if a man squats three hundred pounds, biting into beef jerky with one hand and fighting a hungry bear with the other, his masculinity would still be put into question for ordering a drink that comes in a cosmo glass with a cherry at happy hour. Gender may be a social construct for both men and women, but womanhood isn't lost through social acts; it's acquired or lost through mostly private biology changes with normal shifts in bodily features such as puberty or menopause. There aren't femininity-restoring activities for women because femininity is not something that needs to be earned. For men, it's the opposite. Masculinity is procured through ritualized and often-public social behaviors. This is fairly consistent throughout history and across most cultures all around the world. For instance, in Bronze Age Russia the passage into manhood involved boys killing animals, often their own pet dogs. Currently, boys in the Karo tribe found in parts of Sudan, Uganda and Ethiopia have to jump over bulls completely naked to prove they are men. In Papua New Guinea, boys from the Sambia tribe are separated from their mothers and subjected to a series of rituals, like having sharp grass pressed into their nose until it bleeds.

As Esther Perel put it during our social experiment, "We are born women; we become men." She explained, "There is no word for 'emasculating' for women, or 'sissy' for women. Men's masculinity is predicated on the rejection of the feminine in all societies." In Esther's research, she has found that almost every traditional society around the world "squeezes the fear and the vulnerability out of him to turn him into a man" and "feminine attributes are squeezed out of him so he can be fearless, competitive, powerful and strong."

The second thing I noticed was that hardly any of the men had discussed this with anyone before. All of the men who came to our table, with the exception of those who identified as gay, admitted they hadn't had this conversation with another man. The men I spoke to were doing exactly what they were taught to do: not ask for directions, even when it came to their emotional well-being and happiness. Shockingly, some were more comfortable sharing their vulnerabilities with two random women than with the closest men in their lives. What does that say about how transgressive it is to question or talk about masculinity for men? What started off as a random social experiment quickly became a safe space for men to share what scared and confused them, some for the very first time.

Because I'm part of the *Men Are from Mars, Women Are from Venus* generation, a book that attributed most of men and women's problems to innate biological differences between each other, I expected the biggest problem for men to be women. Given how much emphasis we put on so-called innate differences between the sexes as a barrier to healthy romantic or platonic relationships, I expected men to make a laundry list of all the ways that women drove them nuts. But within a few minutes of our social experiment, I quickly realized that for many of the men we talked to, the hardest thing about being a man was not necessarily dealing with women; it was dealing with other men. This came up with one of the first men we spoke to. He was British, in his midfifties, and seemed a bit taken aback when I asked him bluntly what was hard about being a man. But he didn't pause for very long before he earnestly responded: "Other men." When Esther pressed him to finish his sentence, he responded: "Expectations *about* men *by* other men." He explained that he felt the pressure of "being a leader" and to "have a point of view rather than not know." He also talked about feeling a pressure to speak rather than listen. The gay men we spoke to were even more explicit about the way they felt uneasy in environments where there were a lot of men. For them, the rules imposed by traditional masculinity didn't only make them feel personally uncomfortable; it made them feel unsafe around members of their own gender. One gay couple who came over to us explained that they found themselves constantly and subconsciously sweeping environments for men who could be a threat. "I'm scanning for other guys like me, so other gay guys, and women, and the other thing that I'm trying to look for is hypermasculinity, because those are the guys I want to avoid." They explained that this was the reason they primarily hung out with women. Although we were in the middle of the West Village in New York City, one of the most progressive cities in the world, the rules around what being a "real man" were a significant barrier to gay men freely existing in both private and public spaces.

No wonder men weren't able to be vulnerable about their fears— they're too busy pretending like they didn't have any. When I asked two young men who had recently moved from India to study at NYU, "Do you think masculinity is fragile?" one of them said, "Of course. There's so many expectations, and so many threads holding it together that could go wrong, if one thing [is] different, the whole thing collapses." In that moment it became clear to me that men are so busy maintaining the illusion that "ideal" masculinity is achievable that they have no real language to talk about the ways they were constrained by it. Idealized masculinity is the elephant in the room men have to simultaneously tame and yet pretend doesn't exist. Maintaining that balance between fighting feelings internally and hiding them externally seemed truly exhausting.

This social experiment changed everything for me. As I walked home from the park in the blistering heat I started looking at every man on the street differently, imagining him carrying an invisible shield or armor that most people, perhaps even himself, knew nothing about. I began to call it the man shield. I started trying to guess the shape, material and size of the invisible armor of men I would meet. I would try to show it to the men I would meet. Help them realize it wasn't serving them. The more they tried to hide their weaknesses, the heavier the armor was and the tougher it would be to let go of it.

One guy I was in a relationship with thought I was breaking up with him every time I would ask him to share his insecurities with me. Talking about what made him vulnerable or imperfect felt like an admission of guilt rather than an admission of growth. "I feel like you're looking for problems," he said, interrupting me one day after I asked him about his thorny relationship with his dad. "I know you're a journalist, but I feel like I'm on *60 Minutes*." He eventually came around to realizing that sharing what made him weak wouldn't make me run away; it would make us closer. But this made me realize that the bigger the armor, the less men were aware that it was even there and the harder it would be to help them notice it. This armor allowed men short-term relief from the pressures of masculinity, but the long-term consequences were catastrophic. I was determined to uncover this invisible shield not just with the men I dated but with every man I could reach. I became convinced that this was how we could fundamentally change the world.

2   Manhood Is Never Fully Earned and Needs to Be Renewed Over and Over Again

Once I started paying attention, I could see the pressure for men to prove their masculinity every place I looked. I noticed it everywhere: even in pizza. I became obsessed with a study that found that when male subjects were in the presence of women, they ate 93 percent more pizza. That's almost twice as much pizza eaten to (most likely unconsciously) impress women—because nothing turns women on more than a guy who is bloated and burpy and has pepperoni breath. Don't get me wrong; I love a man who can handle his carbs. Eating carbs together is one of my favorite bonding activities. But why do men feel the pressure to overeat—or, worse, unconsciously do so—to prove something?

Researchers from Cornell University explain these results by arguing that "men will engage in behavior that permits them to 'show off' that they possess extraordinary skills, advantages, and/or surplus energy in degrees that are superior to other men."

In fact, the researchers concluded that "conspicuous eating or overeating as yet another of the myriad activities through which men attempt to establish dominance hierarchies." If you're wondering, the female subjects in the study ate no differently whether they were in the presence of men or women. The pizza study illustrated the way men had adopted behaviors they might not even be aware of just to prove their masculinity. But what happens when, in the expected event that they try, they aren't successful? Bad things.

There are slightly innocuous ways that men will reaffirm their masculinity when it's threatened. One way is to lie. One study from the University of Washington showed that when men were told they scored lower than their actual strength on a handgrip strength test, they were more likely to distort a completely verifiable fact: their height. This baffled even the researchers of the study. In probably the most amazing subdued academic burn, lead author Dr. Sapna Cheryan said, "height is something you think would be fixed, but how tall you say you are is malleable, at least for men." In addition to inflating an observable visible characteristic, having their masculinity threatened made them more likely to report a higher amount of past romantic conquests, identify as more aggressive and athletic as well as stay clear of typically feminine consumer products, because nothing says real man like staying away from a pink razor.[1]

Another study by researchers at the University of South Florida made one group of men braid hair while a control group braided rope. The group that was given the traumatizing task of braiding human hair were more likely to want to hit a punching bag over making a puzzle and were more likely to punch the bag harder. "The most liberal, non-homophobic men in our studies were just as uncomfortable braiding hair as those who hold very traditional beliefs about gender roles," researchers said. "Men's anxiety about violating the male gender role is almost like a classically conditioned response. People have no control over it." The authors explained that being aggressive is a "manhood-restoring tactic" and that "women are not the main punishers of gender role violations." In other words, when men feel less strong, they have all kinds of ways to compensate for it. And most of this isn't conscious or intentional. Given that men are perpetually being told they are not tough enough, they find themselves in a vicious (and apparently carb-driven) cycle.

The studies I've just laid out may seem ridiculous, maybe even frivolous. But they're only the tip of the iceberg in terms of the strategies men use to compensate for this feeling of insatiable masculinity. When the handgrip study was published, the authors gave a stern warning in their press release to contextualize what their data revealed, because the consequences can go above men lying about how tall they are. For instance, the researchers pointed to data that shows that men with baby faces are more likely to display hostile behavior and commit crimes and that when men are told they score lower on masculinity tests, they are more willing to "act aggressively, harass women and belittle other men."

(No word yet on what kind of masculinity-restoring activities occur with men who are told they have small hands, but an interesting case study is currently unfolding in the White House.)

In all seriousness, "the pressure men have to broadcast their manhood at any cost" can have devastating effects. The authors even point to research showing that men who are unemployed are more likely to be violent inside the home. Another alarming study shows that when men are told they score lower on a masculinity scale, they are more likely to blame women for sexual assault.

"Men have a lot of power in our society, and what this study shows is that some decisions can be influenced by how they're feeling about their masculinity in the moment," Dr. Cheryan explained. This means the messages they receive about how much of a man they are, compared to what is expected, impact more than just their mood—it has wide-ranging implications that most men may not have even begun to scratch the surface of. It's hard not to see America's forty-fifth president in those statistics. It's no coincidence that a man who demands a folder of adoring headlines and tweets about himself is also responsible for some of the most overtly violent rhetoric in modern political history. It's hard not to see the link between

Trump's deep insecurities about his masculinity and his propensity to lash out to reclaim it.

While women's femininity can't be taken away so swiftly and they are largely given permission to transgress those expectations (we can wear pants; we can wear shorts; we can be tomboys), men don't have that luxury. But of course, the latitude to transgress applies to different groups of women unevenly. Straight, thin, white, cisgender, able-bodied women have more flexibility than women whose identities don't fit into those boxes. The less marginalized you are, the more accepting society is of you breaking norms, because it doesn't threaten an existing ruling system. Having an identity that fits into the dominant culture protects you. That's why a thin woman proclaiming her love for pizza on Instagram gets her attention and adoration, while an overweight woman doing the same thing invites concern. It also explains why it's fine when straight women kiss each other at clubs, but when queer women show affection in public spaces they risk harassment, discrimination or even death. Women's actions are accepted when the bending of expectations doesn't threaten the existing moral order: it exists within it. The thin woman can stuff her face all she wants as long as she stays tiny. The same concept applies with men bending gendered norms. If a man wears high heels at a Halloween party, it's fun, but if he wears them to work, it's "inappropriate." It's especially preposterous, given that high heels were originally invented and worn by men!

If you stop to really think about it, it's pretty extraordinary that we've decided here in the United States and many other industrialized countries that women can wear a skirt to a meeting, but men can't. Who decided that women and men can wear the same colors, the same materials, but that if there are a few little stitches in the middle separating the legs, it's unacceptable for men? What if we assigned similarly arbitrary rules to what women and men can eat instead of how they can dress? Saying men can wear pants but not skirts is like saying men can only eat square pizza because the round shape, well, that's just for girls. It would be absurd! Yet we accept gendered norms about clothing as truth. We don't ask questions because we assume it's just the way things are, but perhaps it's time to leave some of the rules about gender that regulate the lives of men that no longer serve us behind.

It could be fairly easy to eradicate oppressive norms, because in order to exist, norms need to be applied. A social norm is only powerful to the extent that people are willing to respect it. When a culture sets up specific rules about men, they don't need to be imposed by a higher power because men end up imposing them on one another. They police others in an effort to express their respect of the code that our culture has established.

Transphobia is a striking example of the way that masculinity-restoring activities can quickly escalate and become ritualized violence against others to prove something about themselves. Although there are all kinds of perceived threats to the male status quo, nothing rattles us quite like a man who is perceived to be acting like a woman. And that discomfort is clear in the way transphobia is directed toward trans women. "I think there is a specific kind of vitriol from cis men," my friend Robyn Kanner told me. As a trans woman, she noticed a more vindictive kind of rejection from her male friends after she transitioned. One close male friend in particular saw her identity as a threat to his. "He thought me being trans betrayed his manhood and our friendship," she told me. "My womanhood somehow invalidated his manhood. I tried to keep our friendship normal, but he just pushed and pushed me away." The way that she explained men's reaction to her is that she became what they had been taught to fear the most: a woman. Because men are constantly being messaged that the worst thing they can do is act or behave like a woman, Robyn embodying womanhood became intolerable for him. "Cis men have vitriol towards trans women because they see how a person like them could become something they resent becoming."

We see this reaction modeled in our popular culture. Men's back-lash against Caitlyn Jenner being recognized as one of the Glamour Women of the Year in 2015 was a stern reminder of the way trans-phobia and misogyny often combine forces and work hand in hand and deny the humanity of transgender people. "Was there no woman in America, or the rest of the world, more deserving than this man?" said James Smith, whose deceased wife had been one of the Glamour Women of the Year in 2001 after she was the only fe-male police officer to die in the 9/11 attacks. Smith was so incensed he returned his wife's award in protest. Joe Rogan has obsessively dedicated entire stand-up routines and episodes of his podcast to Caitlyn Jenner's genitalia. InfoWars "reporter" Joe Biggs described the military covering sex reassignment surgery as paying "$100,000 for some guy to chop his dick off and tuck it in." When men take huge issue with being forced to witness transgender people daring to exist within their vicinity, the focus of their rage is disproportion-ately toward trans women, the justification being that they are not acting like "real men." All transgender people are disproportionately marginalized and misgendered, but the weaponized vitriol reserved for transgender women, particularly those of color, feels particularly venomous when it's coming from cisgender men. Why are these men so bothered by what another human being chooses to do? Why do they perceive it as such a threat?

This profound discomfort with men having flexibility when it comes to gender performance is at best cumbersome and at worst lethal. The vast majority of people who kill trans women are cis men. And the murders of trans women are especially graphic. To name one particularly disturbing case, in 2016 a former navy sailor was found guilty of murdering Dee Whigham, a woman he was on a date with. After she revealed she was trans, he stabbed her 119 times, slashed her throat, took a shower and then left her for dead. This is only one of many cases that have been part of this rise in violence against trans women, particularly when it comes to women of color. When the number of reported murders of trans women almost doubled from 2014 to 2015, gender theorist Judith Butler told *Broadly* that we need to pay attention to the identities of those being murdered but also those doing the murdering. "Killing is an act of power, a way of reasserting domination, even a way of saying, 'I am the one who decides who lives and dies.' So killing establishes the killer as sovereign in the moment that he kills, and that is the most toxic form that masculinity can take," she explained. For Robyn, cis men's violence against trans women is a clear act of reasserting their manhood in the most quintessential masculine way possible. "They do it because it targets their masculinity—anytime their masculinity is targeted they go to the tool they have and know how to control: power."

3 Masculinity Is Under Attack

There are many symptoms of what I call the masculinity moral panic. The perceived fear of men acting like women is so strong that it's also used to bully cisgender men out of having a thoughtful, nuanced conversation about masculinity. When we create a cultural environment where men can't ask questions about masculinity, any interrogation of masculinity is interpreted as an admission that one is not a real man.

We've seen the panic take many forms. For instance, when Oregon University proposed holding a "healthy masculinities conference," conservative writer Todd Starnes warned that "universities across the fruited plain are trying to convince men to grow lady parts." As I'm writing this book, I'm noticing that Fox News host Tucker Carlson has been increasing the severity of his fearmongering, dedicating entire segments of his show to the idea that "men seem to be becoming less male." He even went so far as to launch a male-empowerment series, which coincidentally aired every week of Women's History Month in 2018, where Carlson concluded that men "are pretty close to being destroyed" by women because "manhood is under attack."

This is nothing new for the network, which has been quietly preparing for this moment by peddling a gender panic for years. One particularly memorable segment that aired on the morning talk show *Fox & Friends* back in 2014 with hosts Elisabeth Hasselbeck and Clayton Morris featured the colorful chyron "'Wussification' of Men: What Happened to Guys in America?" The segment included author Nick Adams telling viewers about the need to "educate everybody about the importance of being a manly man as opposed to being an effeminate metrosexual." In what seems to be a strangely accurate prologue to the 2016 election, when Hasselbeck asks him if this feminization of men is a "threat to national security," Adams argues that "wimps and wussies deliver mediocrity, and men win. And what America has always been about is winning." In one simple slogan: make masculinity toxic again.

But nothing makes the current new wave of the masculinity moral panic more undeniable than the practically overnight celebrity status of Jordan Peterson, a clinical psychologist and professor of psychology who became a bestselling author after publishing a book called *12 Rules for Life*. In the book, as well as in online lectures, Peterson hands out advice like "say only those things that make you strong" and instructs each member of his primarily young male audience to stop being "a girlie man." Peterson glorifies men who display aggressive behavior, arguing "the best men I've ever met are very dangerous." Peterson is opposed to encouraging men to practice more empathy, saying "there's nothing more horrible for children, and developing people, than an excess of compassion." But he *does* argue that women should have compassion for men they don't want to have sex with and that having sex with those men could prevent national tragedies. For instance, he asserted that the domestic terrorist who described himself as an incel who rammed his van into people on the streets of Toronto in the spring of 2018 could have been prevented if women agreed to have more sex with more men.

"The cure for that is enforced monogamy," Peterson told Nellie Bowles of *The New York Times* when he was asked about the incident. "That's actually why monogamy emerges." In addition to collectively blaming women for terrorist attacks like the one in Toronto, Peterson also manages to make women responsible for Hitler's and Stalin's genocides, positing that their mothers must *really* be the reason they executed and killed their own people. "Was something amiss in their crucial relationships?" Peterson writes in *12 Rules for Life*. "It seems likely, given the importance of the maternal role in establishing trust." As a serious intellectual, he has also taken a very important political stance against the Disney movie *Frozen* because of its radical agenda of letting female characters have this dangerous thing called agency. Peterson is skeptical that a princess can save herself, because consciousness is something that belongs to men. "In any case, it is certain that a woman needs consciousness to be rescued," he wrote in connection with the movie. "And, as noted above, consciousness is symbolically masculine and has been since the beginning of time."

He also opposed a Canadian bill mandating the use of transgender pronouns for transgender or nonbinary people. In a video that received millions of views where he is seen debating this issue at the University of Toronto (where he teaches), he complains, "I am not going to be a mouthpiece for language that I detest, and that's that!" before crossing his arms over his own body the same way my niece does when I won't let her dip her hot dog in her orange juice. According to a *New Yorker* profile, when a transgender student got the courage to come see him after a lecture one day and asked why he insisted on using the wrong pronouns, the student says that he answered, "I don't believe that using your pronouns will do you any good, in the long run."

In addition to receiving millions of hits online, Peterson's sold-out book tour has been composed of primarily young men who often wait in line for hours to speak with him. Currently, his book is Amazon's most read (and most sold) nonfiction book, which makes him one of the most read Canadian authors alive. Profiled by almost every single major newspaper and magazine, Peterson has been called "the most influential public intellectual in the Western world right now" by *New York Times* columnist David Brooks. Although Brooks calls Peterson's advice "harsh" he also claims that for "millions of young men, it turns out to be the perfect antidote to the cocktail of coddling and accusation in which they are raised."

To his credit, Peterson has tapped into the truth that men are lost, but he has capitalized on this moment to advise them to "toughen up" and double down on the ideology that got them here in the first place. In addition to believing that parents should raise their boys to pursue what I would call faux masculinity, Peterson believes that parents should avoid any discussion about equality with them. In fact, he advised parents to pull their kids out of school if their teachers dare teach them about the injustices that exist in the world. "If you have your children in a school and they talk about equity in his class and they talk about equity, diversity, inclusivity, white privilege, systemic racism, any of that, you take your children out of the class," Peterson told Tucker Carlson on Fox News. "They're not being educated; they're being indoctrinated."

The masculinity moral panic has long been an undercurrent of our cultural landscape, but because of the rising power and place of women's movements in popular culture it's been experiencing a new and stronger wave. The magnitude of anti–sexual assault movements like #MeToo and #TimesUp has seeded fear in the minds of young men that they are being discounted, replaced and denigrated, while women gain more momentum and recognition. This mirrors the same kind of backlash we are seeing as white supremacy is increasing as movements like #BlackLivesMatter get traction and white people are predicted to become a minority by 2045. The message these men seem to be absorbing is that if marginalized groups have more rights, they will have fewer, which is of course not at all how human rights work.

Because the fear of being emasculated is so potent, parents often end up pushing unhealthy ideals of masculinity on their own children because they are led to believe that this protects them. When I discussed this with a progressive and self-described feminist dad, he told me about a recent incident where he went to visit his parents with his daughter and son. When he saw his 5-year-old son holding the bouquet of flowers they had brought as a gift, he swiftly reprimanded him, ordering him to give them to his sister. The man said he felt bad doing it but felt like it was the right thing to do. Of course, as a father he isn't trying to harm his son; he's trying to save him from the abuse society reserves for boys who transgress the male code. The system works because it's not questioned. The system works because men think they are passing it down out of love, when of course denying boys the full experience of their humanity is what truly loving them would look like. The problem is not boys; it's us. Flowers don't harm boys; it's the labels we ascribe to those things that do.

When you take a moment to let it sink in that it's 2019, but we are still terrified of letting boys hold flowers, Jordan Peterson and other masculinity moral panic warriors as a phenomenon makes a lot of sense. Their voices are resonating with so many men because those men are experiencing real pain and they are in desperate need of guidance. It would be easy to assume that this speaks to the strength of Jordan Peterson's message, but unfortunately, it's nothing new. It's an old message—but it's now reaching a crowd that is desperate for a justification to explain the pain they are in. Ultimately, the masculinity moral panic speaks more to the sadness and need for guidance among young men—it offers a simple solution to a complicated problem.

The bill of goods it is selling is a short-term fix for men. The more nuanced and time-consuming project of challenging the system requires more energy, but it will also reap more rewards. Instead of offering a path to healing from noxious notions of masculinity, Peterson conditions his young male fans to further entrench themselves into it. Instead of persuading men to have compassion for themselves and others more, he is instructing them to lean into rugged individualism, fear and rigidity. Instead of embracing vulnerability, he instructs men to run away from it.

Although most of the feminist criticism around this masculinity moral panic is that it's insulting to women, I would argue it's just as insulting to men because it's rooted in a deep-seated lie about men: that they have no agency over their attitudes and behaviors. Which brings me to my next point.

4   Men Are Slaves to Their Bodies and Their Nether Regions

Let's get this out of the way right now: men and women share more commonalities than differences. The concept that we are more alike than we are different is called the Gender Similarities Hypothesis. It was coined and discovered by Janet Shibley Hyde when she performed a review of forty-six meta-analyses of peer-reviewed studies that examined sex differences. After closely studying dozens of research papers, she found that when it comes to psychological characteristics, women and men are more alike than they are different over the entire course of their lifetime.

Although she did find differences in motor performance (how far and how hard one can throw), she found almost insignificant differences in psychological traits like aggression, language ability and mathematical skills as well as assertiveness and self-esteem. Most interestingly, she found that in studies designed to suppress the importance of social norms, people were more likely to engage in the opposite way we would expect their gender to act. For example, when subjects were told their gender would not be identified in the results and wouldn't be known by researchers, men acted in ways that were more passive while women were more aggressive, implying that social perceptions shape our behavior and heavily restrict our perceived or actual freedom to act willfully.

Hyde's research prompted the American Psychological Association to release a statement warning against the dangers of extrapolation of biological differences. The APA, in reaction to Hyde's research, backed up her assertion that: "The claims [of gender difference] can hurt women's opportunities in the workplace, dissuade couples from trying to resolve conflict and communication problems, and cause unnecessary obstacles that hurt children and adolescents' self-esteem." The APA also argued that "studies show that one's sex has little or no bearing on personality, cognition and leadership" and that "Mars-Venus sex differences appear to be as mythical as the Man in the Moon."

But using biological essentialism to pigeonhole people into gendered behaviors is not new. In fact, it used to be fairly common and acceptable to assert that women's behaviors could be explained by their hormones. Although many people still believe that women are more emotional, hysterical and unstable because of their menstrual fluctuations, saying it publicly now causes quite the backlash. Believing in biological determinism has been around for a long time and it's always been a popular position both inside and outside of academic circles, but the false truths that it produces are dangerous. For instance, in 2008 when Bill O'Reilly posed the outrageously sexist question of what potential downsides of having a female president could arise, his guest Marc Rudov answered, "You mean besides the PMS and the mood swings?"

Although some people still believe this, at least now it's widely perceived as sexist to engage in that kind of dismissal of women's behavior and agency. But if it's unfathomable to blame a woman's behavior on her hormones, why is it *more* fathomable to blame a man's hormones for his? If we believe that women can experience hormonal fluctuations and still exert the self-control not to let it run their lives, why don't we think the same applies to men? If we stigmatize those who use biological determinism to make assumptions about women as a class, why do we tolerate it when it happens to men? Although we've spent time and energy debunking a lot of the myths about women's nature by defying stereotypes like the idea that women are not as rational or high achieving or as able to lead as men, what about the myths about men?

No hormone gets a worse rep than testosterone. The fact that men on average produce more testosterone than women is used to justify the worst social ills. Testosterone has been blamed for everything under the moon: theft, crime, violence—even the 2008 stock market crash. Neuroscientist, author and former Wall Street trader John Coates has argued that "testosterone shifts traders' risk profiles to become overly aggressive, causing bubbles," and advised that we put more women and older men in banks because they have a "very different biology with less testosterone." One article in *The Guardian* by columnist Tim Adams headlined "Testosterone and High Finance Do Not Mix: So Bring On the Women" argued that men should be ousted from the industry entirely because "hormonally-driven young men should not be left alone in charge of our finances." Although these might be well-intentioned arguments, it's hard to believe we are talking about full-grown adults and not children who have no choice but to act on every bodily and emotional impulse.

But the most persisting and damaging myth about testosterone is that it makes men predisposed to being violent.

The idea that men are biologically predisposed toward being more violent than women may be one of the oldest and most consistent lies we tell about men. One of the most egregious examples of that is how it's used to excuse rape. Evolutionary theorists have relied on the myth of a fixed male biology to explain why men rape women. Entomologist and evolutionary biologist Randy Thornhill seems to love this theory so much he dedicated a whole book to it! In *A Natural History of Rape: Biological Bases of Sexual Coercion*, Thornhill argues that men are evolutionarily adapted to rape women because the potential reward of reproduction is worth more than the costs of the harm to the victim. Of course, Thornhill fails to account for men who rape other men, as well as the many male victims of rape who are sexually assaulted by women. Still, this flawed perspective was called an "intelligent and eye-opening book with a noble goal" by professor of psychology and bestselling author Steven Pinker. It's also still taught in schools (I had a professor who made this part of our curriculum in college) and is still frequently peddled in popular culture.

But very little data actually shows that violence against women has anything to do with testosterone. Sex offenders don't have higher levels of testosterone than men who aren't, and there's no evidence showing that rapists who are castrated have lower sexual recidivism rates. Men who become violent with their partners do not have higher levels of testosterone than the regular population. In fact, scientists who have looked at the effects of altering hormonal fluctuations of domestic violence perpetrators have found that the far more effective solution to curbing abusers' behavior was to help change some of their damaging and deeply held beliefs, such as their sense of entitlement. When Thornhill's controversial book came out, many experts in his own field dissented with the theory. Dr. Patricia Adair Gowaty, a distinguished professor and an evolutionary biologist at the University of California, told *The New York Times* in a review of Thornhill's book, "As sociobiologists we have become enamored of some ideas in the absence of credible and critical data." Rape theories are "intuitively attractive and they fit many of the experiences we have," but she warned against the lack of "adequate scientific controls" in many of the studies. In other words, Gowaty argues that it's all too easy for her colleagues to "prove" the theories that they already believe are true, while ignoring the data that would disprove them.

To be clear, there is a link between violence and testosterone, but while scientists have tried to find a *causal* link between testosterone and violent behavior, their results suggest that testosterone is not the cause of violence, but it can be the result of it. In one study conducted by researchers at Knox College, men who were instructed to hold a gun had levels of testosterone increase one hundred times more than men who were asked to hold a game of Mouse Trap. Holding a gun even made men pour more hot sauce into a glass of water that researchers told them another man would be drinking. In other words, testosterone seems to follow rather than precede violent behavior. Testosterone plays a crucial role in triggering key developmental features, like facial hair, deepening of the voice and muscle growth (it's also, fun fact, produced by the ovaries and it's necessary for their proper functioning!), but there's no unanimous peer-reviewed evidence that it causes violent behavior.

We are not slaves to our hormones—numerous factors go into our choices; one of them is wanting to fulfill expectations. Some research is starting to show that other people's perceptions about our gender are better predictors of our violent behavior than our actual gender. One of the most fascinating examples of this is a study where researchers asked women and men to do a world-conflict simulation. When they were told that researchers knew the gender and name of the subject, women dropped fewer bombs than men, but when the subjects were granted anonymity, women actually dropped more bombs than the men. Maybe if we didn't reflexively expect and require women to be so peaceful, and men to be so violent, they would act very differently.

While there is a dearth of research proving that testosterone causes violent behavior, I'm not arguing that hormones and testosterone don't have an effect on men (or on women, for that matter). That would be ridiculous. But I do believe testosterone's toll on men's behavior has been enormously overblown and widely misrepresented in scientific research as well as in popular culture. Instead of teasing out the nuanced and perhaps even positive effects of testosterone, it's often used to justify the worst behavior in men. Research is starting to give us a much more complex understanding of its effects on the human body.

FORGET EVERYTHING YOU KNEW ABOUT TESTOSTERONE

For instance, researchers from Pennsylvania State University studied the effect of testosterone on men and found that "popular perceptions of the effect of testosterone on 'manly' behavior are inaccurate." The researchers urge the scientific community to address its bias in studies about testosterone and account for more variables and factors in the research that focuses on it: "We need to move away from such simplistic notions by treating testosterone as one component along with other physiological, psychological and sociological variables in interactive and reciprocal models of behavior." Their paper finds that testosterone alone can't explain men's behaviors, but that we need to incorporate the way testosterone is acted upon depending on social systems, arguing that "social environment plays a key role in understanding behavior-hormones associations." This mirrors research by the late Christoph Eisenegger at the University of Cambridge that concluded that the biggest impact of testosterone is not that it made men more physically aggressive but instead that it motivated men to be more competitive and eager to achieve higher social status. This explains why research shows that men's testosterone will rise during more passive activities like a game of chess, despite there being no physical element required for it, and why there is no testosterone difference between socially dominant but nonaggressive prisoners and physically aggressive prisoners. If testosterone predicted violent or aggressive behavior, you would likely see a difference between violent offenders and nonviolent offenders, but there is no testosterone difference between men who are attempting dominance through injuring others and those who don't. Maybe if we didn't generalize all men as inherently violent, we'd appreciate what makes so many deviate from the norm.

Although I encountered very few studies focused on the positive effects of testosterone on men (if anyone wants to fund one, please be my guest!), some are starting to show that it can lead to prosocial behavior. For instance, one German study conducted on ninety-one men found that being given a small dose of testosterone actually made men more honest. When they were instruced to play a game with a monetary reward and the researcher left the room, those who had received testosterone were less likely to cheat on the game and more likely to tell the truth than the control group. Researchers believe that because the financial reward was small, being found out to be a cheater was a greater threat to their social status than getting the money. Because testosterone is ultimately about competing for greater social status, it made the men more honest, not less. Another study found that giving men a small dose of testosterone made them more generous toward a negotiator with whom they were instructed to make a deal. Because being generous can be status enhancing, testosterone increased their kindness toward their collaborative negotiator. The researchers conclude that "a potential interpretation for our findings is that testosterone administration affects a concern for self-image [25], or pride [16]," i.e., it enhances behavior that will make a subject feel proud, and leads to the avoidance of behavior considered "cheap" or "dishonorable."

To put it simply, the way men are affected by testosterone depends on social perceptions and norms that we create; its effect is variable and heavily determined by our social environment. Testosterone encourages men to seek status, but the way one's ranking is defined is entirely up to us and the social norms we agree upon. If being more turbulent gives a man higher status, then this could make him more turbulent—and our society absolutely does reward this type of behavior. So, if we didn't assume that men are aggressive and, more importantly, we didn't expect or praise that conduct, testosterone could serve as an agent compelling men to engage in more prosocial behavior. Testosterone does make men more likely to compete and seek status, but it's the way they learn to do that which makes them violent. If we didn't reward or expect those behaviors, it's worth asking if men would be even on average more violent than women. Testosterone doesn't create behaviors, but it can make certain behaviors more likely, and a person's choice to engage in said behaviors is heavily associated with the social messaging they receive.

Although there is a lot of research on testosterone being associated with dominance through the lens of risk taking, there is little research untangling that from aggression. Most research lumps all of those things together, failing to isolate violence and competitiveness. It's a shame that most of the studies focused on testosterone seems to start from a negative framing about men. Most of the research out there assumes that competitiveness inherently leads to violence, which is just not always true in the modern civilized world. If more researchers were interested in the positive impacts of testosterone, perhaps we would come to very different conclusions about it and men's behavior.

But it's not all bad. Emerging data is starting to change the essentialist lies about testosterone. Researchers at the University of Michigan at Ann Arbor discovered that where a man is raised heavily influences his levels of testosterone. When they created an experiment where male subjects were accosted and insulted by a passerby, the men who were raised in the South were more likely to react aggressively and have an increase in testosterone than those raised in the North. The researchers' conclusion: testosterone doesn't make you fight; you release it when you feel like you need to fight. In many ways, it's the social environment that dictates biology, not the other way around.

And the effects are found across the world. Researchers from Durham University came to the same conclusion when they contrasted boys born and raised in Bangladesh with those born in Bangladesh but who moved to the UK as children. The researchers found that testosterone levels were determined by the subjects' social environment rather than their genetics. Boys who grew up in the UK consistently showed higher levels of testosterone. Researchers concluded that testosterone is not determined by biological factors but "instead reflect[s] their surroundings when they were children."

Further, although one's biological gender does not easily predict one's behavior, one's belief in biological essentialism sure seems to. Research shows that one of the easiest ways to predict one's tolerance of prejudice is not their gender, but rather how much they ascribe to biological essentialism. Research performed in Denmark and Australia shows that subscribing to the idea that men and women are biologically predisposed to act and think a certain way increases a person's likelihood of "predicted lack of support for sex-role egalitarianism and support for gender discrimination." The data also showed that "high essentialists were more likely to respond negatively towards a power-seeking female political candidate relative to a male candidate." Gender equality also seems to be a better predictor of each gender's preferences for the other gender. One mass survey performed in ten countries across the world shows that our preference for the characteristics that align with evolutionary theory fades away in societies that enjoy more gender equality. Using the Global Gender Gap Index (GGGI) showed that the more gender-equal a country was, the less people seemed pulled by what traditional determinist biology would predict. Men in Finland preferred a smart woman. Women in Germany preferred a man who can clean the house. In societies with less gender equality, both women and men put a prime value on more traditional characteristics. Embedded in the very theory of evolution is the idea that humans evolve in and are affected by their environments. Therefore, social environments shape our wants and needs and even what attracts us in a mate.

NO, THE PATRIARCHY IS NOT NATURAL

It's often assumed that evolutionary theory explains the existence of patriarchy as a main organizing principle in society, but the truth is that many evolutionary theorists do not see male dominance as inevitable. In fact, apart from humans and chimpanzees, male dominance is not found consistently across the animal kingdom. As Valerie M. Hudson argues in *Sex and World Peace*, male dominance is not innate in human societies—it was constructed during the shift from hunter-gatherer to agricultural production where resources, and therefore family members, became property. This justified the dominance of men over women, children, other men and of course nature, which becomes separate rather than a part of the beings who inhabit it. Patriarchy is not the natural order of things. It's not that we can't help it; in fact, it's the opposite: we helped create it, which means that change is not only possible, it's probable.

Another lie we tell about men is that their brains are only partially responsible for their behavior because their private parts have their own agenda. Robin Williams summed up this popular notion when he said, "The problem is, God gave man a brain and a penis and only enough blood to run one at a time." Annie Potts, an associate researcher at the University of Canterbury School of Humanities and Creative Arts, calls this the myth of "the man with two brains." In her book *The Science/Fiction of Sex*, she argues that it shows up often in popular culture with expressions like "thinking with your dick" or even "boys will be boys," but she writes that "this 'penis-brain' culturally invested with a primal 'carnal' intelligence, operates in contrast to, and thereby resists, the man's rational cerebral thought." This emphasis on essentializing gender differences down to biology makes the narrative that boys and girls are from different planets the only acceptable narrative. After all, *Men Are from Mars, Women Are from Venus* was the bestselling nonfiction book of the 1990s. It's seen as the defining book for relationships between men and women. It's responsible for re-entrenching in popular culture the myth that women and men are fundamentally different because of biological differences and was written by John Gray, who had a degree in meditation and took one correspondence course in psychology.

THE LIES WE TELL ABOUT TESTOSTERONE MATTER

Massively popular pseudoscience that asserts unchangeable differences between men and women worries neuroscientists because it becomes a self-fulfilling prophecy. Because we believe these are innate differences, children learn that they are expected to exhibit certain traits and then go on to exhibit them. "People say men are from Mars and women are from Venus, but the brain is a unisex organ," said Lise Eliot, professor of neuroscience at the the Chicago Medical School of Rosalind Franklin University of Medicine and Science, while speaking at the Aspen Ideas Festival. "The default assumption is that these differences are hard-wired . . . But male and female brains are not much [more] different from each other than male or female hearts or kidneys." Neuroscientists have found that since the brain is so malleable, especially in children, those small differences are exacerbated and exaggerated by the way we socialize children differently.

Eliot finds that boys are not less emotional or empathetic than girls; they simply show less ability and comfort expressing those emotions because they are encouraged not to. Her research finds that social interactions have a lasting impact on the shaping of our brains. This means that regardless of gender, our brains are not as hardwired as we previously thought. When *Men Are from Mars, Women Are from Venus* was written, the field of neuroplasticity had not entered the mainstream discourse, but now that we know the brain can change itself, claims that we are trapped by our own behaviors are ludicrous.

The biggest irony is that although masculinity panic warriors aggressively instruct men to be "tough" and take personal responsibility for their lives, isn't the ultimate passivity suggesting that men are victims of their supposed brain wiring and can't change? As Eliot told *The Guardian,* "There is almost nothing we do with our brains that is hard-wired. Every skill, attribute and personality trait is molded by experience." Although masculinity panic warriors claim men can overcome weakness and failure, they do not think men have the same flexibility or endurance to change the wiring of the gender stereotypes they've learned. I think Deepak Chopra said it best when he said "most people think that their brain is in charge of them. We say we are in charge of our brain." Isn't that what true freedom for men could look like?

*Sex is the language through which men have license
to ask for love, tenderness, surrender, sensuality,
affection and more.*

—ESTHER PEREL

5   Men Don't Need Intimacy

The penis-brain myth isn't just untrue; it also fuels another dangerous common gender stereotype: that women crave intimacy and men
just want sex. It leads to two kinds of shaming behaviors: women
are shamed for wanting sex and men are shamed for asking for intimacy. Sex and intimacy are both essential parts of the human experience. To say that women love to snuggle and talk while men just
want sex is simply not true.

But the idea that men are exclusively after as much sex as possible isn't only reinforced in movies and films—perhaps the ones most
responsible for perpetuating this idea are those who work in the
field of evolutionary psychology. One of the most commonly believed evolutionary truths about men is the "scatter-gun" theory,
which argues that men are on a quest to drop their seed in as many
women as possible, while every woman is looking for a stable partner
who will provide for her offspring. It's born out of Darwin's theory of
sexual selection, which he argued made women more "coy" and
choosy, while men have far fewer standards because they have less to
lose. This concept is often peddled by masculinity panic warriors and
is known within evolutionary psychology as the Bateman principle,
named after a geneticist who proved this theory by studying . . . fruit

flies. Although it's still highly regarded, the theory has been called into question by numerous researchers, primarily women (go figure), who are still a very small minority in the field (go figure). One of the scatter-gun theory skeptics is Dr. Zuleyma Tang-Martinez, a professor at the University of Missouri–St. Louis. "Bateman's conclusions and predictions have become axiomatic and, at times, have gone unquestioned even when modern empirical data do not conform to this model," she wrote.

This stereotype goes so far that we don't just believe that men want more sex; we also believe that all male species want more sex, even though this is a gross exaggeration and simplification of the wide range of differences across the animal kingdom. A lot of this is coming from popular culture, but it's fueled by evolutionary science, a field still overwhelmingly dominated by white men. Biologist and author Joan Roughgarden summed up her male colleagues' choices of research to the BBC by saying "it's almost like they are using this locker-room logic—counting which males 'score' the most." Roughgarden has been highly critical of the oversimplification of human behavior and sex differences as immutable. She remarks that sex differences are not as large as some research suggests and that in trying to preserve this narrative, the diversity of the animal kingdom is significantly flattened and underappreciated. Dr. Tang-Martinez, who dissents from many of her colleagues, warns about the often-unacknowledged phenomenon of "confirmation bias" among her colleagues in the fields of neuroscience and biology, where researchers end up commissioning and performing research that confirms what they already believe to be true, which is of course shaped by the social environment they were themselves raised into.

The men-want-all-the-sex myth isn't just untrue; it fuels the idea that men don't need other forms of physical or psychological intimacy. While it's often widely assumed that men want more sex and that women want more emotional intimacy, if the data could talk it would say something a little more nuanced. The way society controls women's bodies and female sexuality is widely documented and difficult to refute. From the Salem witch trials, to chastity belts and promise rings, to male politicians curbing access to abortion and access to birth control, it's not shocking that women have developed a discomfort around asking for sex. But on the other side of that coin, and somewhat less widely discussed, is how men frequently feel uncomfortable asking for affection. Besides the fact that we expect men to always be up for sex (pun definitely intended), if we don't always give men the space to ask for or experience emotional intimacy, physical contact can become the most acceptable way for them to express or receive love. In either case, men and women aren't asking for what they want.

In other words, she suppresses her own needs because she's taught that the needs of others are more important—he suppresses his needs because he's taught he doesn't have any.

Although some would argue that the male demand for sex workers powering the sex industry proves the veracity of this myth, sex workers frequently cite that the biggest part of their job has nothing to do with sex at all. Janet Mock, who has been open about her experience in the industry, said that stripping was much more emotional labor than physical work. In her book *Redefining Realness,* she says her job was more about "crafting open roads in conversation that would stimulate him, inflate his ego and make him feel centered and listened to." In an interview for *The New York Times,* she says: "Everyone talks about the tricks that we were doing, which was great and glamorous and looked like a Nelly video. But for clients, it was more about the quiet stuff: sitting and letting someone rub your thigh, and you nodding and listening."

If we accept the premise that many men are at least in part seeking sex workers for intimacy, it's no surprise that a new booming market is one that took the sex out of sex work: the cuddle industry. It's real and it's sort of like Uber for snuggles. Someone meets up with you and will nuzzle you for a set amount of time for a set amount of money. The rules are that it must be consensual and explicitly nonsexual. Although women are known for loving to cuddle, most of the clients seeking out the service aren't ladies; they're straight men in their fifties. To say that women love to cuddle and men want sex is simply not true. One study from the Kinsey Institute in Bloomington observing the preferences of ten thousand heterosexual couples also found that kissing and hugging was more important to men than to women in relationships. So perhaps we are more alike than we are different: we are all seeking human touch. If women aren't given permission to want sex and men aren't given permission to want intimacy, then how do we know what everyone *actually* needs?

And the myth that men don't need intimacy impacts the way that men approach sex. "Sex is still largely defined by men," masculinity professor Michael Kimmel told me over Cobb salad one afternoon. "If you're not sure, just look at the terms we use to define it," he explained as he scooped a bit off his plate. "I nailed her; I hit that; we banged . . . They're all violent." Dr. Kimmel explained that sex is often pursued as a form of conquering: "I scored!" he exclaimed. Of course, implicit in the language is that if one conquers, the other is therefore defeated. What a sad way to view the most natural and intimate act human beings share.

Kimmel's point about the violence and conquering embedded in sexual pursuits for men was echoed in the conversations I had with men, but what I found fascinating was how much and how many men confessed hating the language that they had themselves used. "I still catch myself stuck in some of the negative sometimes violent metaphors from my teenage socialization," Wim Laven told me over Facebook when I asked men about this myth in a public thread. "The language is a pretty good example, not just the words used like 'score' and 'tap' but the words not used. I still can't think of more than a handful of times I've heard a guy use the words 'make love' when talking with another guy. [Sex] is always a discussion of a physical and non-emotional act." The framing of sex as an act of conquering didn't only lessen the act of sex; it also impacted men's own enjoyment of it. Men told me that in order to have any conversation about sex they found themselves squeezing any of the intimacy it has from it.

Men in the thread also complained that idealized masculinity had brainwashed them into focusing exclusively on quantity at the cost of the quality of their sex life. "As a younger man, I believed a lot of the extremely toxic 'numericals' that are a part of sexuality for most men," Patrick Davis said. "IE, 'how many girls did you f*** last year, etc.?' or even how many times you had sex in a given night or weekend." And of course, the way men *talk* about sex impacts the way they *have* sex. Men talked about being wrapped into the ideal of the right or manly way to have sex, whether it was in the size of their erection, the intricacy or number of positions, rather than being present during the act, which honestly would probably increase enjoyment for both partners. "To be honest, you're thinking as much about how much you're going to brag about the sex than actually enjoying it," Patrick said. Sadly, because of the dynamics that traditional masculinity sets up, many men approach sex as something to get from a woman rather than give to a woman. As Michael Kimmel put it to me:

> For so many straight men, sexual adequacy is measured by whether or not she comes (he takes his pleasure for granted). But does that mean he is as selfless as she is? No!! So much of women's sexuality is organized around her relationship to HIM. So much of men's sexuality is organized around his relationship with . . . other men. Sex is often homosocial competition. Women are, in this model, the currency of the male conversation. So instead of him being focused on himself— which would at least be about a sense of self, however selfish, it's more that he is outside of his own pleasure, trying mightily (and often vainly) not to feel so much that he comes, trying

to prove that he is a great lay by making her come, and all the while thinking about his rising status among his bros.

This male anxiety about performance in sex is reflected in the online searches men make. Men Google information about their penis more than any other body part. "Will my penis shrink?" was the most researched age-related concern for men. While many women certainly care about girth, for every one woman who Googled something about penis size, 170 men did.

From my conversations with men it seemed that while sex was an omnipresent and required part of manhood, because traditional masculinity didn't allow any real conversations about it, it created barriers to enjoying the act that's supposed to be a fundamental part of being a man. Men said it prevented them from having a rich relationship to sex. "Toxic masculinity doesn't have open discussions about what sex is, how to please your partner, how to find the right partner," one user wrote. "Toxic masculinity keeps people from talking, keeps people from reflecting on their own sexuality and emotional needs. Toxic masculinity is the utmost devolved form of the male psyche and it doesn't want to nurture or empower those around them. It is egoic, and it takes and it gives nothing back." Men also said that they felt like this culture of conquering meant that they used sex for personal gain or as a form of currency to gain status with other men, which explained why so many women reported feeling used in the context of sexual intimacy. "I have had periods in life, particularly after a divorce, where many women (unfortunately) paid for my hurt and anger," one user explained. "Those sexual interludes were void of intimacy."

As I listened to men describe their insecurities and their inability to share them with other men and how it affected their presence in the bedroom, it explained a lot of the frustrations I heard from women. One of the most frequent complaints I received from the heterosexual women I spoke to was that their male partners felt disconnected during sex. They didn't feel present in the act and focused on what to *do* to their partner rather than how to *be* with their partner. Women told me that the men they sleep with often treated them as unidimensional, as if all women enjoyed the same thing in the same way, when in fact what works for one woman may not work for another. The truth is having sex with a woman is a lot like driving a car: it's important to pay close attention to sounds, bumps and signals. But repeatedly, I kept hearing from women that the men they were intimate with weren't tapping into those signals because they were focused on their own performance. So ironically, it seemed like because straight men were so focused on having great sex, they were having a lot of bad sex, at least from her perspective.

> *Shame corrodes the very part of us that believes we are capable of change.*
>
> —BRENÉ BROWN

6   Male Shame: What Is It Like to Feel Like You Need to Prove Something You Never Quite Feel Like You Have?

When the expectations set by society for men are rooted in lies, it creates expectations they can't fulfill. Through my conversations with men, it became clear that the most common consequence that all the masculinity myths share could be summed up in one word: "shame." Men felt shame that they weren't attaining the unrealistic tenets of masculinity, and that shame was rarely discussed among themselves because that's precisely how shame works. In other words, shame creates lies about how men should think and act, and when men don't reach these impossible expectations they feel additional humiliation. The best way for me to put it is that traditional masculinity creates a male shame spiral.

The experience of male shame starts early. A Perry Undem survey showed that three-quarters of boys reported feeling they have to prove that they are physically strong and play sports and that 82 percent of them reported hearing a man in their family or their peers humiliating a boy by telling him he's acting like a girl. A third felt a pressure to hide their emotions if they felt sad. Given this intense pressure, it's no surprise that research on 343 male college students published in the *Psychology of Men & Masculinity* journal showed that when men experience gender role conflict, defined as the gap between how they view themselves as men and what society expects of them as men, they experience heightened levels of shame.

The way we raise boys creates shame that leads to inevitable dysfunction into adulthood. This became clear when I asked men about how these masculine ideals impacted their adult relationships, particularly with women. "Shame. That's what defines you when you try to deal with women," Hilmar Bjarni Hilmarsson wrote. "Shame if you don't provide enough, or if you feel weak or even just feel too much. Shame that you need them but shame if you don't have one by your side either if you're single. Shame when you think of what you've done, in the past, when you didn't know what you do know. A lot of shame." When I asked him how that showed up, Hilmar said it came from feeling like failure was not an option. "It's shame or anger really, but the anger usually is feeding off the former. And because men aren't allowed to admit to failure, because the matter of their failure is shameful, they keep it locked inside. That lays heavily on many of us, where we keep silent rather than talk about it because we even lack the language and concepts to articulate our pain at being perpetrators and enablers of something we understand hurts us and others but can't seem to stop," Hilmar said.

In other words, idealized notions of masculinity didn't just encourage men to repress their emotions; it created shame around feeling them in the first place. "I am guilty of self-censorship when it comes to openly displaying emotion," Brad, a commenter, said. "When my wife asks me how I feel about something, I lack even the basic vocabulary or recognition beyond superbasic stuff like 'frustrated,' 'bored' or 'yeah—I like that.'" Another commenter, Toby Morgana, who identifies as trans, wrote that he learned a lot about the pressures of being a man when he transitioned. "During the early months of my transition, I thought being a man meant heavy drinking and speaking over everyone," he wrote. "I was engaging in a lot of posturing and trying to seem like nothing was wrong." Brian echoed a similar sentiment: "Guys in my family were basically expected to suppress everything else. My 77-year-old father now refers to me as the sensitive one in our family. Sometimes I think it's a dig and other times I think he's envious." Men's lives were rooted in so much covering up that I wondered if they even knew all the things they had been hiding all this time. For many men, coming to terms with the way they were brought up opened their eyes to all the repressed feelings that had been inside of them all along. As Ashton Hynes put it, "When you understand toxic masculinity, it's like that 80's movie where the guy gets those glasses that allow him to see monsters all around him he never noticed, you know?"

This idea that masculinity mysteriously strips away the basic human need for vulnerability, closeness, intimacy and connection is not only untrue; it also leads to an internalization of shame when men have those needs and an inability to properly manage them. This means that some of the aggression we associate with men may not be due to their nature; it's due to the way we raise them. The patriarchy doesn't just convince men that they don't have emotional needs; it also leads men to feel embarrassed when those needs naturally occur, which leads those feelings to come out in other, less productive ways. This is clear from the research. One study on male college students found that a fear of emotion was correlated with increased likelihood of aggression and hostility. In other words, men and boys end up expressing more aggression because they lack the social permission to express their emotions in the first place. Showing violence becomes more acceptable than showing feelings. The conclusion from the researchers was that gender role socialization encouraged men not to show emotion and made them less tolerant of uncomfortable emotions and less likely to handle them.

In order to indoctrinate men into being "tough," we teach them to deny parts of themselves. And keeping things in is glamorized so that men are obedient to the code and stay quiet. We all grow up being taught that a cool and collected man keeps emotions on the inside, so bottling up feelings and thoughts becomes a practice so common and so ingrained that it becomes second nature. I think many men can spend their entire life not even knowing what emotions they're hiding. Shame is both the connection and the consequence between all these myths because what shames us ends up defining us. The idealized masculinity pact is a vicious cycle. It makes men feel shame and then enforces the omertà rule making that shame impossible to talk about. And this all comes back to men's inability to ask for directions. If you spend your whole life being told you aren't allowed to get lost, going deeper into the woods becomes easier than admitting you're going the wrong way.

To learn more about male shame, I turned to Brené Brown, who is considered the foremost expert on the topic as one of the few academic researchers who has observed and researched it extensively. Brown distills shame down to a fear of one thing: disconnection. As humans, she argues, we are all hardwired for physical and emotional connection, but shame convinces us that we need to hide certain parts of ourselves to preserve connection and avoid rejection. But just like fire needs oxygen, shame needs silence to grow. The less shame is talked about it, the stronger it becomes. "The less you talk about it, the more you got it," Brown told Oprah on an episode of *Supersoul Sunday*, that I've listened to roughly 17 times. "Shame needs three things to grow exponentially in our lives: secrecy, silence and judgment." All three of these elements had shown up in my conversations with men. The fact that male shame is not often discussed makes it that much more powerful and harder to shake.

While women experience a whole host of shame that comes from expectations placed on their gender like motherhood, racialized beauty ideals, having the perfect slim yet large-breasted body, always being pleasant and smiling for others, we've started having ongoing and fairly public conversations around these unrealistic ideals. Women have begun to develop the language to have those conversations. The way traditional masculinity hurts men is slipped under the rug, so men don't talk about it and it, therefore feeds that shame loop. Masculinity, under its current definition, is antithetical to vulnerability, the element that Brené Brown says is essential to a functioning and successful relationship. Because men can't show vulnerability, they can struggle to develop healthy relationships with themselves or others. "Through my research, I found that vulnerability is the glue that holds relationships together," Brown says. "It's the magic sauce." But men are not expected to be vulnerable; they are expected to be strong, and our culture has determined that those two words are antonyms rather than synonyms.

The other reason men are silent about feelings is because the realm of emotions is still not considered their prerogative. Being a man is still almost exclusively defined by bringing material stability, and emotions can almost be seen as an obstacle to that security. We'll be talking more about this when we discuss fatherhood later in the book, but the focus on men materially providing for others as a focal way to understand manhood is what prolific feminist author Susan Faludi calls "ornamental masculinity." It's a superficial and stereotypically macho ideal that depends on capitalistic values of athleticism and aggressive domination. She compares it to the ornamental femininity described by Betty Friedan in *The Feminine Mystique* that was rooted in stereotypical ideals of white feminine materialistic domesticity and subservience. "Men don't want to live in a world run on retail values any more than women do," Faludi has said. "Like women, they want to be needed and useful participants in society." But if your value is dependent on economic rather than emotional stability, how does that translate into a world where economic resources are precarious?

When you combine men's identity being defined by how many material resources they can accumulate and how rarely they ask for help, you get a pretty dark cycle of shame that can lead men to engage in extreme isolation. Although there isn't enough academic research on shame, let alone the specific way that men may experience it, according to a growing number of researchers and mental health experts, it is more corrosive than other human emotions because it leads to withdrawal, which can have dramatic consequences and creates a vicious cycle of further detachment. Shame is not just a feeling; it's a barrier to functioning. It doesn't just make you feel bad; it makes you dysfunctional. Shame creates lies about how men should think and act, and when men don't fulfill those roles, they have additional shame. We see it play out in one of the greatest and most-ignored crises of our times: homelessness. We largely see it as an economic problem, because it is. It's a result of a lack of economic mobility and opportunity as well as a housing crisis, but it's also enabled by the lies we tell about men.

When I tried to find data about the link between shame and homelessness, I came across almost nothing. When I researched homelessness, an issue that is twice as likely to impact men as women, I was shocked to find that very little research has been dedicated to the intersection of masculinity and shame, despite the fact that the number one reason[1] homeless people don't seek out the support of friends or family is "because they were too embarrassed about being homeless." In fact, even research that investigates the link between gender and homelessness is rare.

Part of the reason for the lack of research is because homelessness doesn't receive the academic research and attention it deserves. It's even worse at the policy level. Very rarely do we hear politicians discuss their plan to address homelessness as a main plank of their campaign. If we just take the 2016 election as a sample, Hillary Clinton had a plan for homeless veterans and youths, but it wasn't a front-facing topic like many other issues in her campaign. Donald Trump didn't have a single policy proposal addressing homelessness, and when two of his supporters beat up and urinated on a homeless man's face, he didn't even immediately condemn it. Self-described Trump supporters Scott and Steve Leader, both in their thirties, stole the man's blanket and sleeping bag and broke his nose with a metal pipe. While in jail, one of the brothers said it was "okay to assault" the victim, because he "was Hispanic and homeless." I tried to find one single presidential debate where homelessness was addressed and I couldn't find any. Although there are 554,000 homeless people in the United States, they are rarely seen as a voting bloc because many of them never make it to the ballot box, often because they don't have the proper ID that the state requires.

Although homelessness cuts across all socioeconomic and ethnic groups, the majority of homeless people are single men. In fact, single men are one of the fastest-growing demographics in groups of homeless people. While family and veteran homelessness is on the decline, single-male homelessness is actually increasing. According to governmental data, 51 percent of homeless people are single men, 25 percent are women with children and the rest tend to be families. Since 2001, there's been a 40 percent drop in homeless veterans because of the attention of Veterans Affairs to correcting the situation. Single men haven't received that kind of national policy attention, despite the fact that states like Hawaii and many counties in California have declared states of emergency because of the explosion in their homeless populations in recent years.

Given the high incidence of men who end up in the streets, it's curious that so little research is interested in understanding why men are more vulnerable to becoming homeless. So I went looking for answers by speaking to my friend Kevin F. Adler. In addition to being a sociologist and author, he's the founder of Miracle Messages, an award-winning volunteer-led organization that helps reconnect homeless people with their friends and families by assisting them in recording a message for someone they lost touch with. After a person experiencing homelessness agrees to record their message, the team of "digital detectives" attempts to locate those friends and family members to show them the video and let them know that the homeless person wants to reconnect. They also have a paper-based form and built a 1-800-MISS-YOU hotline to assist with reunifications.

Kevin, whose own uncle experienced homelessness, built his organization around his theory of what he has termed "relational poverty" on the streets: "That homeless people are not problems to be solved, they're people to be loved." Although more affordable housing is the most crucial way to curb homelessness, Kevin argues that many people who live on the streets have social networks, but can't access them out of shame about their situation. "Many are single adult men, and many of these individuals are incredibly isolated, and lonely," he told me. "When we ask them if they want to reconnect and they record a message, the most common reason why they change their mind is 'I feel dirty,' so, in other words, an internalized sense of shame, fear, self-loathing and a result that they feel like they're not lovable and don't want to put that burden or shame on their family." The little bit of research I could find confirmed that shame is a significant moderating factor that prevents men from reaching out to the very support systems they need. A study by Micheal L. Shier, Marion E. Jones and John R. Graham (2011) found that it's common for homeless people to cite embarrassment as a reason for not getting in touch with their support networks. Given this internalized shame, it's no surprise that the average time apart for clients Kevin reconnects is twenty years. He says it takes them on average less than a month to locate the homeless person's loved ones and 82 percent of the time they are excited to reconnect. When I asked Kevin what was the number-one cause of homelessness, he mentioned the lack of affordable housing, the rising cost of housing, wage stagnation, income inequality, mass incarceration and the lack of support for mental health and addiction issues. But Kevin also emphasized shame and how relational poverty is often forgotten.

"Shame keeps people from engaging in resources that may help them overcome problems."

One of the few research papers about masculinity, shame and homelessness was written by a doctoral student at the University of Iowa, Kevin L. Fall. He wrote that shame is both central and rarely an admitted factor in the homelessness crisis, particularly when it comes to men. His research finds that "shame appears to be a dominant theme in homelessness," and that "beginning in early childhood, shame seems to play a contributory role that directs children toward a path of homelessness."

Fall describes it as a shame loop that renders a lot of men helpless in the face of homelessness:

> Painful shame feelings lead to one of two coping strategies. Men may either isolate (i.e., social withdrawal or avoidance) or act out in masculine ways that can include compulsive work, substance abuse or aggression. When men adopt maladaptive coping strategies, they encounter difficulties in interpersonal and emotional conflict that further intensify feelings of shame and reinforce one's sense of inadequacy, thus contributing to the aversive cycle.

It's especially sad when you think about the way homeless men are portrayed. They are called hobos, bums and worse. Many of these words are often said to their face. Jordan Peterson, who advises men to "avoid helping people with things they can do for themselves," mocked a tweet by then-premier of Ontario, Kathleen Wynne, because she called affordable housing something that people deserve. This kind of thinking portrays homeless people as lazy or violent when very often they've been victims of violence themselves. In fact, homeless people are thirteen times more likely to have been victims of violence than people who are housed. Although there are many causes of homelessness, lack of parental support and childhood trauma can often lead to homelessness later in life. In fact, child abuse and trauma can often be a precursor to homelessness. One sample of 212 homeless men found that 36.8 percent had been physically abused, 10.8 percent had been victims of sexual violence and 19.3 percent had experienced a combination of both. If you have been incarcerated, you are also much more likely to become homeless. Being incarcerated for twenty-seven days means you are 11.5 times more likely to have experienced homelessness.

Given how important it is for men to be providers—this is often the defining characteristic for men—it follows that when they are unable to fulfill that expectation, they experience the kind of shame that throws them into isolation. When I think about Jordan Peterson's attitude toward homeless men, it makes me furious. In fact, it's not just his comments about homelessness per se but also the entire model that Peterson spews about what a "real man" is that exacerbates the gap between the current life of a homeless man and the expectation he has of what a man should be. For many of these men, the shame is paralyzing. And hiding on the streets with that shame may become an easier alternative than having to show themselves to the people they love, people who often miss their family members and desperately want to reconnect. The shame of being lost shouldn't prompt men never to ask for help.

How powerful of a vector shame can be became clear to me when I spoke to Charles Lyons, a 25-year-old young professional who works in project management in New York City. He told me that shame was central to his reluctance to ask for help when he found himself homeless over the course of a cold East Coast winter eight years ago when he was only 17 years old. He had a difficult childhood in rural New Jersey, where he grew up witnessing violence and abuse. When his family was evicted from their home a week before Christmas, he slept in his car in a Walmart parking lot. Although he was crest-fallen to be spending Christmas Eve alone in his car, he remembers looking at the pine tree air freshener hanging on his rearview mirror as a reminder that at least he had a symbolic tree. "I could have asked for a place to stay with my friends, but I didn't want to ruin their holidays," he told me when we grabbed coffee. Now that he is housed, he has chosen to dedicate his life to helping those who aren't. He's spent the last few years helping the homeless and disenfranchised find jobs, and he noticed something interesting: it was primarily women who seemed comfortable enough to ask him for assistance. "I've hardly ever had a man directly ask me for help to get a job," he explained. "I've had many women call me crying, desperate for a job, but men will often ask rather indirectly." Charles says that's born out of the way society shapes us that "views women as incapable and views men as supercapable." He says we tell men, "You're a man; go figure it out," and this in turn often means "people are less likely to provide assistance to a man." He remembers absorbing this very mantra when he was homeless. He didn't think about *who* could help him; he just thought about *how* he was going to help himself. "I didn't think who can I turn to . . . it was like I gotta figure this out somehow," he explained. "Pride plays a very big role from a very young age. . . . Men are told that if you don't have anything, well, at least you have your pride." He also noted the link between men's identity and their work. While women often are desperate for work, it's to provide for their children; for men he noticed it was related to their sense of self-worth and identity. "When we have no work, we have no purpose," Charles said.

Let's be clear: while shame perpetuates the cycle of homelessness, it's not the primary contributing factor. That would be a gross oversimplification. Homelessness is a systemic problem that receives a fraction of the consideration and airtime it deserves from policy makers and the general public, and what those who aren't housed want above all else is access to affordable housing. Nonetheless, the data points to the role of shame perpetuating and exacerbating the crisis, so this aspect deserves more attention, too.

When we don't think about male shame we are not productively addressing the world's biggest problems, because many of them are rooted in that shame or exacerbated by it. According to Brené Brown, shame can start to dissipate through the act of talking about it. As she poignantly wrote, "Self-disclosure helps heal pain." In other words, the more we talk about our shame, the more it dissipates because it can no longer hide. Shame's ability to warp the universal truths about gender is as powerful as our refusal to address those myths. If we were to discuss and challenge the myths that dictate men's lives, perhaps men would realize that the shame they're carrying was never theirs to begin with.

> *The strongest men are the ones that*
> *also understand their weaknesses.*
>
> —VICTOR PINEDA

AMUSE-BOUCHE:
Victor's Story

The minute I met Victor, I knew he was a ladies' man. Charismatic, confident and flirty, he hit all the playboy boxes. Yet he tells me it still surprises him when people refer to him as "alpha" or a "wolf pack leader." Victor lives with a disability, which means he gets around in an electric wheelchair and uses a machine to help him breathe. Although he's not society's image of a prototypical woman-izer, I can tell you from experience, he's always the most charming man in the room.

"I project and learned to project some type of strength because I have a physical weakness," he said to me. Knowing that people would make assumptions about his body, he compensated for it with a rock-hard psyche. "Because I weigh ninety pounds and have thin arms and thin legs, there is a perception that I am fragile and weak or in-capable. There has to be for me a moment where I can project strength in order to circumvent the pejorative social construct that would limit what I can do." Victor knows he's not alone. "A lot of men with disabilities have to confront this idea that they don't see us as sexualized or fully human."

Victor developed a strong sense of self to make him immune to societal perceptions about disability. "I don't have the typical male body that you see in magazines, underwear commercials, billboards, but it doesn't mean that I don't feel like my body is attractive, beautiful and able to feel desire and pleasure. Masculinity is anything you want it to be. The problem is when you think it's prescriptive."

Victor wants more men to get to know themselves. "I think most men are oblivious to the multiple identities and cultures they carry," he explained. "We need to be able to have a space to find our most authentic selves by being aware of things that we might be carrying." He recently joined a men's circle that encourages males to get together and discuss the issues they grapple with. "If you want to create a conscious intentional identity, you need these spaces. You can't adapt an identity without being aware of its implications."

One of the changes Victor wants to see is men evolving from the ideal of independence. "Humanity is about meeting people, creating social value and a collective tribe or community. There is always going to be an individual within a group. If you are a man, and you think you're an island, that will come back and bite you in the ass." He explains that living life without needing others is simply unsustainable given that the survival of the human race depends on it. No wonder one of his favorite quotes is "People who need people are the luckiest people in the world," a lyric sung by Barbra Streisand in the song "People."

Victor explained that the limiting definitions of manhood meant other men felt uncomfortable with his disability. "I think there are layers of curiosity, and some of those questions can be uncomfortable. It's hard to think of themselves as asking for help or think of themselves as having to negotiate their needs or desires though another person, needing another person; those are really difficult questions for a lot of men to ask themselves." He explained that disability is just life manifesting itself and this can be scary for men who are faced with what they don't have the imagination to think about.

When we spoke about the role models that exist for men, he said there were plenty, but that we often failed to see how they represent masculinity differently. "Real power doesn't come through coercion. It comes through deep understanding, compassionate leadership and having a way to express a level of morality and ethics that makes you bigger than just a man." Victor referred to the fact that some of the greatest leaders were those who embraced issues that we traditionally associate with femininity like empathy and human dignity, leaders such as Gandhi and Dr. Martin Luther King Jr.

Victor's main problem with our current view of masculinity is that it demands an obfuscation of any sign of weakness, which by definition makes you less strong. "You have to have an understanding of your core weaknesses to celebrate your strengths," he explained. "The strongest men are the ones that also understand their weaknesses. If you're the captain of a rugby team, if you know your team has a vulnerability of weaknesses, you are a much better captain by recognizing that than ignoring that. You're a better man by knowing your weaknesses rather than ignoring them."

He cautioned against men denying parts of themselves. He explained that right now, men are either chauvinistic pigs or the equivalent of white soft bread. "I would hate to see all men taste like white rice. And I'm sure women would hate that, too." Victor's advice for men was simple. Let the world see all of you.

PART II

I Love Men

*It does give you a good feeling to know that there's
something that you can do to help you become the
master of the mad that you feel, and not have to hurt
yourself or anybody else.*

—MR. ROGERS

7   The Great Suppression

*It had no name, but it was everywhere. I would hear about the crisis af-
fecting men and women's intimate relationships wherever I turned.* I
heard it in my group texts with women, in the conversations I would
overhear in coffee shops, and it even flooded my Instagram feed.
Women had always complained about difficulties in their romantic
relationships with men, but something felt different. Suddenly it felt
like women were done. They had put up with men who were emotionally inconsistent or unavailable for too long. Women were fed up
and had reached their limit. They were desperate to love men, but
according to them, men had become impossible to love. In other
words, women were no longer willing to raise the men they wanted
to date. But women's frustrations were just one side of the story—
men were frustrated, too. The women in men's lives were asking
them to be more sensitive in private, but men were still expected to
hide the fact that they were even capable of feelings in public. Their
girlfriends were telling them to open up, but society was still telling
them to man up. They didn't know which man to be and, honestly,
I didn't blame them.

Women's pain was real. "Hi! Today, please meditate on how easily
we accept women's pain as collateral damage in men's self-discovery,"

read a viral tweet by writer and author Carmen Maria Machado. Her tweet came on the heels of a widely read *New Yorker* column by Pulitzer Prize–winning author Junot Diaz where he revealed disturbing serial mistreatment of the women he had intimate relationships with due to what he said was unresolved childhood trauma. A few days later, my phone started buzzing with different female friends sending me the same message. It was a meme of a young woman surrounded by half a dozen hungry dolphins with the label "men who need therapy" inscribed over the dolphin pack. When I shared the image on my Instagram with the caption "If your girlfriend has become your therapist, don't date her, pay her," it took no less than two minutes for me to receive an alarmed text message from my boyfriend at the time: "Is this for me?" It was.

It wasn't just me. Other women, too, were complaining about the men in their lives being so emotionally stunted that they had given up dating men altogether. Women were deleting their online dating profiles, spending their free time in women-only social clubs and opting to rent or buy real estate alone rather than wait for the right partner to build a permanent home with. I heard echoes of this dissatisfaction from almost every straight young woman I spoke with. "I just started realizing I have such rich relationships with the women in my life," my sister said. "Why would I lower my standards when it comes to my relationships with men?" Other friends had fundamentally rearranged their priorities. "I'd rather spend time at work than working on some guy's emotional growth," one friend told me. When I came out as queer to my friends and started dating women, I could see the envy boiling inside my straight female friends. While they were doomed to what they considered a pool of undatable men, I had, well, other options. My friend Meredith even designed a T-shirt that read: "Sadly, still straight." It seemed like women's expectations were evolving faster than men's abilities to fulfill them.

Women weren't only deserting the dating world over this; they were also leaving the men they had married. One friend left her husband because he would tune out and watch television every night, refusing to even go on a date or go to couples therapy with her. Another walked away because he had hidden a drug problem from her and, once she found out, refused to get help. Another woman told me about a controlling husband who blamed her for trying to leave after he got physical with her. "If I had cancer you wouldn't leave me, so you shouldn't leave me if I do this," he told her one night after she tried to end the relationship. "I looked up all these therapists. I did all the work. I made sure they took the insurance and said I would go with him," she told me. When she did and he was given anti-anxiety medication, he refused to take it because he was offended it had even been prescribed. This was more than emotional problems; these women were left dealing with their husbands' unresolved mental health issues. Many women didn't feel married; they felt like rehab centers.

"Depression in men often doesn't look like depression in women," journalist Julie Scelfo told me. She began studying the issue a decade earlier. "It manifests itself in other ways like anger, drug use or alcoholism." In 2007, she wrote a lengthy cover story for *Newsweek* on men and depression, and it turned out to be the most-read story of the year. "I remember the editors were surprised because it was the early days of the shift to online reading and they hadn't expected the story to be that popular." It didn't get a lot of clicks right after it was published, but people kept reading it through the year and they weren't just reading the story; they were writing to Julie about it. She found herself inundated with emails and letters, but the vast majority of them were not from men—they were from women. Julie was floored that so many women had been moved to get in touch and that nearly all of them described their frustration and loneliness in similar terms. "He doesn't want to do anything," one letter said. "I feel like I have to choose between my life and my marriage vows," another wrote. "If I leave him and go have my own life I feel like I'm a bad wife. But if I stay, I die inside." Julie was astonished, yet, in some ways, unsurprised. She began thinking of this vast corps of unhappily married women as "married widows."

One conclusion Julie had reached from her research is that men are dealing with a mental illness but are unaware of it. She had been intrigued by a study undertaken by Michael Addis at Clark University in Massachusetts in response to the fact that men were reluctant to admit they were depressed. Instead of advertising support groups for those "suffering from depression," researchers told her they hung up signs describing a meeting designed to help with "the stresses of living." The result? Men from all walks of life showed up in droves. "Men don't admit they are depressed," Julie said. "But stress doesn't have the same negative connotations." In other words, for many women, their relationship problems were actually undiagnosed mental illness.

Many women said that when they tried to bring this up with men, they would either get angry or shut down. "The only time I could get him to have a real conversation was after he had had a few drinks," one woman told me. All of these different women's stories sounded eerily familiar. In fact, I kept hearing the same thing over and over again. Men were experiencing emotional and in some cases mental health turmoil and didn't have the language to understand, let alone talk about, it with their partners. The male code has instructed them to keep it all on the inside, and that's exactly what they were doing.

I call this crisis the great suppression. Men grew up disowning their emotions. It's a kind of emotional estrangement so pernicious and so embedded in the way we raise them it's almost invisible until it's too late. No wonder men weren't able to manage their feelings: as boys, they had been taught they didn't have any. Emotional expression and management was a crucial skill that simply hadn't been properly instilled in men. In fact, boys who show it get reprimanded. *Boys don't cry. Be strong. Don't let him know it hurt you. If you like her, pull her pigtails.* Of course when you don't share your feelings, they don't simply go away; they just come out in different ways. The way some men tend to bottle up their feelings has been observed by researchers. It's called emotional restrictivity, and it's something that is learned, not innate to their biology. Research by clinical psychiatrist Jeroen Jansz from the University of Amsterdam found that it's not that men didn't have as many emotional abilities, but rather that they didn't practice them as often as women. He breaks down modern masculinity into four components: autonomy, achievement, aggression and stoicism, and concludes that stoicism particularly encourages a disconnection from feelings, vulnerability and pain, which increases the disconnection from emotional states for men. Jansz's research shows that this blocked emotional state has disproportionate impacts on men's health. And now that their female partners were no longer willing to do men's emotional labor for them, it was costing them their relationships, too.

What women were asking for from men was pretty simple: emotional labor. A study from the University of Virginia examined five thousand heterosexual couples and found that the most satisfied women had partners who had one thing in common: emotional engagement. Researchers found that a woman's happiness in a marriage is correlated with how much "emotional work" her husband performs. Feeling understood and connected to her husband was the strongest predictor for a woman's level of marital satisfaction. But for many women, that just wasn't happening in their relationships or marriage. And while many of their mothers had put up with their partner's unwillingness to address their emotional turmoil and take responsibility for their mental health, this generation of women was beginning to wonder why they should. Women were walking away from emotionally abusive and deficient relationships because, for the first time in time in history, they could. Women are more educated and more employed than at any other time in history. Single women without children have the smallest wage gap with men (although women of color still make far less than white women). An increasing number of women have more money and decision-making power, and it was only a matter of time before this trickled down to their romantic relationships. The more independent women become, the less likely they are to tolerate relationships that don't meet their needs.

While women are demanding that men be more emotionally fluent, men are still receiving a very different message about what their role in the dating world is. In my many years of sipping frighteningly overpriced vodka sodas in the company of questionable yet carefully selected members of the straight male community, I've noticed several interesting trends, not the least fascinating of which is our collective insistence on one gender paying for the other gender as an ultimate sign of respect. I'm not exactly sure when we all agreed that men who are on dates with women should get the bill, but I know for a fact it wasn't when women were allowed to have opinions or credit cards, which feels simultaneously several and not enough years ago. It's curious that while we've let go of many norms and even laws regarding relations between women and men, this one has held on for dear life. Overconfidence in our own imaginary gendered rules has meant that although every heterosexual man knows that he is supposed to pay on a first date, only a fraction know they're supposed to ask the women they date follow-up questions.

When I talk to men about what they have been taught about dating women, it's as if they had been prepped for a business transaction rather than an emotional one. Of course some women really care about arbitrary financial rituals like buying dinner or drinks, but women who will go on another date with a guy exclusively because of how much he spills on dinner are becoming an endangered species. They still exist, but they are being slowly replaced by the proliferation of a new kind of woman who has her own savings account and a banker named Todd. She doesn't want a sugar daddy, she wants good company; but herein lies the problem: men have been taught hard-and-fast rules about how to be the former but, curiously, not on how be the latter. While we obsess over whether men should pay for dinner or pull out chairs for women, we muddle the real issue, which is that the new friction between men and women on dates exists outside of these rituals, not within them. When we talk about modern dating, the debate is not whether men should pick up the check or not but rather the more challenging question, which is: If women can also now pay for their own food, what do men do?

In other words, if your job is no longer to pay for the date, what's your job on the date?

The truth is dating is hard. It's hard for women, it's hard for men and it has become increasingly and unnecessarily painful for all of us because of shifting gender norms, which have come to modify the rules about dating. But it's not like we've all settled on a whole new set of rules. Men are getting mixed signals. On the one hand, they are being told that women want to be treated as equals, that they are starting to have more spending power and status in society, which means that men attempting to do things for them is condescending, unwelcomed and outdated. On the other hand, men are being told that being a man means being a gentleman and the main way to show respect to the opposite sex is through chivalry. Because those two messages conflict, men are justifiably lost.

This pressure on men became clear to me when I sat down with conservative commentator Tomi Lahren and two of her friends on a sticky, hot day at a bar in Dallas, when I interviewed her for my podcast. We disagreed on everything from institutional racism, immigration to climate change and men were no exception. Specifically, I wanted to ask her about a video she made that was titled "Is It Just Me, or Have Men Gotten Really Soft?" In it she worries about the "helplessness of today's young men" and how undatable it makes them. "It seems few can change a lightbulb, let alone fix a flat tire or change oil, and that makes for pretty slim pickings for the females out there looking for a match." The video received millions of views, resonating with a lot of people (and of course angering some, too). A few weeks after our encounter, she also tweeted: "As I watch millennial men struggle to lift their bags into the overhead bin I am reminded how f'd we are if there's a draft." When I asked her to explain her position on modern masculinity, it was pretty clear that she didn't welcome a conversation about alternative masculinities; in fact, she was personally insulted by it:

> I think being twenty-four and dating or watching my friends date, it's very obvious; watching TV, it's very obvious. I think we've gotten to a point where masculinity has become a negative thing, it's become an offensive thing to be a man. It's one thing to be tolerant of those that are metrosexual or maybe a little more feminine, it's one thing to be tolerant of them; it's another to glorify them.

When I pushed back at her use of the word "tolerant" to describe her attitude toward men who display more traditionally feminine characteristics, she explained, "We've gotten to the point now where masculinity has now become something that is offensive to people, and I'm offended by that. I know that masculine men are offended by that as well."

Her friend John, a towering six-foot-something buff guy in his late twenties with a buzz cut, wearing a tight-fitting shirt that showed off his muscular stature, nodded enthusiastically. You could tell this topic fired him up. He felt strongly that when we had conversations about new ways of being a man, it meant his way of life was under attack:

> I was raised that you always hold the door, you pull a chair, you treat her with [respect]. When some of those neo-feminists come out and say, "Oh, you think I can't do it myself?" It's like no. I know good and well you can do it yourself. I just want to do it for you because I love you [. . .] Some of these people out there are just so adamant for the sake of it being classified as equality that we shouldn't do that. Then you have the birth of the new-age man . . .

When I stopped him to define what he meant by a "new-age man," it got fiery:

> If we want to boil it down to fashion, we could go that route: skinny jeans, very metrosexual, very effeminate. It's cool if you want to do that; if that's your thing, do your thing; be happy with it. But don't you dare turn around and demonize my class of people that want to be like the old-school type of men. Not criticizing or belittling women, but just being the old-school alpha male that "if you come near my woman or you insult her, I'm going to knock your teeth down your throat."

Let's just say it went from skinny jeans to knocking down people's teeth and throats pretty quickly. For John, chivalry wasn't personal; it was political. And it was clearly not a topic John felt on the fence about. It felt like a conduit for another larger conversation about masculinity being redefined. He clearly was holding on to a definition of manhood that his father probably subscribed to and older generations of other men held on to as well. For John, the proliferation of what he called "beta males" signaled much more than a threat to courtship and dating; it presented an attack on the family. Judging by how heated he was about the topic, this evidently was hitting a nerve that went beyond just paying for dinner:

> It's the respect thing of "she is with me." I love her and I respect her and I want her to be protected. [. . .] I believe that a child needs a mom and a dad. You need the compassionate mother figure the child runs to, but you also need a disciplinarian, the father figure, to raise that child.

When I asked him what he would do when the modern world couldn't guarantee these rigid and more traditional roles, the ideological system he spoke so highly of started to fall apart. I asked him what would happen if he lost his job or got injured or if he had to become a stay-at-home dad. For the first time in our conversation he went a bit quiet. "The way I was raised, no, I could never be a stay-at-home father. I'd have to go out and work. I can't fathom the idea of a woman supporting me. It's just I want to take care of her; that's how it should be." He chalked it up to a fear of being "reliant on somebody else" and him not being able to fathom the idea of not "bringing anything to the table." It made me sad to think that John didn't think he could bring something valuable to the table as a man in a relationship unless it was money.

My conversation with Tomi and her friends crystallized a pretty clear double standard: that while we're comfortable with women existing outside of the bounds of femininity, we're not comfortable with men existing beyond the bounds of masculinity. "I think alpha women need an alpha male, because I know personally if you're not, if you're a beta, I will walk all over you," Tomi explained. "Not because I want to, but because that's what happens. I need someone that's a little stronger than me; otherwise they can't handle me. I'm sure it's your same experience," Tomi said as she looked to her friend Laura, who was nodding her head vigorously.

"When I get off [work], I'm still an alpha female, but I want to be able to feel like I'm actually taken care of, and that if for some reason I can't defend myself, he's going to be able to take care of me," Laura said.

I found it interesting that Tomi and Laura could dip in and out of the gendered ideals about their gender but didn't appear to think that the men were entitled to the same luxury. It's almost as if men needed to remain ultra-entrenched in masculine norms so that it was okay for the women to transgress the normal bounds of femininity and be assertive and dominant in their daily lives. To my surprise, two women who said they subscribed to traditional gender norms called themselves alpha, which is the opposite of a term traditionally associated with femininity. Interestingly, being a beta male was an insult for men, but being an alpha female wasn't for women. They both talked about getting their own paychecks, being assertive and strong, a clash with at least what's considered traditional ideals of femininity, and yet when they talked about men there was no flexibility for their gender roles, no room for error.

They seemed to feel less concerned with how their changing roles were perceived and more worried about how these changes could impact men. In fact, the two women seemed more worried about how men felt about changing gender dynamics rather than how they felt about it. Tomi said she was the one who often paid because she was wealthier than many of her peers, but she was worried about how the men would handle that. "It's emasculating for a man. I feel like it gets to a point where it's emasculating for a man if a woman pays all the time," Tomi said.

It's at that moment that I realized why chivalry annoyed me. Although it's presented as something that men do for women, it's really something men do for themselves. Why would John insist on doing something that a woman didn't want him to do if it were *really* all about her? John didn't express anger that women were able to open doors; he expressed anger that he couldn't do it for them. It wasn't about women not being allowed to be strong; it was about him not being able to show them that *he* was. In other words, the moral panic about chivalry "being dead" wasn't about women being too empowered; it was about men feeling like they were giving up an important part of their identity, perhaps the only part of their identity that they felt they had left. It was a sense of: If men can't open doors for women anymore, what do they do with their hands? While it's interesting to have these conversations and vital to address the shifting identities of men, if we abandoned the old rules, if we let go of men's obligation to open doors and pay the checks, perhaps we could have a more interesting conversation about coming up with other ways for men to be men and show respect to women.

While I was speaking with Tomi and her friends, I felt personally conflicted. Although I disagreed with the premise of chivalry, the truth was that I actively participated in this culture by letting men pay for dates, gifts and trips. Hell, a part of me even came to expect it—just like them. In fact, I had developed a steady pattern of dating men who went above and beyond in the chivalry department. One guy I was in love with sent me an intricate s'mores-making machine (yes, this exists) after our second date because I had mentioned in passing that I love marshmallows. One particular boyfriend would send me giant cookie cakes with romantic messages, enormous edible arrangements and ridiculously large flower bouquets at my office. I thought these grand gestures were expressions of love and maybe he did, too, largely because that's how our culture classifies this kind of behavior. People's reactions would also form my own perception and opinion about his romantic gestures. Women would walk by my desk and smile, but I could tell it was laced with envy. These same women would express confusion if I didn't place the large bouquet on my desk because I was uncomfortable with the attention it was attracting.

It took me a while, but I came to realize the reason why this particular partner's grand gestures bothered me was because they weren't ways to draw attention to me; they were ways to draw attention to himself. It was a way to exert control inside the relationship and to impact how he was perceived by others. It took me some time to figure this out. For the longest time, I blamed myself for feeling uncomfortable, and not being appreciative, failing to realize that the problem was not me. When I asserted myself and kindly asked him to stop sending lavish packages to my office, he kept doing it. This summed up the ultimate paradox of chivalry: If the act really was for me, why did he do something I specifically said I didn't like? When he continued to send things to my office, all I could think about was that scene in *Friends*, where Ross shows up at Rachel's new job when she's working late with a picnic and a loud electric pepper grinder when what she needs is to be left alone so she can meet her deadline and not get fired. When Rachel asks Ross to leave, he gets upset *at her* for not accepting his gifts, failing to realize she didn't ask for them in the first place. Just because someone wants to do something for you does not mean that you have to accept it. It's simple, but because of deeply entrenched gender norms it took me thirty years to figure it out. Of course grand gestures can be romantic, beautiful and absolutely perfect for the person on the receiving end of them, regardless of gender. We should all do things for our partners to show them that we love them. But ideally, both partners should be giving and receiving and gender shouldn't be dictating your role in the relationship; the people who are in the relationship should.

When I realized this, I cut chivalry out cold turkey. I learned the most about chivalry when I stopped participating in it. It wasn't until after going on a self-imposed chivalry cleanse that I really started seeing the ways it was setting up my relationships with men to fail or at least unnecessarily struggle. I couldn't see its effects because I knew nothing else and it was ingrained in my own perceptions about relationships between men and women. I approached every relationship moving forward by splitting everything as equally as possible. It certainly made some men uncomfortable, especially at first. They would always say they were appreciative, but I could tell it made them uneasy because suddenly they were giving up a form of control. Ultimately, though, it freed up a power dynamic that I hadn't even known was there all along. Because I was expected to accept all these gifts, I was also expected to accept everything else. It made me more reluctant to ask for what I needed and made me less assertive in the relationships. It made some situations more uncomfortable because we weren't falling back on familiar gender dynamics, but ultimately the result was a healthier relationship between two equal partners undefined by roles and rules that someone else had made up. It also felt good to release the men I was dating from the financial pressure of providing and paying for everything. It was only when I quit chivalry that I realized how unfair it was to men and how much I had bought into the idea of a gendered stereotype for men when I was so against them for women.

I wasn't the only one on the abandoning-chivalry gravy train. We are witnessing a tidal change where women are giving less importance to old chivalrous rituals. Only 17 percent of women now expect the guy to pay on the first date. Even several men I spoke to were rethinking their relationship and participation in chivalry. Michael Barnes said that coming to terms with the lies about masculinity changed his outlook on it. Growing up in the South, he felt a pressure to perform being a gentleman, but he realized that this implied doing things for one gender rather than all genders. "I make sure to not do things solely for women, such as opening doors, offering to buy drinks, giving hugs, et cetera," he explained. "For me, degendering my generosity was a way to honor a fundamental aspect of myself and a way of balancing how I treat people. I consciously felt a need to have it be clear in my public interactions that I didn't just do these things for women, but that I did them for people, regardless of gender or other aspects of identity, because this is just what I do." He wanted to remove the intrinsic transactional aspect and instead approach every relationship from a place of equality and generosity. "I didn't want my actions to be construed as just being connected solely to heterosexual desire or attempting to get something in return for being a nice guy," he said. "Women might think that I'm being a certain way because I'm expecting something in return or that I have notions of women needing to be taken care of or provided for. This also helps to redefine my relationships with men and model better/wider definitions of masculinity and platonic intimacy." When Michael decided to rethink his approach to romance and chivalry, he didn't just notice an improvement in his relationships with women but also with men because he found himself treating everyone with more respect regardless of their gender.

Of course, some chivalry is just actually courtesy. Opening doors for people, offering to help them with their bags and giving special gifts are lovely acts of kindness that I want to see more of, not less. But if a man is nervous about whether what he's doing is patronizing or polite, just think of one simple rule: if you wouldn't do it for a man to not do it for a woman. Modern chivalry is not about what you do; it's about why you do it. More importantly, when you are attempting to perform traditional symbols of chivalry, intention matters more than the gesture. It's crucial for men to at least reflect about why they're opening doors for women. If you're opening the door to be nice because a woman is carrying a bunch of bags (and because women still get burdened with domestic labor that largely goes unpaid), then you get ten points. If you're opening the door for her because she's the weaker gender, rethink that. In fact, the only rule you need to live by is that if you open doors for women, you need to open doors for men, too. Think about how great your biceps will look! If you're only doing it for one gender, you're probably doing it for the wrong reasons. You can be as chivalrous as you want, as long as you're applying the same rules for everyone. Being polite can never backfire. Why does intention matter? Because intention informs actions and the belief that underlies even a perceived "good" action can in fact perpetuate harmful stereotypes that make all genders worse off.

I know what you're thinking, How could a "good" action have any "bad" consequences?

There's a phenomenon called benevolent sexism, and there's a likelihood you've participated in it before. I have a master's degree in gender studies and heck, I do it all the time. Benevolent sexism is sort of like the Macarena: you don't remember when you learned it, but for some reason you're really good at it. Benevolent sexism is the grand equalizer. While women are less likely to participate in hostile sexism, when it comes to benevolent sexism, the gap pretty much disappears. Just like breathing, we all do it.

Benevolent sexism is when someone advances a favorable attitude toward women, but it's actually rooted in sexism. In the world of dating it shows up when a man orders for a woman, refuses to ever let her pay, insists on walking on the side nearer the street, must lead when they walk in a crowded place, et cetera. This may seem normal, perhaps even justified, but the reason is never rooted in equality. The logic is rooted in an inequality that women require protection from men, but the result appears to be preferential treatment for women. Benevolent sexism is like misogyny with a wink. It may seem inoffensive, but it replenishes the well of sexism every time we do it.

DON'T BUY INTO THE BS BARGAIN
(THE BENEVOLENT SEXISM BARGAIN)

Even once you have her, once you're in the relationship and are exclusive, the tension we explored in dating doesn't go away. Benevolent sexism is bad for men because it makes the women they're in relationships with less happy. One study from the University of Auckland in New Zealand found that women who hold benevolent sexist views had lower marital satisfaction. When women think they need to be "protected" or "cherished" (can you spot the world leader whose favorite playbook this is from?), it increases their likelihood to view any type of conflict with their male partner as contradicting that worldview. It makes sense. If you expect your partner to treat you like a princess, any disagreement or criticism (which is normal in any healthy relationship) is perceived as uncalled for. Benevolent sexism enforces a belief system that's just not realistic. Study coauthor Matthew Hammond has said that "expectations built from ideas in society about what men and women 'ought' to do will be hard for reality to match." In fact, subscribing to conventional norms means that any deviation from that can feel destabilizing. It also proposes a bargain that's impossible for both parties to adhere to. It imposes a rigid structure where women invest in the relationship more (put their needs second, perhaps stay at home or forgo a career) and where men are expected to deliver outside the home to make women feel "protected" when, as we all know, life is not always that simple. Men get laid off, men get injured and the benevolent sexism complex doesn't make space for real life. Another researcher who has examined this phenomenon, Pelin Gul from Iowa State University, has said that "as researchers, we're not looking to give relationship advice, but understanding the detrimental and beneficial aspects of men's benevolent sexism could help women and men have more satisfying relationships."

Now it's important to note that the research shows that men in BS relationships reported being happier in their relationships. The increase in conflicts in their relationships wasn't enough to make them miserable. Because they're getting the good end of the bargain (ultimately the BS model reinforces their dominance), they report being pretty satisfied. But the happiness a man might get from benevolent sexism is sort of like the happiness people experience when they eat a lot of cake or get a lot of likes on a selfie. It's impermanent. Can happiness be *truly* sustainable if it depends on fixed roles that could change (and that according to most structural economic indicators *are* changing)? What happens when the roles that the men are expected to take in the relationship aren't available? What happens when "the man of the house" loses his job? What happens if he gets sick? What happens when a thing called life happens and when he is no longer available because of external factors that are out of his control?

Despite the data showing that traditional chivalry and benevolent sexism aren't leading to healthy heterosexual relationships, there's a panic about preserving these traditional gender roles. Because our culture is invested in the myth of a gender war, a fixed system where women's and men's interests are in opposition rather than in concert with each other, it creates a tendency for pundits and even so-called thought leaders to blame women's problems on men and vice versa, failing to see that perhaps the root of both women's and men's problems could be the same ill: unvarying and unwavering patriarchal gender roles.

Instead of giving up our obsession with distinct gender roles, there's a tendency to further entrench ourselves in them. This insistence on preserving the past is led by many people, like contrarians Jordan Peterson and Ben Shapiro. But Suzanne Venker, the niece of anti-feminist conservative lightning rod Phyllis Schlafly, has also been particularly vocal on the issue of relationships between men and women. Venker's a writer responsible for extremely subtle headlines such as "Chivalry Is Dead Because Women Killed It" and "Men Called. They Want Their Balls Back." Without any visible supporting data, she argues that young men are not settling down because the opposite sex's rise has "undermined [men's] ability to become self-sufficient in the hopes of someday supporting a family." She writes that "men want to love women, not compete with them. They want to provide for and protect their families—it's in their DNA. But modern women won't let them."

It's a common argument made by conservatives—that women's empowerment comes at the cost of men's happiness in relationships with them. The same logic underpins those who worry that women's increase in income capacity emasculated their male partners. I always find this argument particularly droll because I have yet to meet a man who doesn't like more money. Ali Wong points this out in one of my favorite stand-up routines, where she describes a sudden and rapid increase in income after her first Netflix special came out. "My mom is very concerned that [my husband] is going to leave me out of intimidation." Her response is pitch perfect. "I had to explain to her that the only kind of man that would leave a woman who makes more money is the kind of man that doesn't like free money."

Women being able to play the role of the provider releases men from shouldering all that pressure alone. More money is only a problem for men in a society where their identity has only been defined by what they do rather than who they are.

But Venker is so nervous, she goes so far as to argue that progress in gender roles is not just bad for men; it's bad for women, too. In one piece she wrote for Fox News titled "Society is creating a new crop of alpha women who are unable to love," she says divorce would be less common if women were more subservient. It led to an atrocious Fox News breaking-news alert on thousands of people's phones that read "men just want a woman who is nice." When the notification went out, it unleashed a slew of confusion amongst many internet users, wondering if they had traveled back in time. "That's what men like," Venker argued in another piece. "Women who are easy to love." This kind of fearmongering around women emasculating men highlights a persisting discomfort with women gaining more power in their relationships with men and the absence of a role for men outside of being the provider. Instead of seeing equality as a way to expand roles for both women and men and an upgrade from previous more fixed and traditional arrangements, it's framed as a threat to the "natural" order. In her own words, Venker believes there is "something special about men being men and women being women." She doesn't welcome ameliorations in relationships; she wants a preservation of an old, restrictive and, frankly, outdated world order.

The biggest flaw in Venker's logic is that she thinks fluid gender roles are prescriptive rather than expansive. Calling into question the ideals that idealized masculinity has instilled is not about telling men to act more like women or women to act more like men; it's about letting everyone be whoever they want. It's about letting personal preferences, not collective ones, guide women and men's relationships with each other.

Besides, the idea that women have too much empowerment is an oxymoron. Unlike what the nieces of staunchly anti-feminist figures would have you believe, there is enough freedom and liberty to go around for everyone. Freedom is in fact like breadsticks at the Olive Garden; it's unlimited. Contrary to popular belief, every time a woman earns her basic rights and freedoms, a man does not lose his manhood. When one human gets out of the cage, it's a great day for humans and a bad day for cages. White people weren't oppressed by the civil rights movement, and sales of hamburgers didn't decrease when cheeseburgers came along. People weren't like, "Screw this; cancel hamburgers because I can put cheese on this bad boy"; they were like, "Wow, this development is an improvement for all hamburgers." Freedom is like pancakes at IHOP: you can't run out.

And last, Venker's argument is not just offensive; it's factually incorrect. Men who see their female partner as their equal are the ones who go on to have the longest and happiest marriages. When relationship scholar Dr. Gottman performed a longitudinal study on 130 straight couples, he found that men who were the most likely to embrace their "wife's influence" were the most likely to be satisfied and stay with her. This key characteristic in men most heavily dictates the success of a relationship. While recognizing their partner's influence is associated with male happiness in a marriage, unhelpful ideals of masculinity teach men to deny it. In fact, submitting to a woman's demands is a common way that we humiliate men for being emasculated or, in more crass but overused terms, "pussy whipped." It's another example of how being a "real man" comes to literally sabotage an otherwise good man's relationship.

Although the lies about masculinity are often learned and passed on from other men, Suzanne Venker and Tomi Lahren embody the way women have internalized them and are often guilty of reinforcing them, too. And it's not just coming from conservative women. Brené Brown discusses women's discomfort with male vulnerability in her audiobook *Men, Women & Worthiness: The Experience of Shame and the Power of Being Enough*. She says that while women often ask the men in their lives to open up, women can't always handle it. Brown tells the story of a man who came up to her after one of her lectures, eager to encourage her to speak about men's experience of shame and vulnerability. "My wife and daughters . . . they'd rather see me die on top of my white horse than watch me fall off," he told her. "You say you want us to be vulnerable and real, but c'mon. You can't stand it. It makes you sick to see us like that."

When I asked men how traditional masculinity presented itself, more than one man said they felt this pressure from the women in their lives. Jeff Shackelford was one of them. "I seemed to be drawn into a more masculine persona by the women I dated," he said. They had their expectations of how men acted or how 'tough' they thought men were supposed to be. This led me to trying to fill a role, so to speak."

Matt Cusimano said that coming out as pansexual showed him the ways in which masculinity is policed by all genders. When he dated queer men (more on this later) he found that building and developing intimacy was harder with men than women. However, the women he dated felt threatened by his sexual orientation being open to men as well. "Broadly speaking, I'd say my most repressed emotions have been tied into my queerness," he said. "Women have often said that my queerness is somehow not masculine, unsexy and perhaps threatening to their goals of secure and stable monogamy." Because we all associate masculinity with a repudiation of the feminine, when that disavowal is not perceived as complete, we start to question a man's entire identity.

Matt isn't imagining things. It isn't uncommon for women to harbor an irrational fear that their male partner is gay. In fact, when Seth Stephens-Davidowitz analyzed Google searches for his book, *Everybody Lies,* he found that the number one question women ask about their husbands is whether he is gay. It reflects a fear among women that we don't see with men who are in relationships with women. There are eight times more Google searches from women asking if their husband is gay than those asking if their husband is an alcoholic, although the latter is much more likely to be the case.

Women are ten times more likely to ask Google if their husband is gay than whether their husband has depression.

Even when men said they had made the effort to unlearn toxic ideals of masculinity in their lives, they complained about it hurting their potential for relationships. Many men told me about staying away from meeting women in public because they knew other men had made that that kind of environment harder for them because women were less likely to give them the benefit of the doubt. In the same thread, Tim Hourigan said the omnipresence of destructive idealized versions of masculinity makes his life as a man more difficult when meeting women in bars or starting up a conversation with a stranger, even if it's not with the intention of flirting. "[It] makes it more likely I'll be seen as a threat, because of the behavior of my peers," he explained.

Men explained that they felt like they were walking around on eggshells because toxic ideals of masculinity had created a hypersensitivity that had come to poison their interactions with women. They were being prejudged before they even opened their mouth. Alex Bell wrote that he needed to make up for the crummy actions of other men:

> It impacts me by feeling I need to compensate for the effects of toxic masculinity in my own behavior and interaction with women. It means that I try and go out of my way to ensure that my comments or behavior won't be taken as flirtation or sexual come-ons. I even hesitate to initiate innocent invites to activities or events in fear that my invite might be misinterpreted.

This becomes a pernicious trap for men in the dating world because any attempt to deviate away from it is viewed as a transgression punishable through homophobic gender policing. If a man shows any resistance to traditional notions of masculinity, especially in his intimate relationships with women, it's used as proof that he isn't actually attracted to them. It can be used as evidence that he is somehow a fraud. "Everything is gay; if you dance you're gay; if you sit a certain way you too are gay; if you pronounce your words correctly, congrats, gay," Diosan Borrego said. "Especially Latinos." This kind of policing relies on the age-old marginalization of queerness and its inherent devaluation in our culture.

While homophobia can often be felt by men who aren't gay through gender policing, for men who are part of the LGBTQ community, it has more severe implications. Every queer man I spoke to said that "toxic masculinity" had made his dating life immensely more painful and difficult. My friend Carlos Maza said it was a problem most men in gay relationships deal with but don't talk about. "It largely defines gay men's dating lives," he said. "It limits the way that we ask for what we need in relationships. It limits the way we express hurt and desire. It of course shapes the types of sex and physical intimacy we idealize. It looks slightly different but basically all the ways toxic masculinity fucks with straight men: imagine if both partners were doing it *to each other*."

In other words, toxic masculinity doesn't go away in men's gay relationships. In fact, it can be magnified. The overt discrimination against effeminate men on online dating websites came up continuously. Every single guy I interviewed told me about the "masc for masc" phenomenon on many men's dating profiles. "Masc" is a shorthand and colloquial term for masculine, which in this context is synonymous with a way of presenting yourself as virile and unfeminine. "Being *masc* is the ultimate in both the heterosexual and gay world," my friend Pete told me. "The same hierarchy gets internalized in gay men. It's a recipe for disaster as gays are not so 'masc' in the traditional context."

Damaging stereotypes about Asian men being more "feminine" or less brawny mean that they face additional marginalization or mockery within the gay community. "We're conditioned to think

that the masculine, muscled all-American white man is the ultimate image of manhood," my friend Tri Vo explained to me. As
an Asian-American gay man, he's seen how corrosive and limiting these ideals can be. "When a guy looks for a partner while
his head is filled with all this toxic masculinity and stereotypes,
it's likely he won't consider men of color to be at the top of his
list ¯_(ツ)_/¯," he said over text. Even gay dating apps have become a breeding ground for racism. In fact, at the time this book
is being written, a class action lawsuit from Asian-American men
who claim that the app Grindr allows racism to fester on its plat-
form is ongoing. The case was spearheaded by Sinakhone Keodara,
who got fed up after encountering several profiles with racist undertones like "not interested in Asians" or "not attracted to Asians."
Unfortunately, encountering profiles with racist undertones or
overtones was not an experience unique to Asian-American men;
in fact, the African-American queer men I interviewed had also encountered anti-black racism. Although gay dating apps can be the
first real safe space for many queer men, less traditionally masculine men and men of color can experience overt discrimination.

Just how central and damaging idealized masculinity can be to
men's intimate relationships showed up in a conversation I had
with Shalini Mirpuri, a couples therapist in Gainesville, Florida,
about the most recurring problem area for men who enter couples
therapy with their female partner. "I always find myself repeating
'try to listen instead of trying to be right.'" She explained that men
tend to try to rationally solve an argument, rather than pay attention
to the emotions of their partner. If they were to shift to how she was
feeling, rather than who was right, they would solve problems much
faster. Interestingly, for men in gay couples the most recurring
problems were relating to internalized homophobia and stereotypes
regarding masculinity, which were mirrored in the conversations I
had with queer men. When I asked Mirpuri about couples counseling

for lesbians, her answer fascinated me. She said theirs were the easiest kind of relationships to tackle because of the absence of power dynamics she has seen with straight couples. She said the problems were down to personality issues, rather than the typical struggle for control in the relationships she encountered with straight and gay couples. Of course, this is not to say that power dynamics are never present in lesbian relationships; there are many ways these relationships can be toxic, abusive or violent. But the absence of toxic masculinity seemed to have an appeasing effect on relationships, or perhaps the presence of it seemed to be associated with conflict.

As a queer woman who has dated both women and men, I can anecdotally say that same-sex relationships can be much easier because there are no predetermined rules or roles. The first time I went on a date with a woman, I was floored. It was the first time I actually felt like I could be myself on a first date. There was no insecurity jungle gym to navigate. Queer relationships tend to be more fluid because each person is free to be who they are or want to be in the relationship based on their preference rather than predetermined roles defined by society. In a way, they are a social experiment for what relationships could look like where gender is not the most immediate organizing factor, as it often is. When you imagine what it would be like if we assigned roles in relationships based on arbitrary characteristics like hair color or earlobe shape, you see how ridiculous it is that we do it with gender. How weird would it be if we determined that the person with the darkest hair in the relationship should always get the check or that the person with the most detached earlobe always gets out of the elevator first? It's just as senseless to assume that a characteristic like your gender should determine your role in relationships. Of course not all couples fall into traditional gender roles, but even the existence of that predetermined structure requires an acknowledgment of the structure you are deviating from.

It's worth thinking about what deprogramming ourselves could mean for heterosexual relationships.

This utopic absence of predetermined structures is how scientists explain the curious happiness gap between cohabiting gay and straight couples. Although you would expect that couples who don't have to spend a day in court to fight for their right to order a cake for their wedding would be better off, the reverse is often true. Despite experiencing ongoing discrimination, persecution and stigma, gay couples in the United States report higher relationship satisfaction and lower levels of conflict than straight couples. One study from The University of Queensland that looked at more than 25,300 people in the UK and 9,200 in Australia found that gay participants felt happier and more positive about both their partner and the relationship, leading researchers to conclude it was because "relative to heterosexual relationships, same-sex relationships tend to have more equitable domestic work arrangements, less defined gender roles, and a greater sense of social connectedness to a community." Their joy is contagious and trickles down to the rest of their family unit. The kids of gay couples are happier than those of straight couples despite the fact that they often experience bullying because of their family arrangement.

We might not all have the luxury of being born gay, but all of us have the power to use them as inspiration. By letting go of preordained gender roles, responsibilities and power dynamics, men and women could dramatically improve their relationships.

But of course saying "just let go of toxic masculinity" to a man is like saying "just relax" to a person having a panic attack. Men will only break free from the masculinity trap when they have a safe alternative, but for the time being they're growing up receiving the message that they are being surveilled and that any deviation from the ideals created by rigid masculinity will be grounds for embarrassment and rejection from men as well as women. The change is first and foremost individual, but it also has to be collective. No one is free from gender norms, and the messages that men receive about their gender is setting them up to fail, particularly in their intimate relationships.

Emotional vulnerability is not a sign of being weak; it's one of the essential and key strengths of any healthy relationship. But if men are getting the message that showing emotion is bad, so-called feminine or weak and that it means they'll be less valuable in the dating world and they'll publicly be shamed for being "soft," the results can be catastrophic for their intimate relationships. The paradox is that demanding that men be tough actually makes them weaker emotionally. Expecting men to be emotionally intelligent in their relationships is like expecting people to know how to do a butterfly backstroke when they've been instructed to never get wet. If you get the message that being in touch with your emotions means being weak, you'll repress any feelings that come up, often unconsciously, which only magnifies them. Ending the great suppression could be one of the greatest gifts to people of all genders. Men could access their full humanity so that the people they love don't have to do it for them. As my sister often says, if we all took responsibility for our own feelings, the world would be a much brighter place.

Boys learn quickly that it is unsafe to
be an outsider.

—WADE DAVIS

AMUSE-BOUCHE:
Wade's Story

Wade Davis grew up playing a game where a football was tossed up in the air and the person who caught it was "the queer." He didn't know he would later become an NFL player. He also didn't know he would later come out as gay. "Boys learn quickly that it is unsafe to be an outsider," he confided to me. As the first Diversity and Inclusion consultant for the NFL and one of the very first openly out players, he knows firsthand how hard it can be for men in sports to be different when conformity is currency. That's how he explains why so many men end up falling in line with a stereotype they may not even like. "The reward for stereotypical and even toxic masculinity is acceptance in the dominant group," he explained to me.

Wade is one of the biggest feminists I know, and his journey into becoming an ally for women arose as a natural path. "Being gay connected me specifically to what I had read about women's experience. It means you are hypervigilant. Similarly, for women, safety is not always there." The marginalization he experienced as a result of his skin color was additive. "Being a black man familiarized me with what it means to be oppressed." He explained that coming to terms with his gender wasn't as obvious as his other identities. "The male thing was the last space for me to interrogate. I was existing thinking that being a man was separate and I didn't think about what it meant to exist as a man." He talks about the lack of interrogation around masculinity as a form of self-inflicted avoidance. "There's a subtle depression. As men we don't know how much of ourselves we are repressing." Wade recounts being flabbergasted the first time he traveled to India and saw men publicly showing affection to each other in Mumbai by hugging or holding hands, especially given that India has some of the strictest laws when it comes to penalizing homosexuality. You would think countries that punish gayness with death wouldn't be more progressive on public displays of affection between men, but somehow it felt like a strange homoerotic fantasyland. One of Wade's friends who was native to India explained that because homosexuality was so overtly policed, affection between men wasn't. Because it was believed no gay man would dare do something in public that indicated his homosexuality, public affection between men was largely accepted. Because being gay is not considered an option, these men were free to be close to each other out in the open. "In America where gay marriage is law, men don't want to show affection to each other," Wade explained. "The idea of being thought of as gay, to many, is worse than being gay."

Homophobia at its core is a banishment of the feminine. "The root of homophobia is sexism," Wade said. He explained that straight men are uncomfortable with gay men because they believe gay men are performing acts that only women should. "You're giving another man a blow job; that's what women do," Wade said. "Heterosexual men go straight to the sex act. Which is why they hate women also. You will never meet a man who is homophobic and also not sexist. If you hate women, you're bound to hate anything that acts like one." That's why Wade believes it is so important for gay men to be feminists. There is so much commonality in that struggle and interconnectedness.

Wade said that marginalized groups working toward a common goal is the only way to combat the rise of groups like the alt-right.

"These men feel unsafe because everything they've been taught to believe is cracking: heterosexuality is cracking, [a] white world run by white men is cracking and everything they've grown up to believe that was black and white is cracking," he said. "Put a tiger in the room and watch people do anything to survive, even if it's against their own interest. We have dropped a tiger inside of white men."

True friendship is seen through the
heart, not through the eyes.

—NIETZSCHE

8   Bromance

If you want to get men to talk about masculinity, ask them about urinals.

I learned this pretty quickly after striking up the topic with groups of men and realized that while women use the bathroom as an opportunity to bond and catch up, for men it's a strategic game of chess. Men described a whole host of rules about the process of urinating, the most fascinating of which was the importance of the buffer urinal between men, regardless of their relationship. I was told that when there was no space for the urinal buffer, a man would take the stall. If the stall wasn't available, they would forgo the urinal buffer or sometimes form a line. Where they peed was critical, but where they looked was also consequential. Any eye contact was a huge faux pas. Pulling out your phone was, too, although it depended on who I asked. The rules surrounding conversation were also important to respect. For some men, it was unconscionable to maintain a conversation once both were engaged in the act; for others, it depended on the level of proximity. If it was a friend, sure. If it was a coworker, absolute silence. When I asked men if they would pee next to a friend if they entered the bathroom together, I didn't expect the diversity and intensity of opinions and responses.

For some men it was absolutely forbidden, while for others it was a no-brainer that they should be next to each other. The most fascinating part was that no one had explicitly taught them these rules, but transgressing them came at great cost. They didn't know where these social directives came from, but they knew the consequences of not respecting them. The fact that going to the bathroom could be such a minefield for men reveals something interesting about how intimacy is handled and negotiated between men. Upon discovering just how guarded men had to be around each other in public bathrooms, I started to wonder about all the other parts of their lives that required the same kind of vigilance.

As it turns out, this mandatory empty space that men are expected to hold between each other is not only present in washrooms; it's also visible in men's friendships. Although there is a disproportionate focus on the toxicity of female friendship in pop culture and movies like *Mean Girls,* when researchers have studied male friendship they've noticed a strange phenomenon. While women tend to build activities around their friends, men approach friendship in a more transactional way, building friendships around activities. Whether it's watching sports, playing sports or socializing as part of a club, men are focused on the doing more than the being, especially when compared to the way women do friendship. Men are even more likely to focus friendship around joint activities and are more likely to speak about those activities when they are interacting with each other. While women prioritize smaller groups or one-on-one interactions with their friends, men tend to engage in larger all-male groups, which obviously makes intimate bonding less likely.

Given the code of male friendship, it's no surprise then that straight white adult men are the demographic with the least amount of friends. Add divorce and aging, and the pool of friends shrinks even more dramatically. This has caused a quiet crisis where men are left yearning for intimacy but unable to ask for it. It's what I call the male intimacy paradox: while men report wanting more vulnerability from their friends, they aren't asking for it. Half of men report that they don't speak about their personal problems and report craving closer connection with those male friends. And this is regardless of class, sexual orientation, race and even relationship status. The barriers to same-sex intimate friendship are fueling an epidemic of male isolation.

When I spoke to my male friends about how they felt about the friendships in their lives, it opened up a Pandora's box. "[Toxic masculinity] limits my friendships because it keeps things superficial," Chris Connolly told me. "It creates a dynamic where it's impossible to be tender, confused, scared, aggrieved, lost . . . In other words, impossible to be fully alive. The sad truth is that it's actually deeply, deeply alienating." He explained that overcoming idealized masculinity is rooted in this idea that men pretend like they have it all figured out when they are around each other. "I'm learning to express myself more fully around the softer and messier emotions that are often seen as taboo for men. This includes learning to confront and accept the ways in which I myself embody toxic masculinity despite my best intentions," he explained. "So the biggest barrier I face in connecting with other men is the fear of vulnerability lurking beneath this 'got it, thanks' stance that I'm referring to." Chris said that this pressure to never ask for help or admit weakness had trained him to develop a shell when he's around his own gender:

> When it comes to being around other men, I can physically feel the fear pushing away that vulnerability. I change my posture and stance to be more rigid, guarded, almost militaristic. My tone of voice changes; the muscles around my mouth change. All of these are deeply learned behaviors that guard against the possibility of vulnerability—the possibility of not having a clue what the fuck I'm doing, or of being scared, or of being wrong

or of having acted like an asshole. Even if we as men reject toxicity, we are so scared to be found out that we end up burying
it deeper.

This defensive behavior Chris is talking about is not innate; it's
learned. We see this behavior really crystallize in adulthood, but this
is not how boys start out. In fact, the way boys and girls approach
friendship is very similar, until they become teenagers, when platonic
same-sex relationships take a turn for boys. Niobe Way has spent
years studying this phenomenon. In her book *Deep Secrets: Boys'
Friendships and the Crisis of Connection,* she features heartbreaking
interviews about boys experiencing a deep loss when they enter adulthood as men: a loss of intimacy and connection with other men. I
heard similar stories when I brought it up with men. "I definitely experienced a rude awakening in high school," my friend Ed Kennedy
told me. "When I came to high school I was repeatedly rebuffed by
men, both from acquaintances and friendships. . . . I remember so
clearly getting shut down and not understanding at all."

When I researched the strange intricacies of male friendship, it
was pretty clear how this happens: if idealized masculinity instructs
men to never be vulnerable and to avoid intimacy with other men
and to never admit needing anything from anyone, it makes sense
that deep friendship would become difficult to develop and sustain.
In fact, everything that boys are taught creates an environment that
would make male-on-male friendship almost impossible. That's why
I often heard men repeat the same thing over and over again: that
most of their friends are guys but that their closest relationships
were with women. "Even with [the men] I am close with, it's still frustrating to not have the openness I have in my female friendships for
things like conflict resolution, emotional depth and support," Ed told
me. "The vast majority of my male friendships tend to stay at the ac-
quaintance level." He said that when he tried to dig further in his

friendships he was often stonewalled. "When there is deeper emotional talk, it just tends to put the guy in coach mode and be like 'Hey, buddy, I know it's tough, but we keep our personal problems off the field.'" This explains why, for the vast majority of men that I've spoken with for this book, their closest confidant is a woman, often their romantic partner, if they are straight.

While women face each other and feel comfortable with physical proximity, men have to remain cautious, which then makes emotional connection harder. If you want to know how our culture feels about two men having emotional intimacy, look no further than the term we use to speak of it: a "bromance." Male friendship is so fraught that we as a culture have invented a special term to characterize the extraordinary phenomenon of two men having dinner together.

Men have the ability, the need and the desire to form deep and intimate friendships just as much as women. A quick look at history shows us that men were not always so guarded when it came to creating bonds with other men. Let's just say that male friendship in America wasn't always so self-conscious. If you look through nineteenth-century photos of men, you'll notice right away that male friendship has undergone a massive transformation. It used to be common for men to seek a photographer's services to capture them holding hands, sitting on each other's laps and being physically intimate. Because it is so rare to see men enjoying that level of physical proximity, you'd assume the men in the photos are romantic couples rather than friends. The physical proximity men displayed in the photo studio reflected the comfort they had with the emotional intimacy in their everyday interactions. It wasn't uncommon for powerful and highly regarded men to show great proximity with other men. Theodore Roosevelt, for instance, was known for using affectionate language in his letters to other men. Abraham Lincoln famously (and yet platonically) slept in the same bed as his best friend, Joshua Speed. It would be impossible to see anyone show no visible sign of shock upon hearing the news that Donald Trump regularly shares his bed with another man.

Frederick Douglass said that his friendships with other men helped him survive slavery. "I must say, that I never loved, esteemed, or confided in men, more than I did in these," he said about the men who were enslaved and would socialize after long, grueling and painful days. "They were as true as steel, and no band of brothers could have been more loving."

Male love was also foundational in the American colonial and Revolution periods. Richard Godbeer, a professor of history at the University of Miami, wrote a whole book detailing the sensitive and tender ways men related to each other during these pivotal moments in American history. In his book *The Overflowing of Friendship: Love Between Men and the Creation of the American Republic,* he says men would refer to each other with affectionate pet names like "dearly beloved" and "lovely boy" without restraint. "Pre-modern American men embraced a range of possibilities for relating to the other men that included intensely physical yet non-sexual relationships," Godbeer writes. This approach didn't just define men's relationships; it also impacted and guided entire value systems that placed a greater emphasis on fraternal collaboration and family over a more centralized patriarchal authority model.

This historical snapshot of our views and comfort with male intimacy offers an interesting commentary on the evolution of friendship and how that can be influenced by social pressures. But it begs the question: If men used to be this comfortable being this loving with each other, what exactly happened to male friendship in America?

Homophobia happened.

Although the term "homosexuality" was coined in the late nineteenth century, it recently went from being a behavior to an identity that was associated with a mental disorder. This transformation was abrupt and had wide-ranging consequences on men. Showing affection toward another man became a feared label rather than an innocent action and men adjusted themselves accordingly, especially because such behavior could come with criminal charges and repercussions with the introduction of sodomy and decency laws. Godbeer notes in his book that the way we currently approach both friendship and sexual orientation, although we assume it is just rooted in nature, would be confusing to the patriots or anyone living in the colonial period:

> The modern assumption that most people are attracted—sexually and romantically—to either women or men would have surprised early Americans. . . . Male friends often referred to the pleasure that they took in touching and holding one another; they delighted in the proximity of each other's bodies . . . Sexualized love was just one in a rich repertoire of possibilities open to premodern men as they explored their feelings for male friends.

Justifiably, when homosexuality was penalized, men began to want to protect themselves from that threat. But times have changed. Thanks to the tireless work of LGBTQ activists, homosexuality is no longer a crime; it has been removed from the *Diagnostic and Statistical Manual of Mental Disorders* (*DSM*) and, despite continued systemic discrimination, even some of the most hard-line conservatives now openly support same-sex unions. So in other words, although homophobia is less politically sanctioned, it has left vestiges that impact current male behavior and habits. The male affection shortage in America is almost like a kind of post-traumatic homophobia. Society has begun to move on, but the male code hasn't. Don't get me wrong, homophobia is alive and well, but despite a majority of men being tolerant of homosexuality, the skeleton of homophobia is still the pillar of mainstream masculinity culture, because the rules haven't been rewritten. Masculinity is mirroring old and archaic views that have been themselves debunked. Adhering to old laws of masculinity in modern male friendship is like saying no to a free upgrade. Why wouldn't you?

The consequences of not addressing post-traumatic homophobia are dire. And, this is not just an American problem. It has created a full-blown loneliness crisis that's become so severe that governments in Denmark and the UK have started to intervene. British research shows there are 2.5 million men who have zero close friends in the UK. That's roughly 7 percent of the male population. A report from Australia found that one in four men can't name a single person outside of their family whom they can rely on and that 37 percent feel like they aren't getting the emotional support or connection they need. Data also shows that the more a man subscribes to ideas of self-reliance, the less satisfied he is in his friendships. Men who didn't have strong relationships with their fathers and men who are unemployed or face disability or illness are particularly at risk of emotional disconnectedness. When I traveled to Iceland, several men described it to me as a public health crisis that was being heavily debated in the public sphere. And this goes further than just friendship; we see more isolation when it comes to social ties to family, too. British research shows that almost one in four men have one monthly contact with their children (regardless of their age) or less.

When I brought up friendship to men, it was often something they hadn't always given a lot of thought to, until significant moments in their life. While I observed that for many of my engaged female friends, a common problem when planning their wedding was narrowing the number of bridesmaids, men I spoke with had the opposite issue: they had trouble finding a best man. Although some men end up having numerous friends at their side, it's oddly telling that in the oldest heteronormative tradition, women had multiple female friends at their side, while men are expected to have just one, and that even that seems hard to find. Many of the men I spoke with recounted a similar experience of having to write an "awkward email" to an old college buddy they had lost touch with to see if he would be free for the wedding.

FRIENDSHIPS AREN'T JUST FUN: THEY MAKE MEN LIVE LONGER

An increasing volume of research shows that people who sustain a higher number of close friendships enjoy a greater life expectancy. Heck, there's even research showing that having more friends makes you less likely to catch a cold. Friendship even has a larger impact on longevity than family ties. Just like smoking or subsisting on nothing but Oreos and margaritas, having no close friends is bad for your health. Loneliness is one of the greatest threats to a person's health. Similar to cardiovascular diseases, it is associated with weaker immune systems and can cause early death. One analysis on 2,320 male survivors of a heart attack found that men with a lot of close friends were less likely to die than those who lacked social connections three years later. What friendships can accomplish for health is unparalleled and can't even be replaced by a romantic partner. One study on Swedish men showed that having one close relationship (usually with a romantic partner) didn't do much to lower the risk of getting a heart attack or fatal coronary heart disease—having a strong social network did. In fact, social isolation was as significant as smoking in the leading causes of coronary heart disease. So although marriage is good for men's health, research is almost unanimous that homosocial relationships between men contribute more to emotional well-being than any romantic relationships can. In fact, study after study has shown that the more socially isolated you are, the more likely you are to die early. TL;DR: seeing your friends might be more important than taking your vitamins.

In fact, the longest-standing research on happiness from Harvard shows that the health of one's relationships is a better predictor of longevity than one's cholesterol levels. Researchers monitored the happiness of 724 men for seventy-eight years, bringing them in every two years for blood tests, brain scans, in-depth interviews and filling out detailed questionnaires about their work, family, marriage and relationships. The first cohort was chosen from Harvard's classes of 1939–1944 and originally included John F. Kennedy. (The only downfall from the study is that it only featured white men, but apart from the stark lack of diversity, it is still an interesting sample for the purpose of understanding male happiness.) The biggest lesson from the study is what has been found with more diverse sample groups: that loneliness literally kills men. Although the number of friends mattered, the quality of friendships contributed the most to well-being. Those with the most meaningful relationships had the longest life expectancies. A strong relationship with a spouse also acted as a protective force against loneliness, especially in old age. Subjects who were the best at dealing with their emotions in a healthy way (without resorting to denial, avoidance or projection) had the strongest support system, which was also correlated with longer life expectancy.

Other research concurs with the fact that having good friends protects you from early death. Emerging meta-analyses performed on 49,000 subjects even conclude that friendships and social connectedness are the highest predictors of life expectancy, above all other behaviors like smoking, heavy drinking and being overweight. Psychologist Susan Pinker calls it the "village effect" and wrote a book about the "social contract that we need to survive and thrive." She argues that women's friendships make them live longer almost everywhere. She notes women outlive men across the world by six to eight years, except on the small, remote Italian island of Sardinia. She explains that this island contains six times more centenarians, in equal parts male and female. She expected to find a difference in their positive attitude or approach to life, but what she found was a difference in the way they organized as a community. In fact, she explained that it was hard to interview subjects because they kept getting interrupted by friends, family, the priest or a shopkeeper. After conducting in-depth research on the island, she concluded that it was the strength of their social ties that explained why the men lived as long as women. She argues "social isolation is the public risk of our time" and posits that this can explain the gap in life expectancy for men and women.

This tendency to rely on a support network rather than simply on oneself gives women an edge across the entire animal kingdom. Research on female baboons in Kenya shows that those with more friends live longer—up to two or three years longer. Separate data shows that the offspring of female baboons with lots of social connections have a higher survival rate. Separate research on female cancer patients finds that friends can mean the difference between life and death. According to data collected by the *American Journal of Epidemiology*, women with breast cancer have a higher rate of survival when they have many close friends. In fact, women who were isolated were 64 percent more likely to die from cancer and 69 percent more likely to die from any other cause. The research is clear: friendships are indispensable, and the fact that women are more skilled at building and sustaining friendships gives them a comparative advantage over men in society.

TO UNDERSTAND THE POWER OF MALE INTIMACY, LOOK NO FURTHER THAN THE AIDS CRISIS

Striking research on gay men who lived through the 1980s AIDS epidemic uncovers just how dramatic the impacts of loneliness on men's health can be. In the late 1980s, men who weren't aware of their HIV status joined a study. Many of them were infected, and about a third of them developed AIDS and one-quarter died. Researchers tried to tease out what explained how long one lived after being infected by HIV.

What they found was that one factor made them more likely to die: being in the closet. The conclusion was that closeted gay men were more sensitive to rejection and this biologically made them more vulnerable to disease. The conclusion of the study was that an "unwillingness to disclose emotional experiences" was associated with weakened immune responses. Lead researcher Steve Cole, who was just a postdoctoral student at the time, is now a professor of medicine and psychiatry and biobehavioral sciences at the David Geffen School of Medicine at UCLA and director of the UCLA Social Genomics Core Laboratory. He has become an expert on distinguishing the link between health and social identity, advocating for more attention to the impact of social isolation on human health. He argues that humans are more social than any other species and that social ties and community are essential to survival. When speaking about his research, Cole described being in the closet as "walking around with a time bomb" for these men because it required constant policing of their identity and prevented deep connections and friendship, which are essential to well-being. You don't need to be gay to feel the pressure to perform straight stoic masculinity. The toxicity that forces gay men to act like straight men is the same toxicity straight and queer men feel having to act like straight men all the time. This type of policing sometimes is a means to survival or sometimes merely a path to acceptance, but it is always harmful.

Men's health isn't the only part of their lives that is impacted by a lack of intimate friendships; it also has repercussions on their romantic relationships. When men are missing something from their male friendships, they often go looking for it in a romantic partner, but this can set up a tricky dynamic.

If men can only access true intimacy with their significant other, it puts an awful lot of pressure on that person to provide support and makes that relationship more challenging if there are no other confidants when it comes time to talk through challenges of the relationship. Sure, your partner should be a source of support, but if they are your exclusive source of assistance it can be problematic. I know that if I'm having problems with my partner, I immediately can talk through it with my friends, but so often when I've dated men, I've asked, "Have you talked about this with anyone?" and the answer would be a shrug. The lack of male affection might explain why some men become angry and violent when they do not get the intimacy they feel they're owed from women. It's also partly why breakups and divorces can take a much larger hit on men than on women in heterosexual relationships. While the woman may have other relationships she can rely on for support, her partner has often lost the sole source of support he had. Although the stereotype is that men take breakups much more lightly, men are more likely to suffer both physical and mental health issues and have suicidal thoughts than women after a breakup.

When I spoke to men about this, it became clear that heterosexual men had been implicitly discouraged from being intimate with other men and instructed to prioritize romantic relationships with women. In fact, sexual conquests make a man rise in the male hierarchy. When I brought up the topic with Tristan Garcia, he confided that he had *never* gone out to dinner in a public place with a male friend. Ever. Tristan described an unspoken rule with his peer group that money for dining out is to spend on dates with women, not other men. He said going out to dinner felt too intimate. He even confided that he purposely dressed down when he met up with men, and described being fascinated by the fact that straight women get glammed up to go to brunch or have dinner together. Tristan explained subscribing to a certain casual dress code when he met up with other men because if he were to show up with a clean button-down shirt or with cologne on he was afraid he would be mocked for having given so much thought to his appearance. He explained that a straight man could show up with such attention to clothing only if he was meeting with a woman afterwards.

So, given how vital friendships are to well-being, how do men, and frankly all of us, go about making more lasting friendships? Everyone struggles with friendship, especially as we get older, when schedules and obligations can get in the way. Although it can be tricky to prioritize friends when there is so much competing for our time and attention, I wanted to leave you with a few rules you can try out to improve your own friendships. Regardless of gender, everybody needs a bit of help navigating making and keeping friends as an adult.

MY FIRST TIP: REMEMBER THAT FRIENDSHIP ISN'T A THING YOU HAVE; IT'S A THING YOU DO

Close friends who know you inside out aren't something you get; they're something you earn. Friendship is like your Uber rating: you can't expect it to be good unless you really pay attention to it. If you're rude, careless or late, it will suffer. As Emily Dickinson put it, "My friends are my estate." Your friends become the house you live in, so make sure you maintain it properly. Missing a birthday or an important event in their life isn't the be-all and end-all, but be careful how many times you let that happen. Friendship is a garden you must tend to. You can't just go in there when you need something, because if you only show up to harvest, not sow, you'll be sorely disappointed.

MAKE YOUR PARTNER YOUR FAVORITE FRIEND, NOT YOUR BEST FRIEND

When I asked Esther Perel why married people didn't used to call their partner their best friend as is so common today, she paused and said, "Because they had best friends." Although both men and women are taught to view their partner as their everything, the consequences can be more dire for men than women. If you had a best friend before you got in a relationship, that person should keep that slot and you should tend to that relationship just as much as you used to tend to it. Of course as we grow older, our lives change, we have kids, we travel, we move away, but it's important to maintain the bond. We all struggle with schedules and obligations, but making a point of calling at least one friend every week is a good way to ensure that friendship is ritualized. It could be an unscheduled FaceTime or a weekly text-in where you see how a friend is doing. Put important dates for your friends in your calendar, so you can check in on them when they are taking off for a trip, or going in for surgery or going through a rough time at work.

OBEY THE PRIMARY RULE OF STOICISM: DO MORE LISTENING THAN TALKING

When I asked my friend Daryl why he felt unsatisfied with some of his male friendships, he said: "Men don't listen to each other; they just take turns talking." It stuck with me because that goes against all the rules of communication but also all the rules of the stoic man, the traditional masculine ideal I kept hearing about. Although stoicism is associated with being immune to feelings, its true origin comes from the ancient Greek school of thought that is based on the idea that the highest virtue is knowledge. Epictetus said it best: "We have two ears and one mouth so that we can listen twice as much as we speak." This isn't just good advice for life; it's also great for building friendship. Even if you're the most interesting human being on earth, if you're doing most of the talking, someone else is bored.

FINALLY, PICK THE BEST TEAM

As Tim Ferriss says, "You are the average of the five people you associate with most, so do not underestimate the effects of your pessimistic, unambitious, or toxic friends. If someone isn't making you stronger, they're making you weaker." Be deliberate about who you spend time with. Don't be competitive with your friends' successes, because after all we are all connected, quite literally. Research from Harvard has shown that your friends' happiness and success is literally contagious. Their misery is, too. So don't secretly wish for them to fail at their new job or new workout plan. Misery likes company, but so does happiness.

Remaining silent doesn't make anyone a good man.

—GLENN CANNING

AMUSE-BOUCHE:
Glenn's Story

"I didn't do anything about sexual violence. I never did anything," Glenn Canning said. "And here I am sitting here without my child and I hate myself because that's what it took." Glenn is a former veteran, photographer and writer, and he's also the father of Rehtaeh Parsons, a Canadian teenage girl who tragically lost her life in 2013. She hanged herself in her home in Nova Scotia after, her parents say, she was gang-raped by teenage boys at a party. She was tormented by classmates after a photo of the assault went viral online. In the photo, she was seen bent over a window naked from the waist down vomiting while being penetrated from behind by a teenage boy giving a thumbs-up to the camera. One of the two boys involved who was charged for child pornography told a judge in court that he cried when he heard that Rehtaeh had killed herself. "You should have been crying when she was alive," the judge responded.

Since the passing of his daughter, Glenn has become one of the most outspoken advocates for victims of sexual assault in Canada and beyond. What gets him out of bed every morning is knowing that his daughter's story can inspire others to act, especially when it comes to young men. "The most important thing to ever be done with Rehtaeh's story is having young guys listen to it and say, 'I have to do something,'" Glenn said. He believes too many men remain comfortably ignorant about the prevalence of men's violence against women. "Men have to understand that if they don't know someone in their life who has been assaulted it's because they haven't made it safe enough for them to say they were. The chances are overwhelming that someone that is close to you has had their lives destroyed from sexual violence or abuse."

Although the majority of men don't end up committing sexual assault, Glenn wants to target the men who are complicit in that violence. "Men know their silence is part of the problem," he said. "Every man has a voice and every man has a responsibility to use it. I wish I had done that before my daughter started high school. I'm the most guilty man out there for not using my voice and now it's too late."

As a father, Glenn believes the key to ending violence lies in the way men raise their sons:

> I wish parents raising young men right now would let them know that it is okay to cry. Okay to hurt. Okay to be angry if it's a healthy thing. Violence is never an option, never a resort. Fathers have to be setting examples for their sons. Take your son to a women's march, to an anti-racism event, engaging them in social issues; it was never even thought about when I was growing up. Where did that get us? I'm fifty-five years old; only in the last five years have I started to use my voice.

Today he speaks at different schools spreading the message that sexual assault is a man's issue. He is using his pain to encourage other men to heal:

> A lot of young men have been assaulted. I was molested myself as a child and I didn't address it until my daughter died. A lot of men have been affected by sexual assault and harassment. Men aren't used to saying stuff like that. There's a

blockage in the male psyche that we need to address. This is men doing it. Overwhelmingly it is men doing it; how are we not a part of changing it? It's sad and infuriating.

When I asked Glenn what the biggest mistake a man could make was, he said remain silent about injustice. "I can never forgive myself for that. This issue killed my child. Now I know. Silence is the worst weapon in the world."

> *I'm not gonna be doing the diapers; I'm not gonna be making the food; I may never even see the kids . . . I'll be a good father.*
>
> —DONALD TRUMP
> SPEAKING TO LARRY KING IN 2005

9 Waffles Are His Love Language

I don't know what I did to deserve such a devoted dad, but I became keenly aware that I won the dad lottery pretty early.

Some families go to church on Sundays; my family ate waffles. Every waking Sunday of my life growing up, my father made my entire family a tall stack of waffles—from scratch. If you ask my father any sort of question about the recipe, he will launch into an explanation of the various modifications he's made over the last thirty-five years with a degree of seri-

ousness akin to an expert lecturing the United Nations about the ingredients of a lifesaving drug. When I was in elementary school, waffles were consistently served with fresh-made whipped cream and local maple syrup. One Sunday around 1993, suddenly the whipped cream was replaced by plain yogurt without acknowledgment or explanation. I assumed we were having serious financial problems, a recurring fear I had as a child that was primarily prompted by changes in food rituals. To this day, my dad remains convinced that waffles are a healthy breakfast food. He meticulously altered the recipe mostly to accommodate the women in his life. When my mother became very concerned with the calories we were all ingesting, he replaced butter with canola oil, but just half the oil because it made the waffles "too droopy," he would explain in the same way a scientist would explain how he created the cure for cancer. Every Sunday my father would get up before my sister, my mom and me and start fluffing his egg whites, never asking for any help (mostly because we were lazy and reckless with measuring cups but also because I think he secretly loved doing this for us). The alarm clock I grew up with was the melody of rapid whisk banging that my dad would do to ensure not a single drop of the batter was wasted. As he was the son of two Hungarian refugees who immigrated to Canada with very little, nothing offended him more than wasting resources.

For my dad, waffles were not food; they were a lifestyle. He wouldn't just make a few for Sunday breakfast; he would double the recipe so that we had enough individual waffles to last us for the whole week. My dad also became our family's maple syrup provider, buying it in bulk so we would never run out. Of course, purchasing maple syrup by the pound was also a surefire way to make sure he got the best price. As he often repeated to me and my sister, paying full price for anything was for "losers." About once a month, he would make us run down to get more maple syrup from the downstairs bathroom, which had become a storage room for all the cans of maple syrup, a thing my sister and I just assumed was normal until our friends would come over and start asking very valid questions about it. We both were fortunate enough to experience a childhood where our bathroom was always filled with maple syrup and our fridge was always packed with waffles. Every morning before he would drive us to school on his way to his job at the post office, my dad would eat a waffle like it was a piece of toast, nonchalantly flipping the pages of his newspaper. I had read somewhere that the children of parents who had lived through famine or excruciating circumstances had really good metabolisms, and I could see how he had inherited one by the number of waffles I've seen him ingest over the course of my life. My grandmother had immigrated to Canada after being orphaned at the age of 11, working as a child domestic servant and then at a refugee camp after World War II. Her unwavering grit had clearly trickled down to my father, both mentally and physically. He had a stellar work ethic and inherited a metabolism that made him tall and skinny despite eating dessert for breakfast. Waffles were in fact such a recurring staple over the course of my life that they became a totally nonexuberant breakfast food for me. The way I feel about waffles is how most people feel about stale cereal. Let's just say I grew up with a lot of waffle privilege and I'm still learning to check it.

I had a renewed appreciation for my father when I realized that he'd become somewhat of a legend among my male friends, something that was impossible for him to register since he was born with an ego the size of a small raisin. After my coworker and dear friend Liran spent a weekend at my parents' house in Montreal, I walked by his desk weeks later and saw a Post-it note titled "Questions for Andrew Plank." Most of the questions were about real estate, one of the many random areas my dad had staggeringly good advice in. When I first moved to New York with my then-boyfriend, he was stunned when my dad drove down from Montreal with the mix for his homemade waffles in a reusable plastic ice-cream container (the same one from when I was a kid) and his waffle irons for us to feast on Sunday morning. "New York City is the food capital of the world; doesn't he want to us to take him to a restaurant?" my boyfriend said, laughing. But maintaining rituals even after I had moved away is exactly the kind of behavior I had come to expect from my dad, because our entire relationship had been defined by them.

When I was little, our nightly ritual would end with him making my female stuffed monkey converse with me in English (I grew up speaking mostly French). Although I owned forty-six stuffed monkeys (I was convinced I was Jane Goodall), Emma was my first monkey and she had a special place in my heart because she would never turn down a request for a conversation. Emma would ask me about my day, she would ask me about how I was feeling and when I had full-blown meltdowns she would prop my door open with her head and always crack some joke to make me smile. I remain convinced that if more adults had pretend pet monkeys their loved ones could make talk, we'd save a lot of money on therapy. His care and attention continued throughout my time in college. When I performed in *The Vagina Monologues*, he came to both performances. He recorded the entire play on his camcorder, but, unhappy with the quality of the sound, he came back the next night and heard me say the word "vagina" another forty-nine times. When I ended up in crutches three (Canadian!) winters in a row during college, he made the half-hour drive to downtown Montreal to get me to class and back every single day. Although he worked a full forty-hour workweek at the post office, with an hour commute, he still managed to make me, my sister and my mom feel like we were his number-one priority in his life, mostly because we were.

This story about my dad matters because for far too many children it's not the norm. While we expect moms to be nurturing, we don't always expect the same from dads. My father's parenting style never felt particularly unique or special to me because it was all I knew. But when I would see people's reactions and shock at my dad's behavior, it became apparent to me just how unconventional he was. It highlighted one of the biggest lies we perpetuate about men: they're not naturally good at caring for others, let alone their own children.

I also saw similar reactions from people when I interviewed Canadian Prime Minister Justin Trudeau. Because I had always been keenly invested in the power of positive fatherhood and believed it could be the key to creating a better future, one of the first questions I wanted to ask him when I got to interview him when I was reporting on the 2016 election for Vox was how he balanced being a father with being the prime minister of Canada. The reaction I received from some of my colleagues and friends in the media surprised me. "How refreshing to hear a man asked about this topic for a change!" Emma Gray wrote in HuffPost Women. I'm not one to reject praise, but it shouldn't be surprising for men to receive this question: in fact, it should be totally normal and, frankly, boring.

"I take time to work and I take time to play with [the kids]. Similar with Sophie, have time where I'm working and time where I'm just the goofy husband," the prime minister told me as we sat down waiting for our poutines at a Montreal-style deli in the East Village. He went one step further and said that fatherhood wasn't just a commitment while he was in the home; it was intrinsically connected to his job as a world leader. "I'm in politics not in spite of the fact that I have kids, but *because* of the fact that I have kids," he said. Trudeau explained that he tried to make his children a priority even in his job as he weighed the decisions he made as a politician and that being a father made him better at his job. "Is the time I am away from them compensated by the fact that I'm busy making a better world for them?" Trudeau also spoke about being keenly aware that he was modeling a traditional division of labor to his children given his job. "In a certain sense, highlighting gender stereotypes has been a little more challenging because we're in a family where, you know, Sophie does a lot of great activism and work and public speaking, but she's mostly a mom and I'm the one who is the breadwinner and we live in a place because of *my* job," he explained. "Part of it is modeling. Showing that I'm attentive and respectful, and very much in a partnership with Sophie as much as we are in a marriage. That I respect her."

If Justin Trudeau had been a woman, none of what he said about parenting would be newsworthy. In fact, it would be 100 percent basic if it had come out of the mouth of a woman. It was precisely because it was said by a man that made it sound revolutionary. His candor about the difficulty of balancing work inside the home and outside the home felt revolutionary because I couldn't think of another male politician who had spoken so frankly about it. Saying that he wanted to go beyond the male provider model despite not being in a position to do it was a pretty extraordinary and rare admission from a man, let alone a world leader.

Although many reporters have been trying to shift the narrative, the sad truth is that we don't often hear men being asked about fatherhood because parenting is still not considered a focal point for men. Jennifer Garner expressed this back in 2014 when she and her then-husband, Ben Affleck, came back from a press day with a very different set of questions. Although every single reporter asked Garner about how she balanced her family with her career, Affleck's most recurring question was about how he balanced acting with his libido after spending so much time with *Gone Girl* costar Emily Ratajkowski's breasts. "We're talking about them—they are real and they are fabulous and everyone should take a look and enjoy," Garner artfully said about Ratajkowski's breasts in a speech to a roomful of women at a *Glamour* event. "As for work-life balance, he said that no one asked him about it that day. As a matter of fact, no one had ever asked him about it. Not once." Even Simone de Beauvoir, one of the most recognized and distinguished thinkers of her time, noticed this gross double standard and discussed it in her groundbreaking feminist oeuvre *The Second Sex*, in 1949. "I could not help but comment to my distinguished audience that every question asked about Sartre concerned his work, while all those asked about Beauvoir concerned her personal life," she wrote.

Interestingly, since de Beauvoir wrote her book almost seventy years ago women have progressed immensely, receiving more interest and questions about their life outside the home, but curiously, men haven't received more questions about their life inside the home.

You'll notice that Garner was asked about her job, but the accompanying questions about her role inside the home were only reserved for her and not her partner, Ben Affleck. Thanks to feminists who have fought for women to be perceived as more than simply mothers, the work that women do outside of the home has become accepted and valued. If Simone de Beauvoir suddenly came back from the dead, she would probably be impressed to see that one of the hard-earned victories of the feminist revolutions of the twenty-first century is that our culture has begun to view women beyond simply their roles as mothers. Although plenty of women choose to work only inside the home, the assumption has become that they can do both. Although there is still an enormous pressure to bear children and participate in motherhood, we have largely come to terms with the idea that most women work and that this is a good thing. Society even wholeheartedly celebrates women who pour themselves into it. It's so accepted that Ivanka Trump, the daughter of one of the most reactionary presidents in modern US history, literally wrote a book titled *Women Who Work*. The importance of women's roles in the workplace is celebrated regardless of political party, which for America, one of the most divided countries in the industrialized world, says a lot. It's largely accepted and even encouraged in most industrialized countries that women have ambitions that go beyond the home. But although the gender revolution has been so far remarkable, it has been grossly incomplete: while women have been taken seriously as workers, men have yet to really be taken seriously as caretakers. And embracing the role of men in the home means shifting their role outside of it, or at least adapting the expectations that are associated with it. In other words, if men are to spend more time in the home, it probably means they are rethinking their relationship to the time they spend outside of it.

All this time we were so focused on getting people comfortable with the idea that women work, but that revolution was never followed by a movement saying it's okay for men not to.

THE SILENT PANIC AMONGST MILLENIAL MEN

Although very few young men would admit this to me, the discomfort with this asymmetrical gender revolution reveals itself in the largely silent yet growing anxiety they have toward working women and their role as fathers. Although millennial men will say they are comfortable with shifting and blurring the roles of gender inside the home, when they're asked about the same topic anonymously, their answers tell a different story. No man I spoke to admitted that he felt intimidated or uncomfortable with women's economic and social gains, but their answers in anonymous polls reveal a discomfort with women's empowerment and what it means for shifting gendered norms. Instead of feeling excited about a different kind of masculinity and a different way of being a man, young men are expressing fear around the idea of the role of a man in the family changing. In other words, although men's increased participation in the home might be popular with feminists, it's not necessarily popular with a lot of young men. Rather than seeing the model of the male breadwinner who works outside the home and the female housewife who works inside the home as outdated, they are clinging more firmly to it and to the traditional definition of being a man.

As academic and family studies professor Stephanie Coontz writes in *The New York Times,* "Overall, Americans aged 18 to 34 are less comfortable than their elders with the idea of women holding roles historically held by men." She cites research by Joanna Pepin and David Cotter, who found that more young men today believe in the superiority of the male breadwinner model for their family than in 1994. Although only 42 percent of male high school seniors in 1994 believed the best model was a man working and a woman at home, that figure has curiously jumped to 58 percent today. Even the number of young men 18–25 who disagree with the statement "a woman's place is in the home" has shockingly decreased. Their data also shows more young men today believe that a woman working outside the home harms preschool children. The number of men who believe that a working mother can have a relationship with her child that is as warm as that of a stay-at-home mom is also lower than it used to be. There's also a significant and noticeable dip in support for working mothers between 2010 and 2014. Researchers say that drop has mostly been driven by young men. This signals that heterosexual millennial men, although more likely to be married to a working woman, are less supportive of her than their fathers were of their wives.

When I first came across this data, it felt counterintuitive, so odd that it felt like it couldn't be true. It's particularly shocking because millennial men are more progressive than their fathers in almost every other respect. I couldn't find a single issue they were less tolerant of. They are more supporting of policies to protect the environment, of laws that promote income equality, they're more likely to be supportive of LGBTQ rights and hell, they're even more likely to identify as feminists and socialists. Why weren't they embracing changing gendered roles along with all other radical causes? Why would they embrace change on every front but resist it in the case of their own partners?

The more I thought about it, the clearer it became to me. The male provider/female caretaker model was still the go-to model for men for one simple reason: there was no other alternative. Young men were resisting women being identified with that label because there was no other model for them to embrace instead. All this time we've focused on the changing role of women inside the workplace and inside the home, not realizing that this would also shift men's. We updated what it means to be a woman, but we didn't update what it meant to be a man. We've had articles, books, entire conferences, dedicated to helping women navigate these new shifting roles while expecting men to figure it out all on their own. If young men aren't presented with a viable substitute for that model of the man as the provider, they're stuck idealizing the only model they have. Men were secretly wondering: If she's the provider, what does that make me?

I had a sneaking suspicion that men weren't the only ones subscribing to this outdated version of manhood as defined by providing, and I was right. According to Pew Research data, the expectation to provide is not just something that men self-impose; women also expect it. Although a third of women make as much as or more than their partners, seven out of ten Americans overall think that providing is very important to be a good husband. Providing financially was even more important than contributing to domestic work in the home. Conversely, barely three out of ten Americans believe that it's requisite to be a good wife, although men were significantly less likely than women to believe that providing should be part of a woman's responsibilities. Moreover, the less education you have and the lower you are in terms of socioeconomic groups, the more likely you are to believe that men's roles should be rooted in providing. So sure, men are limiting themselves to a narrow view of masculinity, but so is everyone else around them. It's a cage we're all trapped in. This means that some men might want to live more equitable lives and blur the lines of gendered expectations within their relationships, but the women they are in partnerships with might not always be interested. After all, they've absorbed the same messages about ideal masculinity that men have. As male relationship expert and author Terry Real put it in his conversation on therapist Kathy Caprino's podcast, "Patriarchy does not exist only in men. The force of patriarchy is the water that we all swim in and we're the fish."

NURTURING FATHERHOOD IS STILL SEEN AS UNNATURAL

This myth of the sole male provider largely goes unnoticed for both women and men because we're often told it's part of men's nature. Pop science is often used as a throwaway to justify the low standard we set for men. In fact, every time we have a thoughtful conversation about the involvement of fathers, there's a classic counterargument that active fathering goes against men's nature, which is fueled by the idea that women doing any other role than parenting, like providing financially, is against theirs. The rigidity with which we approach men's and women's roles in the family was clear from the panic expressed by conservative pundit Erick Erikson after Pew published data showing that 40 percent of breadwinners are now female. In an appearance on Fox News, he argued that women taking up the role of breadwinners and, consequently, fathers taking on the role of the caretaker was a threat to the gender role order. "When you look at biology, when you look at the natural world, the roles of a male and a female in society and in other animals, the male typically is the dominant role," he told Lou Dobbs. "The female, it's not antithesis, or it's not competing; it's a complementary role." In another segment, where he was challenged by Megyn Kelly for his comments on Dobbs's show, he protested against those who want to treat women and men equally as parents, warning that they believe "the male and female role are completely interchangeable." Although the backlash to their views on female breadwinners being a threat to society was anti-woman, their assumptions about fathers in the family were just as insulting to men. In claiming that women spending time outside the home was dangerous is the inherent assumption that the father spending more time inside the home is not preferable either.

Given how often this stereotype is reinforced, it's no wonder providing was central to the identity of every man I spoke to, regardless of where they grew up or how they identified. It was virtually impossible to speak about what it means to be a man without it coming up. But where does the idea of the provider even come from? It is associated with being one of the oldest and core defining characteristics of masculinity. The term is used interchangeably with the term "breadwinner" and it's associated with financial stability and premised on bringing in an amount of money that goes toward responding to the needs of the family. The belief that men are solely responsible for monetarily supporting their family came to fruition during the industrial revolution. It wasn't until the early twentieth century that the idea of a "family wage" became an organizing principle of our economy as we know it. As Barbara Ehrenreich remarks in *The Hearts of Men,* this family wage was only available to the more privileged, most often white, male workers, like those who were members of unions or certain professions. Nonetheless, this is the origin of the gender wage gap. "As it turned out, the other side of the principle that a man should earn enough to support a family has been that a woman doesn't need enough to support even herself," Ehrenreich writes. This explains why a woman such as Oprah Winfrey, back when she worked as a local broadcaster, was told that she couldn't get the same salary for the same job as a man because she didn't have a family to support. The argument that men needed to fulfill their role as economic supporters justified the creation and the persistence of what we know as the wage gap today. Women were pushed out of higher-paying jobs, as male-dominated fields became better paid. The fact that female breadwinners now head, according to some accounts, 40 percent of households in the United States has rendered the concept of the family wage completely obsolete and yet it continues to underpin the way families organize. So the concept of the provider came from a different time, but although it felt outdated to me, did it feel outdated to men, too? When I decided to ask men about what the term "provider" meant to them, it was clear that although there's no updated alternative label to replace the term with many men had already begun redefining it on their own. When I asked men on Facebook if they identified as a provider, a captivating thread ensued. "As a parent, yes. As a man, no," Jim Dooley, a 47-year-old father who lives in Eddyville, New York, responded. "I spent most of my life in a blue-collar job, surrounded by, for lack of a better term, regular men and most of my friends would fit that description too." When I followed up with Jim, he told me that he would rather get rid of the term "provider" altogether:

> We should just avoid the word. Just use the word "parent". "Provider" has too many negative connotations . . . The fact that in

the past a man's role was seen as more valuable because he was the one who provided food and shelter seems really sad. It's not only sad that we treated women this way. By undervaluing the work of stay-at-home moms, we were short changing our children, too. On another level, the word "provider" does have a clear definition and I'm sure it has been used to make women feel inferior, both intentionally and unintentionally. And now that more women are playing the role of provider, stay-at-home dads shouldn't be made to feel inferior either. Let's learn from our mistakes.

For other men, it wasn't the word "provider" that they thought needed to change; it was the determiner that precedes it. We often say "the provider" as opposed to "a provider," implying that it's a unique responsibility that falls on the shoulders of one single person. "Provider seems to have a negative connotation to me," said Terrance Kayton in the same thread. "I am a trans man, I identify with being a provider for myself and a partner for my lover, and together we provide for our family. It sounds, to me, that 'the provider' can only be one person and that person has sole responsibility to be the provider." Terrance's uneasiness with the term "provider" led him to come up with a whole new label for himself as a man and parent. "I just made up 'co-provider,' which I feel offers the opportunity for multi-loving parents, partners and families to be seen," he said. Michael McCall added that it also diminished the complexity of the partnership between a couple. "The use of 'the' in describing any role in a mutual relationship is likely dangerous and cheapens what could be a richer, more nuanced collaboration," he wrote. "I think my wife and I have always seen the parental role of provider similarly—to provide our son with guides for finding important things in life and then space to find his path."

Some men also expressed disdain for the term because it suggested a power dynamic between two partners and a role hierarchy that could put a strain on the relationship. "The concepts of providership and dependency are loathsome and don't help build good foundations for partners," Sean David Burke wrote. He said that he found himself working longer hours or taking extra jobs to ensure that he can pay for his partner's experiences instead of focusing on spending time in the actual relationship. "The last thing I ever want is expectations or dominion over any living being, especially a person I love," he said. "Sadly, it has often created imbalance, resentment towards me and a pattern that needs to change." Another dad said that he didn't need a distinct role from his wife, especially since at the end of the day, all the resources are pooled. "As a husband, I make no distinction between what I bring home and what my wife brings home."

Other men said that they rejected the term "provider" because they felt like it was reductive of the plethora of contributions they could make as men. "There's a really odd dynamic where 'provider' is often associated with providing materials like breadwinning despite providing care proving every bit as important (if not more so) than material odds and ends for the long-term well-being of children," Trevor Counceller wrote. "My definition is much broader than either of my parents'." David Cline, who stayed at home and raised his kids for fifteen years, said he didn't view himself as the provider, but that didn't stop him from knowing that he was providing. "I provided stability, love, the ability for my wife to not worry about the boys while she was at work," he wrote. Single dad Joey Braz viewed the term "providing" as a two-way street with multiple and varying different sources:

> "Provider" is a gender- and age-neutral term in my house. I'm a single dad in a three-generation household. I might collect a paycheck, but I couldn't do that if my parents couldn't help w/ the kids, house, etc. I also couldn't do that if the kids couldn't help out, too. We ALL provide each other with love, support,

accountability & instilling of values. Sometimes it's the adults & sometimes it's the kiddos who provide. It might not be how I grew up but that's what family means to me today.

Only one man in the entire thread identified as the sole provider and said he found it extremely challenging because it was never his plan or a preferred situation. "I always wanted to be a co-provider and partner," said Alex Bell. "The idea that others had to be dependent on me didn't feel like an equal relationship. For most of my relationship, my wife and I were co-providers, until a series of car accidents resulted in my wife with traumatic brain injury and unable to work. For the past seven years I have been the main provider. . . . It no longer feels like a partnership. I long for the days that we were equally contributing."

This fascinating thread on providing was illuminating because, although my question used neutral language about whether men identified with the term "provider" and what it meant to them, there wasn't a single man who had a positive reaction toward it. In lieu of a scientific poll on the topic (if any researchers are reading, please feel inspired to do one!), this thread offered an interesting glimpse of the frustrations, contradictions and pressures that men encounter with the concept so often imposed on their identity as men.

Given the anxiety so many men feel about the label, how is it that the overwhelming majority of Americans, seven out of ten to be exact, still use a term that so many men find outdated or insulting? After all, I agreed with the men I spoke to. Providing money is important. Providing care is important. It had always been confusing to me that only one counts as providing. The problem is not the way that men identify with this role but rather our narrow view of what a provider does. How is it that paying for a frozen turkey is providing but preparing said turkey isn't? How is the person buying the book providing but not the one teaching that child how to use it? A pencil has no value if a child doesn't know how to write with it.

There's a gap between the expectations of men's lives and their actual lives, and the most effective way to alleviate that pressure of being a provider for men is to expand and empower the multitude of their roles and, particularly, the richness of their role as caretakers. The ideals we impart on men puts such a high premium on providing that it crowds out any other contributions that fathers can make to their family, which can be just as, if not more, important than financial resources. Distilling the role of men in their families down to a material focus diminishes and lowers the standard for all dads.

Earlier in this chapter, I discussed how the dearth of questions about fatherhood for men in popular culture revealed a lack of investment in their role as caretakers. But even worse is that when stories about fathers do show up, in the rare case that there are depictions of fatherhood in our media landscape, they can be very bad. The way outdated masculinity norms are embedded in the way fatherhood is represented became undeniable to me when I started working in media and would see the kinds of stories about dads that would receive media coverage. Let's just say I knew we had an expectations problem with the way we view men when the biggest news story about fathers in 2016 was that a single dad had braided hair. I imagined headlines about moms following the same framing: "Florida Mom Successfully Feeds Own Children" or "Local Mom Gets Everyone to School on Time and Remembers to Wear Deodorant." Although I support appreciating and celebrating dads, the subtext in many of the news stories was shock that men were average to decent caretakers.

The flip side of being surprised by dads who do the bare minimum is the rush to criticism of mothers who are trying to do the bare maximum. The only thing that rivaled the traffic of a story about an average dad was that of a story about a terrible mom. The hunger for these stories was undeniable. For every news story about an "awesome dad" who miraculously changed a diaper without accidentally murdering anyone, there was a story about a mother criminally breastfeeding her child for as long as she believed was right for her child. A trend that was coined "mom-shaming" started percolating online around 2015. It was a genre of amateur photography of the cruelest form where people would snap pictures of what they perceived as bad (curiously, only female) parenting and post it online. One picture of a woman nursing went viral after someone posted it protesting that she should "cover up," clearly defeating the entire purpose of an already pretty questionable point.

As I watched the bare-minimum dad and the bare-maximum mom as internet trends simultaneously take off, it dawned on me: How could our standard for motherhood be so high yet our standard for fatherhood be so low?

The lowballing of fatherhood didn't feel fueled by ill intent, but rather it felt like the result of the lack of storytelling about fatherhood created a dad-story desert that turned average fatherhood into front-page news. These stories were getting a lot of traffic because people weren't used to seeing representations of men in the home; that's why the rare story about them felt like a National Geographic documentary on an endangered species. The way our society fails to accurately depict fatherhood starts early and goes well beyond the news or the mainstream media. It's even salient in the books we give our kids. Suzanne M. Flannery Quinn noticed when she looked at two hundred bestselling picture books and found fathers were far less likely to be represented as prominent parents. Numerous studies have found an underrepresentation of fathers in children's literature. And then there's television and films where dads are often presented as absent or bumbling idiots.

And even when fathers step out of the mold and prioritize caretaking even momentarily, they risk being humiliated or mocked for it. For instance, when New York Mets second baseman Daniel Murphy missed two baseball games because he wanted to enjoy the full three days (!) of the paternity leave offered by Major League Baseball after the birth of his son, he was ridiculed by former NFL quarterback turned sports reporter Boomer Esiason. "Quite frankly, I would've said 'C-section before the season starts,'" he said on his radio show, suggesting that a woman should undergo surgery to prevent paternity leave (or something). His co-host, Craig Carton, piled on. "To me, and this is just my sensibility, assuming the birth went well, assuming your wife is fine, assuming the baby is fine—twenty-four hours, you stay there, baby is good, you have a good support system for the mom and the baby, you get your ass back to your team and you play baseball," he said. Mike Francesa, a veteran sports reporter who has been nicknamed the Sports Pope, reiterated the same perspective a few days later on the same program. "I don't know why you need three days off, I'm going to be honest. You see the birth and you get back," he said. "Your wife doesn't need your help the first couple days; you know that."

I personally don't know any women who would agree with that statement, but who asked us anyway, these guys seem like the real experts on pregnancy!

Men seem to have taken notice of the terrible way they are portrayed and are increasingly annoyed with it and expressing a craving of different images of themselves in television and films. Dove Men+Care conducted a study in 2015 that showed that although a wide majority of men (86 percent) believed that masculinity means something different to them than it does for their fathers, only 7 percent of men could identify with current representations of masculinity in the media. "Looking at dads in pop culture and movies, I end up being so turned off by the role of the dad and how that type of fatherhood is displayed," stay-at-home dad Christopher Persley told me. Even in the rare case where fathers are shown as caretakers, they are represented differently than moms. As an educator and media critic with his own blog, *The Brown Gothamite*, Christopher pays close attention to positive representations of fatherhood, but he finds himself disappointed more often than not. "The standards are still so low, it's almost like we are just given a pat on the back for being there." Christopher brought up the second *Incredibles* movie, which had just come out at the time of our interview and was being lauded for its representation of a father who stays in the home for his wife to go out and be the superhero. "I wasn't all that impressed with what he did," Christopher said. "Yes, he was there at home with his kids, but he didn't enjoy it. He didn't even want to be there. That's not worthy of celebration for me." Indeed, staying at home was presented as something he *had* to do, not something he *wanted* to do. And that difference matters because seeing a dad enjoying caretaking in pop culture is still far too rare.

The negative messaging about fatherhood in media, television and film isn't just annoying; these messages shape and impact the perceptions and treatment of fathers. Christopher is all too familiar with them. Because fathers are so rarely seen actively and successfully parenting their kids, he finds himself being stared at when he's out in public with his daughter. "I always feel like there are eyes on me as a parent," he said. "So many people question aspects of my parenting." As a black father, Christopher says the criticism and surveillance is particularly pernicious. He says that people will point out the way his daughter Camilla's hair looks to him, assuming that it's a failure on his part rather than the result of a conscious decision to let her wear her hair the way she likes. People often stare or rudely interrupt him while he's having a private conversation with his daughter to comment on his performance as a dad. Even when it's to say something complimentary about him, Christopher finds it invasive. "I know they think it's a positive thing, they feel like they need to comment on my parenting because I'm a dad, but I've never noticed anyone saying that to a woman or a mother. I don't appreciate it," he said. "Even Camilla notices it, so it's challenging to have people engage with me as if my parenting is on display."

Although the situation feels grim for men trying to flip the script on traditional masculinity as it relates to fatherhood, there is hope, especially when we look to other countries that made fundamental changes to their laws and have seen men enjoy more freedom as a result of those policy changes. Although it feels inevitable, it's not everywhere that fatherhood is primarily associated with "providing" and a prioritization of work over family. Denmark is a great example; it's one of the countries that enjoys the most generous parental leave policies in the world. Dads receive two weeks of paid paternity leave after the birth of a child and are entitled to taking up to a full year off. In 2001, the country received a lot of attention for its introduction of its daddy leave quota, with a use-it-or-lose-it father leave that could not be transferred to the mother. It created a new default, which fundamentally challenged assumptions about the way families operate and expectations in the workplace on new fathers. Even though Danish men take far more leave than men in other industrialized countries, because Danish men don't take as much leave as Norwegian and Finnish men (largely due to the fact that the gender wage gap is higher, which means men usually make more than their wives and prefer to remain in the workforce), the government has continued its efforts and commitment to encouraging them to take time to father. For instance, the government recently implemented a new campaign with the tagline *"Orlov—tag det som en mand,"* which translates to: "Paternity leave—take it like a man."

This intentional emphasis on expanding the role of men as fathers doesn't just offer relief for mothers, it also happens to be associated with a more positive definition of manhood. For instance, research has shown that Danish men, especially those who have more education, have become less likely to subscribe to more patriarchal or traditional male gender norms. Given how central men's role as caretakers is in Danish society, it's not surprising that research on Danish dads shows that when men talk about fatherhood, they emphasize their role as caregivers rather than the financial support they give. "I think that being there for your children is the most masculine thing I can think of," one subject in the study said. Denmark's commitment to blurring the divisions of labor around gendered lines appears to have a direct impact on men's perceptions of their role as men.

Expanding parental leave doesn't just mean that more men end up taking it; it also means their role as men fundamentally changes and that they are free from the stigma imposed by constrictive masculinity norms like working over being inside the home. This became clear to me when I started asking my male friends if they'd be discouraged from taking parental leave, and the most interesting answer came from Tobiass Naess, a Norwegian man I met while I was speaking at a conference in Bergen. "In my company, they look at you funny if you don't," he told me. In other words, instead of being stigmatized for taking daddy leave, he knew he would be stigmatized if he didn't. A nation's paternity leave for fathers sets the tone; it changes the default and the impact on behavior is huge.

When I asked Tobiass if he identified as a provider, he didn't even really get the question. "I'm not even sure I one hundred percent get what you mean with 'identify as providers,'" he (adorably) said. This wasn't a language barrier; it was a cultural one. When I explained that it meant providing financially, he said parents didn't really use gender to determine their role inside their families. "Speaking for myself and my social circle—and I guess it's representative-ish for a fair part of Norway—after the first months, parenthood is parenthood. There are really no father tasks and mother tasks," he said. "It's seen as just a normal thing to do to take care of your kids. It's not masculine nor feminine. It's just parenting." After his wife went through a double mastectomy and their third child had to be bottle-fed, Tobiass loved being able to participate in the act of feeding him. "Being part of that feeding ritual of the tiny toddler—that was new. And nice. But I never thought of it as 'feminine,'" he said. "It certainly does not challenge any part of my masculinity, and I struggle to see how it could." Living inside his logic even for a few minutes felt really nice.

Tobiass explained that the men who couldn't take the leave they wanted existed, but they were a minority. "Not taking paternity leave is seen as a little silly/backwards," he explained. "In some industries, male-dominated ones in particular like finance, there is still some adversity to paternity leave. It's a recurring debate. But the debate here is very different from what you have in the United States. Paternity leave is the norm. What's probably interesting is that the paternity leave is supported across the political spectrum, from far left to far right. The difference lies in how much should be mandatory."

The Scandinavian model is dreamy, but the United States is still very far from it. In fact, it's the only industrialized nation without any guaranteed paid parental leave. Very few American companies voluntarily offer time off for their employees, because the government lets them. The vast majority of Americans do not receive any paid time off to care for their children after they are born. In fact, only 14 percent of the companies in the United States offer paid parental leave, for either mothers or fathers. The average American father barely takes any time off after the birth of a child. According to a 2011 Boston College study, three out of four men took a week or less after the birth of their child. That means I have a carton of oat milk that's lasted longer than the average American man's paternity leave. The lack of parental leave for men is a consequence but also the cause of the unfinished gender revolution.

Despite the reservations that millennial men have about the parenting abilities of working moms, it's not women who are reporting not seeing their children enough; it's men. According to Pew, although fathers are spending more time with their kids than ever (they used to spend about 2.5 hours with their kids per week in 1965; they now spend on average 7.3 hours with them), fathers much more than mothers report feeling like they don't see their kids enough. Despite the stereotype of the overworked busy mom who accidentally puts her baby in a briefcase, women are spending, in the grand scheme of things, quite a lot of time inside the home. In other words, men's fear and anxieties about their role as men in the family are real, but women spending even more time in the home won't necessarily solve anything. It's strange that when we talk about work-life balance, we often frame the problem as women not being able to find enough time to see their kids, when the data shows that women spend *more* time with their children today than they used to, not less. Looking at these data points presents a different solution to the problem of work-life balance: instead of focusing on how much time women are able to spend in the home, perhaps we should be focusing on how much time men can.

While fathers in the United States aren't taking nearly as much time off to care for their kids as they would want, some are starting to challenge the very norms and assumptions about them that justify that imbalance in the first place. A small group of men are starting to bravely question the gendered falsehoods about caretaking and the policies that they end up creating. Their activism is pointing out the way archaic masculinity scripts can lead to gender discrimination against men. In the same way that women created meaningful change by challenging unfair laws that don't guarantee equal treatment in the workplace, men have started fighting unjust laws that prevent them from being equal partners in the home.

I had the pleasure to speak to one of them, Derek Rotondo. The 31-year-old millennial dad lives in Ohio. As a fraud investigator at JPMorgan Chase who was expecting his second child, he was excited to hear that his company had just expanded parental leave for expecting parents. "Once our policy had been updated, I was excited to spend time with my new son. But then I learned that I couldn't." Although JPMorgan had increased its parental leave to sixteen weeks, Derek was denied when he asked for it because he's a man. The company told him he could only receive two weeks off because the longer parental leave was only for the "primary caretaker," which was assumed to only be a woman. He was told that a man could not be the primary caregiver unless he could prove the biological mother had gone back to work or that she was "medically incapable of any care of the child." Under the company's current policy, men are automatically considered "non-primary" parents. "I wanted to spend as much time with my second one when he was new, because there is so much bonding and trust that occurs so early." Gobsmacked by what he learned, he decided to take on the giant corporation with a lawsuit claiming sex discrimination. The ACLU has joined the case, arguing that the "policy is outdated and discriminates against both moms and dads by reinforcing the stereotype that raising children is women's work, and that men's work is to be the breadwinner." Cases like these expose how policies that codify gender roles really benefit no one.

When I spoke to Derek about his ideals of being a man, they were multifaceted. Being a good dad wasn't a political position or a partisan decision. Derek didn't fit the stereotype: he didn't seem particularly progressive. All he wanted was to simply be there for his children. His version of masculinity was tied to being a present father, but Derek also subscribed to numerous other ideals tied to more traditional masculinity. Identifying with more traditional or "manly stuff" didn't stop him from wanting to also be taken seriously as a nurturer and caretaker:

> I try to be really good at everything that I do. I am not a big guy, but I can hold my own in a fight. . . . I am an excellent rifle shot and pretty good pistol shot. I'm the cook in my house. I run the finances and wonder why my friends our age are broke. Why should being a dad be any different? I choose to excel at everything that I possibly can. Being the best dad I can be is part of that, and being around is necessary to facilitate that goal.

At the time that this book was written, Derek's lawsuit was still being litigated. When I asked him about backlash he faced because of the lawsuit, he said it primarily was coming from men who thought he should be grateful for getting *any* time off. "Any negative feedback I get is mostly from older men," he said. Frankly, they didn't know what he was complaining about. "You should be thankful you get two weeks; we only had two days," was the typical response he got.

Despite being marginalized by other men, Derek is not the first to question corporate America's stigma against working dads. I got the chance to speak with Josh Levs, a former CNN correspondent who fought a legal battle against Time Warner's parental leave policy in 2015. After his wife had to have an emergency delivery and his daughter was born prematurely, he was told he couldn't take more than two weeks off. Had he been a woman, he would have had access to more time off—ten weeks to be exact. "I'm home caring for my four-pound preemie, my sick wife, and my two boys," Josh told me. "I message work asking whether I have to go back to work right then or whether I can get the ten paid weeks. That's when they said no." He ended up suing his employer and receiving a settlement. He's now an advocate fighting to end the stigma against men taking parental leave. He says it's not just about workplaces giving dads more time off but also about ensuring that they aren't shamed when they take the time. "I grew up with gender equality, but the workplace didn't," he explained to me over the phone. "An overwhelming amount of paternity leave is not used and the number-one reason is stigma." "When men take paternity leave, they are demoted and fired for asking for it. I've spoken to many men who were told they simply could not take paternity leave."

And nowhere is the injustice of offering men less paid leave than women clearer than for gay men. Although both Josh and Derek have female partners who could take some time off, the habit of offering less parental leave to men disproportionately impacts same-sex families. Many gay fathers end up simply combining their sick days (if they have any) to piece together even the smallest amount of time to bond with their child.

Although some skeptics will say that a cultural shift isn't possible in a place like the United States because Scandinavian countries are fundamentally different, we've seen cultural shifts happen at the state level on much smaller scales. In California, for instance, when it became the first state to ever institute paid parental leave in 2004 and then began expanding its daddy leave policy in 2005, men were 46 percent more likely to take time off and took it for longer amounts of time. Men taking daddy leave rose by almost 50 percent and were more likely to spend time with the child while the mother was back at work, which increased the overall amount of time that babies in the state spent with at least one parent present inside the home. In other words, when we make policy changes to parental leave, men like it. When parental leave is available, it shifts male attitudes toward their role as men in their families.

But the unfinished gender revolution is not just about the division of labor when it comes to who takes care of the kids; it's also about the division of labor when it comes to who takes care of the house. The fact that domestic tasks remain still so gender segregated for straight couples is a direct consequence of this incomplete gender revolution. While women have taken more roles inside the workplace, they still perform most of the work inside the home. The housework gender gap exists in every country across the world. Even in gender equality utopic countries like Denmark, men spend an hour less on domestic chores than women per day. In the United States, women still do 40 percent more housework than men. One survey even found that women admitted to preferring to ask their children rather than their husbands to do certain tasks. Sure, men in the United States do more domestic work than any other generation of men prior to them, but they overestimate how much they do and how equal it is with what their partners do. And although the stereotype is that working mothers are more likely to neglect to spend time with their children because they have full-time jobs, the modern working woman actually spends as much time with her children as midcentury mothers who spent all their time at home. And they didn't even have robot vacuums back then!

But again, the message to men is that real men don't clean, cook or change diapers. This lie is often peddled in conversations about heterosexual marriages. It was repeated by author Susan Patton, nicknamed Princeton Mom after she wrote a viral op-ed in the Princeton newspaper instructing college women to "find a husband on campus before you graduate." In a debate titled "Feminism vs. Family" I had with her in 2014, she argued that if (straight?) women were focused on their careers they wouldn't be able to find husbands until their thirties, which means they would be competing with more attractive and younger women in their twenties. Her argument was rooted in biological differences between men and women and was based on the idea that women had a "shelf life" (and of course that men didn't). Suddenly doubling up as an expert on female libido, Patton also claimed that men shouldn't take up more responsibilities in the home because women are not attracted to men who clean up after themselves. "The idea of a man wearing a little apron and dusting in the house," she said. "That's not a turn-on, is it; that's just not a turn-on." She's right. If you're going to sleep with a woman at least have the decency to trash her place first.

If straight women are less attracted to their partner when he participates in housework, it's worth asking if it's because they are really just aroused by slobs or if it's because society arbitrarily assigning certain tasks to one gender and not the other. I like to think it's the latter.

Besides, shockingly, the data doesn't indicate that women run away from a guy who does the dishes. Research shows that more egalitarian distribution of jobs and responsibilities around the house doesn't just benefit fathers and their children; it's been shown to enhance the men's romantic relationships with their partners, too. When roles are linked rather than ranked and tasks inside and outside the home are better distributed, people in those relationships enjoy something else: a more exciting sex life. Although idealized masculinity encourages us not to think of men as contributors inside the home, when they go against this stereotype, not only do they enjoy more egalitarian relationships, they also seem to have more sex. Researchers who analyzed data from 2006 found that straight couples who shared housework had sex 7.74 times a month. This means that a man taking responsibility for housework is literally a turn-on. Interestingly, the study did suggest a bell curve effect, because when men do the bulk of the housework, the amount of sexy time suddenly goes down. This signals that there is a lot of work to do to normalize these kinds of family arrangements.

Judging by the data, when you take traditionally ingrained gender roles away, you end up with more egalitarian divisions of labor and more satisfied partners. According to a 2015 survey by the Families and Work Institute that looked at same-sex and straight partners, there is a clear difference between the two sets of couples. While straight couples tend to follow more traditional separations of labor with men doing more outdoor and time-consuming chores, same-sex couples divided tasks up based on preference and skill, something that feels like a pretty great way to do that. Same-sex couples tend to split the childcare and the handling of sick kids evenly, while for straight couples, women were more likely to take on those tasks. What was the secret to this chore utopia? Talking. Apparently, when gender isn't a determining factor, couples are forced to (gasp!) discuss (gasp!) what works best instead of relying on obsolete gender stereotypes that we've kept around for no good apparent reason. Not falling into expected gender roles guarantees more freedom to all partners regardless of their gender. That's why we see same-sex couples consistently split housework more equitably than straight couples and are happier as a result.

Although it's tempting to blame individual men for not contributing to work inside the household, it's crucial to look at the way laws and the policy environment collectively encourages them not to. Although ensuring that men can take parental leave has a plethora of benefits, many countries still don't have proper laws to guarantee that men can. Women may be asking men to do more, but our policies are sending them a different message. Danish men are not differently wired than American men. There isn't something in the water that makes them more feminist or tricks them into equality. In fact, the data seems to suggest that the easier way to nudge men into doing more housework is to give them more of one simple thing: time off.

The truth is that many men would like to help their partners but can't. And more parental leave could change that. My home province of Quebec isn't only responsible for Justin Trudeau and my dad: it's also become a riveting case study in showing the immediate effect of expanding parental leave on men's participation in domestic work. When the province instituted a "daddy-only" quota of five weeks in 2006 and augmented how much fathers receive (they now get up to 70 percent of their salary through an insurance program), the number of men who took the leave increased by 307 percent. The men in Quebec took longer paid leaves and also spent 23 percent more time doing work around the house than fathers in the rest of Canada. Of course, correlation doesn't equal causation. It is entirely possible that a bunch of French-Canadian dudes were enlightened all at once, but most likely, the very experience of taking daddy leave changes men. When we only or primarily provide parental leave for mothers, it sends a powerful message to men: childcare and housework is not your job.

Finally, parental leave is only one part of the equation when we talk about laws that contribute to fathers not being able to perform all aspects of fathering. Masculinity norms have a hand in both making it hard for men to *be* fathers and also making it hard for men to *have* fathers. One of the most profound ways it shows up is in the mass incarceration and the criminalization of black and brown fathers. It is impossible to look at the issue of parenting without addressing the massive sociocultural and economic structures that can make being a present father an uphill battle particularly for nonwhite men in America. Although there's often a focus in the media on absent black men, the reason why many fathers aren't making it home for dinner isn't because they're stuck at work but because they've been put behind bars. The way our criminal justice system disproportionately punishes men of color dramatically thwarts their ability to parent their children. It reinforces and in certain cases perpetuates a gender binary where women take care of children while men are absent by locking up millions of fathers. Although the fastest-growing prison population is female, men make up the vast majority of prisoners in the United States, 93 percent, to be exact. Many of those men are fathers. A chilling 92 percent of parents who are currently in jail are fathers, and according to the National Fatherhood Initiative, the number of children growing up with a father inside prison has increased 79 percent since 1991. Sadly, fathers who are incarcerated are more likely to have grown up without a father, perpetuating the cycle of fatherlessness. The prison industrial complex in the United States imprisons so many parents, disproportionately parents of color, that it's really hard not to view it as a system that deliberately separates parents from their children.

Given that black people are five times more likely to end up incarcerated than white people, the ramifications on men's economic and job opportunities are massive, which in turn affects the role they can play in the family. If you are a black man in America, you are twice as likely to be unemployed as your white counterpart. However, given the huge proportion of black men who are incarcerated, if we were to count those men as part of the unemployment rate, the unemployment rate for prime-age black men would be an astounding 19 percent. For comparison, it's in the low single digits for white men (1.6 percent, to be exact). And this data doesn't even account for local prisons. We can't talk about absent black fathers without acknowledging how radically different their economic prospects are, given "The New Jim Crow." Michelle Alexander describes in her book of the same name a deliberate system that ensures black people are locked up. "African-Americans are not significantly more likely to use or sell prohibited drugs than whites," she writes. "But they are made criminals at drastically higher rates for precisely the same conduct."

So while black and white fathers may engage in the same behavior, the way they are treated by our justice system differs and has real ramifications on their ability to father. And yet, as Alexander notes, the incarceration system is described by politicians in non-racialized ways, even though at the height of the war on drugs, 90 percent of those incarcerated for drug offenses were not white. The bias against black men exists at every level of our justice system, whether it is police officers, judges or juries who perceive men of color as more guilty, violent and therefore deserving of a punishment like incarceration or even the death penalty in states where it's still legal. As Alexander notes, "The United States imprisons a larger percentage of its black population than South Africa did at the height of Apartheid. In Washington, D.C., our nation's capital, it is estimated that three out of four young black men (and nearly all those in the poorest neighborhoods) can expect to serve time in prison."

But still, despite the fact that one in nine black children will grow up with a parent who is incarcerated at one point during their lives, data from the Centers for Disease Control and Prevention (CDC) shows that black fathers are *more* involved in their children's lives than non-black dads. But poverty organizations are often not so great at targeting or working with fathers, because they assume they are not involved. If a father has been incarcerated, it is much harder for him to get a job. If he's not white, it's even more challenging. Given that a white man who has been incarcerated has a higher likelihood of getting a job than a black man without a criminal record, many black fathers simply can't even pay child support. And the data is clear that when fathers can't contribute they are more likely to interrupt the relationship with the child. If providing financially is the root of male identity, when men can't perform it they experience shame, which leads them to abandon or further isolate themselves from their family. The fatherhood crisis cannot be addressed without a fundamental disruption of the state's intentional and alarming disproportionate incarceration of black and brown American men.

The justification for locking up so many men is inextricably tied to how we view masculinity. Politicians and policy makers often frame it as a way to punish bad behavior and reform men. This approach and obsession with "law and order" as a foundational part of American society is clear from the policies and the words that politicians use to speak about tackling crime. Donald Trump, true to form, is the least covert about it. He's referred to the minority of immigrants who commit crimes as "animals" and "bad hombres" and he's even committed to wanting to grow Guantanamo and "load it up with some bad dudes."

But it's not just Trump—incarceration is often presented as a solution to fixing "bad men," when there is actually very little evidence showing that it's an effective way to reform them or reduce crime. In fact, the prison paradox, a term coined by Don Stemen, a professor in the Department of Criminal Justice and Criminology at Loyola University Chicago, highlights that despite a dramatic increase in the number of people who are incarcerated, it has not been followed by a decrease in crime rates. In fact, data shows a completely counterintuitive trend: increasing incarceration in a community can increase crime rates because it disrupts the family and social bonds that protect us from ending up in prison in the first place. It rips fathers away from their children, making those children more susceptible to being imprisoned, too. Incarceration does not heal men; it's most often a system that further entrenches them into a cycle of harmful behavior to themselves and others.

But racism and toxic masculinity don't just combine to rationalize the incarceration of black and brown men; it individually encourages men to participate in criminal activity in the first place.

Research by Christoffer Carlsson, a professor in the Department of Criminology at Stockholm University, found that men who perceived themselves as failing to attain what was expected of them traditionally as men, like having and providing for a family or having a job, were more likely to see criminal activity as a means to financial independence and self-actualization. Conversely, men who viewed ceasing criminal activity as a way to demonstrate masculinity through self-control and determination were more likely to be successful at getting out of the system. But environments like prisons tend to reinforce traditional male hierarchies rather than dismantle them. Researchers have described the prison environment as requiring that men wear a mask of "hypermasculinity." As Corinne C. Datchi, an associate professor of counseling psychology at Seton Hall University, wrote in her research on incarceration published in *The Journal of Men's Studies:*

> Performances of "hypermasculinity" are strategies for coping with imprisonment, deprivation, and loss of social status that conflict with relationship satisfaction and engagement in family roles; in turn, low engagement in family roles and relationships may result in decreased family support and contact as well as reduced opportunities for accomplishing nondominant forms of masculinities.

Furthermore, the men who end up lining the walls of our prisons are men whom we see as perpetrators, but we forget that the vast, vast majority of them were often victims to begin with.

Masculinity professor, author and community organizer Jackson Katz sees the issue of incarceration and idealized masculinity as completely intertwined. "The prisons of the United States are absolutely filled with chronological adult men who are really little boys under the shell they've created. In part they've created this armor in defense against trauma and abuse they've experienced in their childhoods," he told me. "Boys who have been abused, neglected and traumatized are ten times more likely to become abusive of others, not just girls and women but other men." And as Katz noted, the trauma-to-prison pipeline is not just passed down to boys. "Girls who have been abused are much more likely to become self-abusive and put themselves in situations of further vulnerability." Prison becomes another site of violence for men where instead of being healed they are put through further trauma, and then thrown back into the world to be retraumatized.

But while fathering is made more difficult by the industrial prison complex, becoming a dad can help them escape it. Datchi's research found that present fathering has been shown to have a protective impact on men, decreasing their rates of recidivism. Men who maintain close links with their children while incarcerated are less likely to end up behind bars and more likely to have a job when they get out. Viewing fatherhood as a key role connected to ideal definitions of manhood was also correlated with a reduction in criminal activity. So in other words, idealized masculinity reinforces men's rationalization of criminal activity, while positive masculinity can help them interrupt it.

Masculinity is a powerful vehicle that motivates behavior for men, too, and if it's redefined in a positive way and framed as responsibility for others rather than domination of others the impacts can be tremendous.

Although being a dad can help men survive and potentially escape incarceration, the effects of their time spent locked up are passed on to their children and often become intergenerational. One researcher, Anna Haskins of Columbia University, decided to study the educational impacts of it on the children. She examined detailed data from five thousand children born between 1998 and 2000 and isolated the kinds of factors that could impact education advancement, like socioeconomic status and parental behaviors. What she found was heartbreaking: sons of incarcerated fathers were more likely to have educational delays and end up in special education by the time they were 9 years old. The data also showed that having an incarcerated father has the same impact as missing several months of school on children. Although the children weren't delayed cognitively, it was their emotional and behavioral skills that were lacking in the sons of incarcerated fathers, things like attention, focus and the ability to control emotions. Interestingly, she found no sizable effect on daughters.

In addition to teaching us that nurturing children is not natural for men, outdated masculinity norms also makes us think that boys can't be weak and that they require less coddling and support than girls when, in fact, the data suggests quite the opposite. Many parents, regardless of gender, even believe that too much support can be bad for a boy. That kindness will make him weak rather than righteous. For many parents, the fact that they raise boys and girls differently may be unconscious. Fathers in particular interact differently with their kids depending on their gender. Research demonstrates that fathers smile more at their daughters than their sons. They also sing to their daughters more, use more analytical language, have greater responses to their sadness and happiness and were generally more engaged. Conversely, the fathers of sons engage in more aggressive rough-and-tumble play and use more achievement-specific language. Men are simply replicating how their fathers engaged with them, preparing their children for the appropriate gender roles. Although often unintentional, gendered parenting can have wide-ranging consequences. When boys are raised differently than girls, with less support, affection and emotive engagement, it can stifle their emotional development. These differences in parenting, especially when they occur in the first five years of development, have lasting effects.

The irony is that while there's an assumption that boys are more self-sufficient, they're actually more vulnerable to their environment than girls are. While girls absolutely *do* benefit from adult involvement and input, their success in school is less dependent on it. Boys are more vulnerable when they're raised in a one-parent home than girls and show more signs of disruptive behavior. This effect is magnified by racial disparities. One of the largest studies on income inequality shows that black boys have worse outcomes than white boys in 99 percent of the country. Even when black boys are raised by *actual* millionaires they are as likely to end up incarcerated as boys raised with a yearly household income of only $36,000. The fascinating (and potentially hopeful part) of this research is that one thing seemed to protect black boys from this distressing fate: seeing black fathers present inside the home. Indeed, in areas where there was a high presence of fathers living with their children, black boys didn't fare worse than white boys.

Now this could signal that there are more opportunities for black men in those communities, but it also points to the power of being able to see what you can be. Research shows that positive role models have protective effects on children who have been exposed to adverse life circumstances. Research shows that if you're a young African-American boy, having a role model means you're less likely to be depressed or have anxiety; if that role model is male, you are less likely to engage in problematic behavior. Of course, mentors can't be the be-all and end-all, but their power in changing our society is undeniable. Although boys benefit more from male role models, adult men are less likely to volunteer than women to join mentorship programs. Perhaps this would be a great place for men to start.

The future of boys is riding on the current behavior of men. It's not just about helping fathers be present parents; it's also about ensuring that all men take radical responsibility for the next generation of boys. Too much is at stake for them not to.

AMUSE-BOUCHE:
Mau's Story

Maurice stopped counting how many friends he lost to gun violence when he hit twenty-five. Not twenty-five years old, twenty-five friends.

Being raised in the poverty-stricken borough of the Bronx with a single mother is not an obvious path to the White House, and yet the combination of his mom's persistence and his own grit landed him a job in the Bush presidency, and then to a seat in the Situation Room under President Obama. Sadly, that's not what he felt society expected of him. "When you grow up in the inner city, you have three avenues: be a rapper, be an entertainer or be a basketball player," Mau said. "I chose basketball." Due to his rigorous practice schedule and dedication to the sport, his hard work was rewarded with a spot on Furman University's Men's Division 1AA basketball team. And thereafter, he enlisted in the US Air Force and applied for a special-duty assignment at the White House, in his fourth year of service. Despite having paved a successful path for himself, Mau is all too familiar with the challenges that men of color grow up battling within the United States that set them up for failure. "The circumstances are simply conducive to failure," he explained. "In the inner cities, there is no access to jobs to produce income, healthy food choices and zero health care options. I had a chipped tooth until the age of twenty-five." Mau says that without access to the appropriate care, he couldn't get it fixed and that stifled his confidence when applying for jobs. "I hid behind basketball. In many ways, basketball was my security blanket because of my chipped tooth."

Mau is no longer in the White House, but he has remained tied to former President Obama through his work for his initiative My Brother's Keeper, Obama's MBK Alliance initiative actively working with communities and organizations to scale ladders of opportunity for young boys and men of color, through an emphasis on growing mentorships and lowering youth violence. Having been so affected by his own male mentors, he's dedicated to helping young black men do the same. "I want to change the narrative of what it means to be a man of color," he explained. He had strong male role models in his neighborhood growing up, but he knows those aren't always available to all kids. "Young boys and men of color are expected to fail. The law of expectation, the law that says 90 percent of people do what's expected of them, is very serious; if society expects young boys and men of color to be successful and be great and amazing at things they explore and share, they will do just that, I guarantee! What kid doesn't try and fulfill expectations of him or her?"

When I asked him how mentorship changed his life, he confided that it allowed him to become what he didn't know he could be. Knowing that someone was betting on him made Mau bet on himself. "Looking back, when I realized that someone believed in me made it a duty to believe in myself. It was my duty to take on that challenge." Some of his most meaningful role models were his upstairs neighbors, who both happened to be star basketball players: Billy and John Goodwin. They took a liking to Mau and would offer him guidance and advice about applying for college and how to maintain his high school GPA to get a basketball scholarship and the kinds of groups to stay clear from to protect his road to success. "Only hang out with people with goals like ours," Mau remembers being told by them as a form of protection from the harm of other, more negative influences in his neighborhood. One of the most memorable yet simple character traits that Mau remembers taking away after spending time with John Goodwin was how educated every choice was for him. "I would realize that he would be thinking before he spoke," he said. "In these underserved communities, you have a lot of things that happen abruptly, because of how intense and unfiltered someone's emotions erupt. In a split second, people have arguments and regrettable instances where someone gets hurt and/or gets taken to jail, respectively. People are on edge because of the adverse incidents and trauma of living in these neighborhoods."

Later, when Mau enlisted in the military, his first assignment was to Misawa Air Base, Japan, where he ended up spending four years. That's where he met Sergeant Weston, a 34-year-old master sergeant originally from Jamaica. He was almost ten years older than Mau, who was only 25 at the time, but he would seek Mau out to teach him how to do things like change a tire, fix a car stereo or something as simple as making sure he knew how to refill the windshield wiper fluid. "Those were formative lessons," Mau said. "It took away some fears I had about things I didn't know how to do as a man, never had grown up with a father." Mau explained the sergeant would show him how to do things before he even had to ask. "He saw something in me that I didn't see in myself and emphatically wanted to share his knowledge of those skills with me."

These role models gave him something he could touch and minimized the distance between what he was and what he could be. Mau stressed the importance of his mentors being a tangible source of guidance, each laying the blocks for what he started to understand he could build. "In underserved communities, there is a plethora of disappointment, so you become comfortable with disappointment," he explained. "I don't believe anything before I can touch it." Without the involvement of Mau's mentors, he's remained convinced that he would have ended up on a very different path. What if more boys had that, too?

If you lose your job, you will lose your woman.

—CHRIS ROCK

10   The Mancession

If there's one thing that's defined men over the last one hundred years, it's work.

One of the most poignant and cruel ways that racism operated beyond the Jim Crow era was to exclude black men from certain forms of paid employment and segregate them in the worst-paying jobs, with inhumane and dangerous working conditions. This was central to the last speech Dr. Martin Luther King Jr. ever gave. He delivered it on April 3, 1968—the day before he was assassinated—in front of hundreds of Memphis black male sanitation workers who were holding signs that read: "I am a man." King was encouraging them to remain on strike and peacefully protest subminimum wages and dangerous working conditions. His speech, which prophetically made references to his potential imminent death, was also surprisingly hopeful. "I'm happy, tonight," he told the crowd. "I'm not worried about anything. I'm not fearing any man." Although his speech was all about defending black male workers' rights to higher wages and better working conditions, this has sadly largely remained unchanged. The history of the state's collective attempt at the emasculation of black men through exploitation continues to have ripple effects today as the racial wage gap between white and black men continues to get bigger and is larger than the wage gap between white and black women. Today a white man without a college degree is as likely to find a job as a black man with a college degree.

Despite the deafening lack of progress for black men in America, the "I am a man" signs that men held that day have had a lasting impact on the course of history. The expression became an iconic rallying cry in the struggle for black workers' rights and one of the most memorable slogans to put an end to segregation in the United States. It illustrates just how central work has been in the defining of masculinity in a postindustrial America.

To be clear, work has historically been a central characteristic of the female and male experience. Women have always worked. But the difference is that now women actually get paid for it. The myth that work is a new phenomenon for ladies always cracks me up. "Our grandmothers fought for the right to work," reads Ivanka Trump's synopsis for her 2017 book, *Women Who Work: Rewriting the Rules for Success*. Of course, no one "fought" for immigrant's and black women's rights to work. They were coerced to labor as slaves and later as domestic servants, long before white upper-middle-class women were hired as part of the "productive" labor force. And women, across races and ethnicities, have long been expected—and continue—to bear the burden of domestic and reproductive work, or what economists have adorably called unproductive labor. If you ask anyone who's ever had to grow another human being inside of herself for nine months or change the diaper of a newborn baby after it ate solid foods for the first time, "unproductive" is probably the last word that comes to mind.

To be fair to Ivanka Trump (and the people who will spend $17.99 on her book), it's true that overall female participation in the official labor market has radically changed. It's more than doubled since 1945. This makes women's entry into the workforce one of the most defining social and economic shifts of the last fifty years. The female influx beginning in the 1960s was due in large part to policy changes, such as the greater availability of birth control and childcare, but a seldom-discussed factor is the shift from manufacturing to a service economy. Sure, it became easier for women to work, but their skills were also in higher demand. So it might have been a man's world, but someone needed to serve them coffee, and women rolled up their sleeves. Due to changes in trade, globalization and automation, the jobs that were primarily done by men, like mining and manufacturing, have been moved overseas, leaving those men with fewer options. Fewer and fewer jobs require skills that men traditionally brought to the table.

The economy is changing, and it's revealing a new way that idealized masculinity hits men where it hurts: in their ability to earn a living wage. We often talk about how these changes in work patterns have unparalleled impacts on women, in terms of giving some women more economic independence and opportunities, but the impacts on men and their collective identity are far from insignificant. Young men were raised by fathers whose defining characteristic was being the provider. But fewer and fewer of the men in this generation are becoming primary breadwinners. Men's identities are still wrapped up in financial contributions, and their male currency in how much they bring back home. This jostles the masculine ideal their fathers modeled and taught them to emulate. What makes them men if the main organizing principle of the provider is not available to them? In addition, the jobs that are increasingly available, like nursing and eldercare, are not being taken by men because they are seen as feminine. This creates a continuous cycle of men's choice of jobs being entirely too tied to their gender identity and an inability for them to choose jobs that would ironically allow them to fulfill the central role as breadwinners.

While men have traditionally been expected to provide "brawn skills" (such as physical strength), in this new economy, women have had a comparative advantage. Given their ease with so-called brain skills, like interpersonal abilities and communication, they have experienced a slow spike in working hours, whereas men's have dropped because their skills are less in demand given the shift to a service economy. Since most new jobs require skills that women more stereotypically exhibit, women have had a leg up. Because of an aging population, the largest job creation is projected to be in the realm of personal and home health aides as well as nurse practitioners. What do these jobs have in common? They're traditionally done by women.

Although women still make less than men and bear the largest burden of domestic labor, most of the job losses in America have occurred for men. Economists like Mark Perry from the University of Michigan started calling the recession the mancession, due to the fact that men were disproportionately affected. The truth is that for many of them, the recession didn't end in 2009. More than 80 percent of the jobs that were lost between 2007 and 2009 belonged to men in industries like construction and manufacturing, and female-dominated industries like health care, education and service were where the most jobs were created, prompting some experts to posit that the mancession could have longer-lasting effects on men than the Great Depression did.

Although some politicians have instructed men to blame women or immigrants, they should be blaming robots: they're the ones taking men's jobs. The United States reverting back to being mainly a manufacturing economy is as unlikely as One Direction getting back together. Even if some politicians were to keep their unrealistic promise of magically keeping all factories in the United States, 85 percent of the loss of factory jobs was due to changes in technology and automation, not due to factories moving overseas. In other words, we are producing more with less, which leaves low-skilled, non-college-degree-holding men with fewer opportunities. Men have every right to be angry. But they shouldn't be afraid of women or immigrants; they should be afraid of robots.

The numbers don't lie. One in six American men between 25 and

54 either is unemployed or has stopped looking for work, or so the government classifies them as such because they have stopped receiving employment benefits. That means there are roughly 10 million men of prime working age who are literally missing from the economy. And that number has not been going down; in fact, it's been steadily increasing. The number of men who are unemployed has more than doubled since 1950. The number of men not looking for work has more than tripled. Opportunities for less-educated men have experienced the most significant drop and could be the most important factor explaining the exit of so many men from the workplace. The rise of men who are incarcerated also plays a role since it not only cuts them off from economic opportunities while they are serving time but also limits their ability to participate in the workplace after they get out of the system because employers may not hire them. Because 9 million men of prime working age have been incarcerated at some point in their life, their chances of finding work are much slimmer. In fact, research points to the fact that being incarcerated lowers your chance of finding a job by 30 percent, especially if you're not white.

Despite these economic changes, men are still viewed as workers before they are seen as fathers. The men who are participating in the labor force often rely on women's unpaid labor to do so and women still bear the brunt of it and get severely penalized financially when they have children. This explains why the gender wage gap between men and women is smaller than the gender wage gap between mothers and non-mothers. Men don't experience the same dip in pay and opportunities when they become fathers; in fact, they experience an advantage after having a child, coined "the daddy bonus." According to Michelle Budig, a sociology professor at the University of Massachusetts Amherst, fathers are more likely to be hired by employers and even experience an increase in salary. In fact, men with children are viewed most positively by employers, whereas women with children are seen most negatively, despite no evidence that they are less productive. Because the standard is so low for fatherhood, being a dad is seen as noble and a sign of a good character and work ethic. Mothers, although doing the same or more work inside the home, are not viewed so positively. The irony is that research on workers' actual productivity shows the exact opposite. In fact, data from the Federal Reserve Bank of St. Louis shows the complete opposite: mothers are the most productive employees.

This is not to say that being a father in the workplace is easy. But very often being a mother in the workplace is even harder. The same behavior exhibited by both a mom and a dad is judged more harshly when it's coming from her. For instance, one study from Cornell University found that having "PTA" on your résumé if you're a woman makes you less likely to have a job interview, while for men it makes them more likely to get a callback.

But this reluctance to see mothers as productive is not just observable in bosses; it's visible in society. Staggering Pew data from 2007 shows that only 22 percent of adults in the United States believe that mothers working is good for society, compared with 44 percent who believe it's bad. The irony, of course, is that giving women equal pay would have the greatest positive impact on children across America. According to a paper from the Institute for Women's Policy Research, equal pay would be one of the most cost-effective ways to end child poverty. Their data shows that women making as much as men would lift 2.5 million families with children out of poverty. Women don't need to stop working, they need to be paid fairly.

Being aware of this tendency to view mothers less positively than fathers is important, not just for the managers reading this book but also for men whose coworkers include mothers. As more fathers become engaged in parenting and take on bigger familial roles, this impression should change and in turn not just liberate women from those tasks but also normalize men's involvement in the home.

But as I mentioned in the introduction of this book, the fact that President Trump didn't even envision fathers as part of his original parental leave policy proposal when he was a candidate says a lot about how we view men. No wonder he argued in a 2005 interview with Howard Stern that fathers who change diapers are "acting like the wife." Or that two years later when he had Barron, he bragged that his current wife, Melania, "takes care of the baby and I pay all of the costs."

As a candidate, Trump didn't offer a modern alternative to approaching the changing roles of men; he promised to uphold a fixed system where they would be able to preserve a model of masculinity that no longer exists. He brilliantly capitalized on the gendered shift from manufacturing to the service economy and earned the support of white working-class men largely because he validated their anger. He masterfully made himself into a champion of men, more specifically white blue-collar male workers, with his strong emphasis on trade and keeping factory jobs at home, despite literally riding a golden-plated elevator and starting a trade war his first year in office. Even though Trump cannot magically solve these men's problems, his strategy worked flawlessly. It produced the largest electoral gender gap in history (or at least since we've been keeping track) and experts predicted the largest gender gap in midterm history in 2018. He used coded gender language throughout his campaign, promising American men that he would "bring back jobs," so much so that numerous white women I interviewed justified voting for him because he could guarantee their husbands' jobs and ensure their white sons' economic security, too. In fact, one of the largest bases of support he received was from women without a college degree—62 percent of them voted for him, the vast majority of them of course being white. One white female Trump supporter who admitted to me she hated Trump confided that she voted for him because "the white man has been completely forgotten." Her well-being as a white woman depended on the white men in her household. She said she was worried about her husband's job and her son being unemployed once he's out of college. I think white women wanting to guarantee their own safety and their families' because of Trump's promises about bringing back their jobs was one of the least-discussed motivations for white women's huge support for Donald Trump at the ballot box despite so many of them saying they disapproved of him as a man and as a candidate. It doesn't make them tolerating his racism any more palpable. But, in addition to exploiting racism, Trump shamelessly played off gender stereotypes to garner votes from both men and women, to further entrench the very norms that have left men unemployed in the first place.

WHAT'S A "REAL MAN'S" JOB?

These outdated stereotypes about what a "real man's" job looks like are keeping men inside a structure that is limiting their opportunities to capitalize on the successes and growth areas of our economy. Yes, many industries are declining, but due to these gendered myths men aren't participating in the industries that aren't. Although low education and incarceration certainly have had an impact, they can't fully explain why so many men are missing from the workforce, because there are millions of jobs available to them. Are they not taking those jobs because they can't or because they won't? The question remains: If so many men have become unemployed because their jobs are becoming less and less relevant, why aren't they taking new available jobs? Harvard economist Lawrence Katz calls this phenomenon "retrospective wait unemployment," where men are looking for jobs that they used to have, not a job that they could have. He says that what may seem like an economic problem at first sight might also be a social one. Men don't see themselves taking jobs that are primarily done by women because their model of masculinity doesn't allow for it. They may even feel like they wouldn't be hired if they were to apply for those jobs. And because jobs performed by women are consistently devalued, it makes them underpaid, which ultimately makes them less appealing to men, too.

The lack of options we present to men are so grim that they remain attached to traditionally male jobs like coal mining despite arduous, dangerous and increasingly deadly working conditions. After a stunning investigation by NPR in 2018, the National Institute for Occupational Safety and Health revealed it found the biggest cluster of advanced cases of black lung disease in its history in Appalachia, the epicenter of the coal mine industry. Their report noted that one in five long-tenured miners have contracted the deadly illness. "We can think of no other industry or workplace in the United States in which this would be considered acceptable," the authors of the report warned. Although more than seventy-six thousand coal miners have died from black lung since 1968 according to the US Department of Labor, the number of reported cases is higher than in the 1990s, due to several factors, one of which is the decline in unions, who ensured the enforcement of safety regulations and screening for miners. While men are being infected with the deadly disease at dizzying rates, Donald Trump doesn't just want to send more men to coal mines; he also is actively seeking to crack down on protections, many of which were specifically set up to protect men's health in the industry. For instance, the Trump administration announced it would be revisiting the "Regulatory Reform of Existing Standards and Regulations: Retrospective Study of Respirable Coal Mine Dust Rule," to make it "less burdensome."

You would think that this kind of disregard for the health of coal miners would have the men in the industry up in arms, but in fact the opposite is true. Idealized masculinity conventionally creates a narrative embedded in coal mining as a culture that makes it feeble to question the industry's treatment of workers. Because it's an industry based on the rugged miners or "tough guys," in the words of Donald Trump, any concern for health or the environment is seen as a sign of weakness. This means that when men do raise their voices about the need for better environmental or health protection they risk public humiliation or stigma. Dustin White, an eleventh-generation Appalachian born and raised in West Virginia whose own father was a coal miner and died of cancer, gets this kind of back-lash when he speaks out about the need for change in the coal-mining industry. As the project coordinator for the Ohio Valley Environmental Coalition, he often speaks on the topic at conferences, and the reception he gets from coal miners is often hostile. When he took the stage at the National Academies of Sciences, he was heckled by one of the workers, who shouted, "Where's your dress?"

Shockingly, it wasn't even the first time this exact line had been thrown at him. He told me that he perceived this as an attempt to discredit his masculinity, something that defines the identity of coal mining as a whole and that's exploited by coal companies to keep workers silent about struggles or concerns. But this wasn't always the image of the miner; it was a narrative artificially created by the industry to increase recruiting after years of oppressing their workers, leading to the biggest labor revolution in US history. It culminated during the 1921 Battle of Blair Mountain in Logan County, West Virginia (which remains the biggest labor insurrection in US history), when coal miners wore red scarves (hence the origin of the term "redneck") and many were shot down by "gun thugs" hired by the coal-mining companies to squash their own workers. That's when the industry began an overt attempt to use masculinity as a recruitment strategy for jobs that many men no longer wanted to put their life at risk for. Dustin remembers when he was a young elementary-school student the industry sponsored activities and field trips to get young boys interested in the profession. "Companies changed the narrative and started saying that coal miners were powering the nation and that if you wanted to be like your dad and grandad, if you were a boy at thirteen or fourteen years old, you should go into coal mining to provide for your family because it's the manly thing to do," Dustin said. "Over time they developed this mentality that the miner is this big tough guy. So when it came to environmental issues, before [the companies] hired gun thugs, and now their actual employees were the ones who became intimidating." This marketing strategy worked wonders for the coal industry. Dustin said that any demand for reform of the industry is now viewed as an attack on it, almost unpatriotic, yet men are told to toughen up whenever health consequences come at them. "As men we are told to be emotionally detached, but I am literally watching people I love die." Although these jobs are already dangerous, the reliance on toxic masculinity as a code of conduct makes them an even greater risk for men and is exploited by corporations to avoid accountability. Because of the strength of the gendered marketing strategy, men continue to fight on behalf of the companies poisoning them. He says that although workers don't speak publicly against the industry, when he gets them one-on-one they admit that they feel hopeless because for many it's the only path to economic prosperity, and although they're worried about health, they feel helpless. "All of these men are basically broken," Dustin said.

For Dustin, this issue came to a head when he had to witness his father spending the last few weeks of his life without access to water because of the 2014 West Virginia Water Crisis, which was caused by a chemical used to clean coal being dumped into the Elk River, a source of clean water for three hundred thousand West Virginians. "Watching my father go through that was the culmination of everything I was fighting for." Left without any clean water, Dustin melted snow and boiled water from the creek to keep his father alive. "The Red Cross came only once. I told them my father is dying of cancer and they only gave me one case [of water]." The harrowing way his father had to spend the last few days of his life keeps Dustin awake at night. "The irony of the whole situation here is that this man who came back from Vietnam and had to go into the coal mine because that was the manly thing to do to provide for his family, he didn't have access to clean water because of the industry."

But there is reason to have at least a glimmer of hope for the men currently employed in these male-dominated industries like coal mining. There's emerging data that shows we can make these industries less deadly for men if we tackle the culture of weaponized masculinity within them. New, creative programs are starting to show that when entrenched traditional masculinity ideals are challenged, health outcomes can improve. Oil rigging, for instance, another industry that is heavily male dominated, has dealt with issues similar to those of coal mining, with high levels of accidents and health risks. But when two oil rig companies decided to implement a program centered on giving men emotional vulnerability training, overall accidents went down a whopping 84 percent over a fifteen-year period. The workers, who were essentially offered group therapy and given space to open up about personal problems, stress and anxieties, not only became more productive (they handled more barrels per day) but also became more reliable and efficient. The researchers who observed these changes found that simply challenging the ideals of masculinity through allowing men to be more open with each other and ask more questions made the men engage in less risk on the job.

When men are freed from the box of what a man can or cannot do on the job, their lives dramatically improve.

WOMEN CAN'T BE WHAT THEY CAN'T SEE. MEN CAN'T EITHER.

Our ideas about who we can become as career professionals start in childhood. After all, one of the first questions we ask children is "What do you want to be when you grow up?" When I speak to adult audiences I usually start my talk by asking who has kids. After those people raise their hands, I tell them to keep their hands up if they have ever told their daughter that she can do anything that a boy can do. Most people proudly keep their hands raised. When I ask who has told their son that he can do anything that a girl can do, the room goes silent because almost every single hand goes down. I often ask myself how come we've progressed to a point where we don't think girls should be limited by gender, but boys can be.

I hope by now I've made it abundantly clear that the disappearance of traditional working-class male jobs has meant that we need to rethink what a woman's and man's job looks like. But in a world where men are shunned for adopting any semblance of a feminine characteristic, it is easy to see why men haven't rushed to take jobs in female-dominated industries. Just search the word "nurse" online and see what pops up. There's barely a shadow of a man's image. It's easy to see why they wouldn't be lining up to apply. We often say women "can't be what they can't see," but we often don't apply that same saying to boys and men. If a young man is thinking of becoming a nurse, a simple Google search might be enough to discourage him from pursuing that dream.

That's if he's even allowing himself to entertain that career goal in the first place. If a man is a millennial in the workplace (who will make up 75 percent of the workforce in 2025), he grew up in the golden era of gender-segregated toys. Toy stores had two colors, pink and blue, and very rarely did parents venture outside of the expected toys for their children's gender. The toys we give children determine who they think they can be. The toys we refuse to give can have an even greater impact on their self-actualization. We cannot divorce the limited roles we offer boys from the limited roles men see for themselves. If the vast majority of nurse kits are bright pink and their ads only feature girls, what does that signal to boys who may be interested in this profession?

Although many people believe that toys have always been divided and categorized by gender, that's far from being the case. We assume it's normal because it's the reality we live in right now, but targeting kids with specific toys based on their gender identity is a fairly new phenomenon. Although there was some differentiation between boy and girl games before the 1950s, that differentiation came to a halt after World War II. In fact, research by Elizabeth Sweet shows that by 1975 nearly 70 percent of toys showed no gender marking. But something happened when, in the mid-1980s and 1990s, toy stores went back to a visible division between boy and girl aisles, assigning almost each kind of toy to a specific gender. These drastic marketing changes in toy stores mirrored the dramatic shift in the industry, with large corporations targeting specific genders for their products. For example, Lego, makers of one of the most gender-neutral toys, started creating girl-specific Legos with female characters with large eyelashes and more revealing clothes. A few years later in the early 2000s, Disney created the Disney Princesses franchise, marketing products around Cinderella, the Little Mermaid and other female characters like Tinker Bell. This marked the first time Disney marketed products that weren't related to a film release. It quickly turned into a $3 billion industry by 2013 with over twenty-five thousand products by 2006, becoming Disney's fastest-growing collection in the brand's history.

This has had a real impact on the development of boys and girls, worrying psychologists, including Lori Day, who told *The Boston Globe* that "boys and girls stop playing together at a much younger age than was developmentally typical until this recent gender segmentation." The practice of assigning certain toys to boys or girls persists despite research showing that girls and boys don't inherently show preferences for toys that follow gendered lines. Although it's unclear why we assign pink to girls and blue to boys, research by Sui Ping Yeung and Wang Ivy Wong on Chinese preschoolers found that ascribing certain toys to certain genders increases children's preference for colors that researchers assign with their gender. And they also found that making a toy the color traditionally associated with their gender had no impact on the boys' performance with a tangram puzzle but that calling a toy "for boys" enhanced their performance at it. So in other words, what largely defines their preferences for certain toys is heavily rooted in what they are told is appropriate for their gender.

It bears repeating that gender is largely a social construction. We assign gender significance through social norms and rules, but the differentiation between boys and girls is something we prioritize as a society when in fact there are more behavioral and cognitive differences among boys then there are between girls and boys. These differences matter only insofar as adults give importance to them. In fact, until children reach preschool age, they believe that gender can change and is not immutable. One well-known study showed children three photos of the same baby. In the first photo the baby was naked, in the second he was dressed in an outfit that reflected his gender and in the last he was dressed in a way that reflected the opposite gender. Most of the children aged 3–5 believed that the gender of the baby can change depending on what he or she wears. If a girl dressed like a boy, she was a boy. If a boy dressed like a girl, then he was a girl. However, once they reach 5–6 years old, gender becomes fixed, as it is for most adults. Children start subscribing to the idea that gender is rigid and largely inflexible. But they certainly don't start out believing that. Essentially, by the time they reach age 5, children have completely absorbed the thoughts and views of the adults around them. Children start believing that certain things are just for boys or just for girls and even their preferences start to reflect this newly absorbed adult-imposed gender regime. Furthermore, research shows that children choose toys based on what they think is the right toy for their gender, so the way that a toy is marketed and perceived and the feedback they get from their parents and peers when they play with that toy is incredibly impactful. But what if children could just choose? What if we saw every child as an individual rather than a gender? Maybe if we left kids to their own devices we would find there are more differences in toy preference across one gender than there is between the genders. And besides, imagine if we divided toys on the basis of other markers of identities, such as race or religion. It would be outrageous for toy stores to have a Muslim or Christian aisle to divide up acceptable toys for children of each religion. Why is it acceptable to do it with gender?

I know what some people are already thinking: it's just toys; relax. But although it's tempting to deem toys insignificant, they aren't frivolous. Research shows children primarily learn about acceptable roles and model behaviors through play, so it's unsurprising that the toys that were marketed to them as youths shaped their life choices. The boys who grew up being given trucks and mechanical tools are being asked to apply for jobs that they were never given permission to explore. How different might the world look if instead of giving boys a truck and girls a doll, more would be given the freedom to choose?

Although some companies are starting to make concerted efforts to make toys more gender neutral—Target removed gender-specific labeling in its department stores in 2015, for instance—gender-neutral toy marketing is still rare. The debate around gender-neutral toys in the last few years has focused largely on liberating girls from the sexist pressure to play with princesses, dolls and other pink things. This has been largely dictated by the market. Parents started questioning what the toys that were being marketed to their girls were doing to their confidence and the scope of the roles they saw themselves occupying in society. After seeing its sales dip, the makers of Barbie attempted a last-ditch effort and revamped the decades-old brand, moving away from the thin, white blond doll and putting a bigger emphasis on racial diversity, larger body types and female empowerment. Whether a more "feminist" Barbie can have a positive impact on girls is debatable, but toy companies' increasing concern about what their products are doing to girls is nonetheless a move in a positive direction.

A small handful of companies is applying a gendered lens to the way they market toys for girls but also for boys. The makers of American Girl products, for instance, recently announced their *very* first male doll. According to Mattel, the male doll was among the top requests of their clientele, but the decision caused quite a stir. After seeing the doll featured on *Good Morning America*, Reverend Keith Ogden, a pastor at Hill Street Baptist Church in Asheville, North Carolina, wrote a scathing warning to his parishioners. "This is nothing more than a trick of the enemy to emasculate little boys and confuse their role to become men," he later told *The Washington*

Post. He told another newspaper that allowing boys to play with dolls would corrupt their childhood. "It's not natural for a boy to act like a girl. It's not natural for a girl to want to be a boy," he told the *Citizen Times.* "You've got the government and people who placate this mess instead of telling little boys they can't change their biology." His preoccupation about boys playing with what we have deemed as "girls' toys" is not uncommon. Although a majority of Americans believe that it's good for girls to be exposed to toys that aren't traditionally for girls, fewer are comfortable with that idea when the genders are reversed. This difference is especially drastic among men. A Pew survey showed that while 72 percent of men say girls should be encouraged to play with traditionally boys' toys, only 56 percent say the same about boys playing with girls' toys.

But the closer you look, the more you realize that American Girl is an outsider in the toy company industry. Corporations' newfound concern about the messages they are sending to girls has not been paired with the same concern for boys. The toys marketed to boys have just as many damaging stereotypes about their gender: they tend to be more violent, more competitive and rooted in domination rather than cooperation. In addition to that, boys are often given toys that help them develop spatial and cognitive skills, but they are less often given toys that encourage social and emotional development. Research published in the *International Journal of Diversity in Education* shows that dolls can teach empathy and prevent bias in children of all genders. Why are so few of them marketed to boys and why are so many parents reluctant to let their boys play with them?

This uneasiness with boys playing with anything that could be attributed or associated with girls relies on a steady fundamental belief that cuts across society: that being feminine is a weakness. If what women did weren't so devalued, men would have no problem engaging or dabbling in any of it. If there was nothing wrong with femininity, no one would be worried about men exploring it. In other words, the reason why we as a culture are scared of men acting like women is because we diminish the feminine.

People are so uncomfortable with letting boys explore their feminine energy that when parents risk letting their boys explore outside the toxic masculinity cage, it's perceived as bad parenting or even child abuse. For instance, when celebrity Amber Rose posted an Instagram of her 4-year-old boy getting a manicure, it prompted a severe backlash online. Concerned internet users asked if giving a boy a manicure would be damaging for the boy, rather than wondering if our social norms that make us react in this way are precisely what threatens boys' well-being. Manicures don't screw boys up; our reaction to them receiving manicures is what screws them up. And this isn't even the first nail polish gender-panic incident. Back in 2011, J.Crew's president and creative director Jenna Lyons was featured in the company's magazine lovingly embracing her son who was sporting pink toe nail polish. The caption read: "Lucky for me I ended up with a boy whose favorite color is pink." The Media Research Center called it "blatant propaganda celebrating transgendered children."

Would people have had the same reaction to a parent letting her daughter play with monster trucks? Probably not.

Given this arbitrary rule we've made up that boys and girls play with different things and that if boys play with anything that develops empathy and care for themselves or for a child it can ruin their development or go against their biology, when children choose outside of the bounds of our rigid cultural norms they often get told there is something wrong with them. When I asked men about the toys they wanted as children but were told they shouldn't have because those toys were just for girls, I received a slew of heartbreaking responses. The sheer number of men who wanted an Easy-Bake Oven or kitchen tools and were denied them made me incredibly sad. One man recalled overhearing his parents being worried that he enjoyed cooking. Men had stories about asking for Cabbage Patch

Kids dolls, jump ropes, the blueberry boy from the Strawberry Shortcake toy line, Polly Pockets, anything with glitter, the Barbie Corvette, Rollerblade Ken, Wonder Woman or Black Widow action figures, even hula hoops, only to be told they weren't supposed to like those things in the first place. Can you imagine a boy learning to cook and care for others from an early age? Oh, the humanity! One man talked about the only present on his list for his seventh birthday being a "blueberry muffin dog pupcake," which is essentially a stuffed puppy inside a cupcake. He remembered having a meltdown and crying so much when he didn't receive it that his father finally bought it for him but instructed him to keep it hidden inside the house so no one would see him with it.

Another man recounted being only five when he was playing with a plastic toy shopping cart that happened to be pink. "I carted it around our yard, moving my action figures and the like," he said. "We were having a barbecue and some of my dad's friends were teasing me that I was playing with a pink shopping cart. While I was distracted, they took it to the far back and smashed it. Threw it in the trash." My friend Jose Morales told me about growing up in the Dominican Republic, where he had a collection of soldiers and guns, but he also enjoyed playing with a wider range of toys that included toys that had been originally bought for his sister. "I remember as a kid, since I grew up with my sister, I used to play with her friends and play dolls with them and teatime and the adults would get so upset about it," he said. "The neighbors would talk and the other boys bullied me when they found out. The boys would make fun and call me *maricon*, which is Spanish for 'faggot.' I would get smacked as well. It all became a shameful situation. To me it was just playing, but to them it was not normal." Despite these harmful messages about what boys shouldn't do, Jose later pursued a career in nursing in the United States. Even as an adult he faces the same limited stereotypes about what men can or cannot do. He often gets referred as a "male nurse," and it drives him nuts because that assumes that any nurse is female unless otherwise specified. Frequently he'll introduce himself as the nurse and patients will incorrectly refer to him as "Doctor." Although his parents are supportive of his choices, they aren't immune to believing in some of those same gender stereotypes. "For my father when I explained to him that I was going to nursing school he couldn't understand it," Jose said. "And even three years into it, he still asks me when are you going to finish and do your doctor [degree], so I answer yes, I am; I'm going to get my doctorate in nursing!" He laughs it off, but navigating these unnecessary gender stereotypes is a daily struggle.

It's especially frustrating that we send the message to boys that nursing and teaching are only for girls because those jobs used to be done almost exclusively by men. Although roughly 90 percent of elementary-school teachers and nurses are currently women, both industries were once male-dominated professions. For instance, back in the 1800s, the gender ratio was completely flipped and 90 percent of teachers were indeed male. As Dana Goldstein notes in *The Teacher Wars*, women were encouraged to pursue the profession because politicians and school reformers realized that they could pay them far less than men. Thanks, systemic and deeply entrenched sexism! Goldstein chronicles how the stereotype that women are better teachers was deliberately created to attract more of them to the profession. Women were framed as more nurturing and biologically suited to work with children while men were painted as abusive and dangerous for children. We tend to think that women are more inclined to go into teaching because they are more empathetic when in fact evidence points to men choosing it as a career path before it was deemed a "feminine" profession. The first paid nurses were also male. When plagues hit different parts of Europe, men were the primary caregivers. The first nurses in ancient Rome were also exclusively male. In the United States, it wasn't until the 1900s that men started leaving the profession for higher-paid jobs.

Although both jobs require empathy and care, which are associated with women today, the professions were mostly associated and held by men. Given that so many men used to occupy these jobs, many experts believe that men aren't entering these professions simply because of stigma—and the fact that salaries in these careers are currently relatively low.

And again, similarly to the gender-bending trends in the toy industry, changes in the labor industry have been one way. Although there are many different kinds of campaigns to encourage girls to take on male-dominated jobs like those in science and engineering, the same gender-expectations expansion hadn't occurred for boys. I still remember my dad taking me to a "girls and science" day when I was in elementary school. Parents would be given workshops to help develop mathematical and scientific skills in girls while their daughters were encouraged to try out the professions with a set of games and experiments. Why don't we have "boys in teaching" or "boys in nursing" workshops for both kids and their parents to explore these as professions?

Although there have been some efforts to recruit more men into nursing, they have often replicated stereotypes about masculinity, which is what got us into this segregated job market mess in the first place. One campaign that showed nurses holding snowboards and other manly things with the slogan "Are you man enough to be a nurse?" spread across the United States in the early 2000s. But perpetuating stereotypes about what makes you manly doesn't help men in the long run. It reinforces the idea that empathy and caring for others can only be a driving force for women when of course men have the potential and desire to care for others just as women do.

In the new economy, empathy isn't just a good quality to have; it's a skill that's in high demand. Depictions of care work in advertisements and pop culture almost exclusively feature women. Just like with nursing, do a quick internet image search for "care work," one of the fastest-growing industries, which includes everything from looking after children to providing support for the sick or the elderly, and all you'll see is a bunch of women smiling with one hand on the arm of an old person in a wheelchair (very specific, I know). The vast majority of care workers are currently women, and most are women of color. But a growing aging population has created a significant supply problem for the care work industry that has forced some organizations to make bigger efforts to recruit men. A report presented in 2014 by the International Longevity Centre UK called this a "workforce time-bomb" in an industry where four out of five care workers are female. According to the report, "in order to entice [men] into the care sector, providers will need to use innovative promotional campaigns to address persisting stereotypes and target underrepresented groups."

But changing the way men are socialized won't be enough to convince them to join this growing industry because they're also reluctant about the pay. Data shows that men, especially white men, are more resistant to taking these jobs because they don't pay enough. (Black men are 3.3 times more likely to take low-level care jobs.) Given that care work is a female-dominated field, it's devalued and subsequently also underpaid. For instance, many care workers aren't even making minimum wage, as was the case in an adult care facility in Silicon Valley that paid its employees a mere $6.25 an hour, according to the U.S. Department of Labor. It's also the case with waitressing jobs (also mostly performed by women) that pay less than the federal minimum wage (the minimum wage for servers is an abysmal $2.13 an hour). A report from the Women's Law Center found that care worker jobs rarely pay over $11.00 an hour and that women, even those with bachelor's degrees, are segregated in these jobs. While making a good salary is interesting to both men and women, men tend to place a higher premium on it. Given that masculinity as an identity is wrapped into familial providing more for men than it is for women, this makes a certain amount of sense.

This tension—between the reluctance to enter into the care or service industry and the need to be the provider—was explained to me by Steve, a father I met moments before Trump took the stage at his inauguration in Washington, D.C. Steve had driven all the way from Grand Rapids, Michigan, with his wife and three kids to see Trump take the oath of office. "I have friends who are one step away from the soup kitchen and no one helped them," he told me. At 46, Steve explained that many of his peers who had manufacturing jobs are now unemployed. "Some of my guy friends who are educated, have a good work ethic, cannot find a job." He went on to admit: "Maybe they're being too selective with the jobs they pick." He agreed that men, especially those with families to support, should take jobs that feel less traditionally masculine in order to support their families, but he also recognized the importance of work as an organizing principle for their identity as men. "I'm not sexist, but it's a man thing. Not a lot of people want to do that [kind of work]. I should say not a lot of my friends would want a job like that and make a career out of it." He said he personally didn't object to men staying home with the kids rather than being the primary breadwinner, but that those who did would eventually become the target of jokes. "Our neighbor across from us definitely gets the flak from the other guys because he's a 'stay-at-home mom,'" he explained. "'Waffles and Pop-Tarts are ready, guys,'" he joked. When I pressed him on what was worse, not being a breadwinner or taking a job that is female dominated, he seemed more flexible. "At the end of the day you have to take care of your bills, take care of your household and work hard," he said. "It's difficult, but in some of those situations you have to adapt if you have two or three kids, and you want to send them to a good daycare; you have to."

Despite being the primary breadwinner for his family, Steve was visibly involved as a father. He held his daughter in his arms as he spoke to me and was looking after the two other little ones who were running around him. "When I was little and I played football, my dad worked, so I never saw him," he said. "But when the new Jordans [shoes] came out, I got them. I understood that." Despite his demanding job, he said he was more involved as a dad. "I back them up; I go more to their games," he said as he lifted up his other daughter.

Providing for your family by holding a traditionally female job like waiting tables might not be the first choice for many men, but slowing down technology to maintain the level of manufacturing jobs that existed in the 1960s is not realistic or fruitful either. Valuing the work of women in care or service jobs ultimately would increase wages, leaving *everyone* better off. Giving men more flexibility to explore jobs in industries that are female dominated ultimately means giving men more flexibility in how to be a man—and also in how to provide for their family.

Of course, marketing is everything. It probably doesn't help that we've labeled the fastest-growing jobs in the service and health care industries pink-collar jobs. Data shows that even something as simple as the job description could make a difference in attracting more men. Numbers gathered by Textio, an application that checks for gender bias, found that men are less likely to go for jobs that call for traditionally female skills like "empathy" or having a focus on "families." The effect also exists when the genders are switched as well, where words like "extraordinary" or "premier" make women less likely to apply.

Making every job feel open to all genders should be a no-brainer for any company. And it's even better for the companies trying to hire; not only do they increase the pool of candidates, but they also increase the speed at which they find the right person for the job. Textio found that opting for gender-neutral language helps companies find a candidate fourteen days more quickly than when using feminine or masculine language. That sounds like a figure most managers going through the grueling process of hiring can get behind.

In addition, the desegregation of jobs benefits the customer. Many male patients prefer to have male nurses attend to them and the same goes for social or care workers. Older men often feel less embarrassed or humiliated if they are washed by a male attendant. Teaching may be the greatest example of a profession that would highly benefit from a larger gender diversity of hires. The dearth of male teachers unfortunately becomes a self-fulfilling prophecy for boys. Roughly 90 percent of elementary-school teachers are female, which means that an entire gender is virtually missing from the profession. Many boys don't grow up with role models of empathetic and socially intelligent men, and male teachers could change that. This is especially pertinent for young boys of color, who may go through the entire school system without encountering a person who looks like them. According to the Department of Education, only 2 percent of teachers are black men. It's a worrying statistic because there's mounting evidence showing that having a teacher who looks like you can be incredibly powerful for young children and conversely that not having one can reduce the chance for success. It is well known that having a same-race teacher increases children's test scores and how much they like their teacher. But one study that examined one hundred thousand African-American elementary-school records from students in North Carolina found that the impacts stay with the child long after they've left school and that the effects on children from low-income homes is even longer. Researchers found that the simple act of encountering one single black teacher lowered the likelihood of dropping out of school for low-income black boys by 39 percent. Having a black teacher between grades 3 and 5 increased the likelihood of all children aspiring to go to college. That's why having male teachers and particularly male teachers of color could make an enormous difference for the long-term success of children who are the most disadvantaged.

Letting go of unnecessary and untrue gender stereotypes about what a man's job is would benefit men and their families but also society at large, especially when it comes to those who are the most vulnerable. Having more men in care work, teaching and the health care sector would mean better outcomes for children, the ill and the elderly. When we limit who can work, we limit who can enjoy the fruits of that labor. That's why we must expand opportunities for all.

Everything in the world is about sex except sex.
Sex is about power.

—OSCAR WILDE

AMUSE-BOUCHE:
The Post-#MeToo Rules

One of the most frequently asked questions I received from men while researching and writing this book was how to talk to and approach women in the workplace, given the flood of stories that have come out with the #MeToo movement. Originally coined by Tarana Burke, #MeToo has become a rallying cry for women looking to share their stories of sexual harassment or assault and has led to the downfall of numerous high-profile men such as Harvey Weinstein, Matt Lauer, Charlie Rose and more. Sexual harassment was, until recently, not taken seriously by companies and society at large, and men are held to a new standard. This is a giant step for humanity but could be a difficult one for men. Here are some tips:

RULE 1: TAKE STOCK OF HOW MUCH POWER YOU HAVE
Do you know who almost always knows exactly how much or little power they have in the workplace? Women. Women, especially those of color, know exactly where they stand in the power structure because they are so often at the bottom of it. But one thing that I came across in my conversations with men was that they had

often been told to check their privilege, but they have rarely been told to examine their power. Checking your privilege is passive—it often means taking a step back. But examining your power is active. I'm an advocate of the latter more than the former. I think it's more important to take stock of how much you have and then use all of yourself for good. Also, while privilege is fixed (it's based on fixed identities: being white, male, able-bodied), power is relational. It changes depending on situations and the people you are associating with.

For instance, in the midst of the #MeToo headlines a male friend confided in me that he didn't understand why a female coworker had felt uncomfortable about a romantic encounter they had shared. He didn't understand why she described it as making her uneasy when at the time she didn't protest it. When I asked him more about this woman, I realized this wasn't just a coworker. "I've helped her with opportunities in developing her career," he told me nonchalantly. "So you're more of a mentor she relies on for advancement?" I said. He nodded yes. The more I asked questions, the more I realized he wasn't just a friend or coworker to this woman, but that there was a clear power difference between the two of them. When I asked him if he had ever thought about the fact that he had more power in that relationship, it's like a lightbulb went off in his head.

Because men still hold the vast majority of positions of power and authority in our society, that gendered power dynamic is so frequent it's often invisible to them. But very rarely is it invisible to the women. Power is like social mobility: the people who know the most about it often have very little of it. Because my friend hadn't acknowledged the power dynamic between them, he hadn't been able to see how she may not have been able to say no to his advances. It hadn't occurred to him at the time, but given that the floodgates have now been opened, men are held accountable and have a real interest in not screwing up with them.

RULE 2: WHEN TRYING TO DATE A WOMAN AT WORK, USE THE RULE OF ONE

In a post-#MeToo world, a lot of men are worried this is the end of office romances. As a person who has been smitten with a coworker more times than I'd like to admit, I don't think it needs to be. In fact, almost half of people have at one point dated someone they work with and a third of those relationships ended up in marriage. Women being actually believed when they report sexual harassment didn't ruin romance; in fact, it reset the rules of romance for the better. If you want to make sure you don't cross the line, follow the official policy that was instituted at Facebook and Google: you only get one shot. Office romances are allowed as long as there's no conflict of interest and a coworker only asks another once. If the answer is ambiguous ("I'm busy," or "Maybe . . . let me check") or is a full-on "No," the person is no longer allowed to ask. Dating at work is simple: you only get one shot.

RULE 3: BE AWARE THAT IF THE ATTRACTION IS MUTUAL IT'S NOT HARASSMENT

Many men complain about not knowing if a flirtation will be taken as harassment. But here's the thing: if you're not sure if you're flirting or harassing, you're probably not flirting. Buddhism teaches us about conscious eating, conscious walking, and I think men need a practice of conscious flirting, especially in a work setting. Many men go into flirting with a woman as conquest, like she's a mountain they're trying to climb. But if they only approached flirting by putting her first, they would be able to tell right away if she was interested. The subtle cues are key and paying attention to them is even more important in the workplace since you're both stuck there if things don't work out.

RULE 4: YOU DON'T HAVE TO AVOID WOMEN: JUST STOP HARASSING THEM!

I've spoken to a lot of men (and women) who say they're afraid of hiring women now. Not hiring women to solve workplace harassment is like tackling the extinction of the sea turtles by killing the ones who are left. Refusing to be in the same room as a woman after dark doesn't exactly accomplish ending sexual harassment. It's discrimination. Women are not the problem. The men harassing them are.

RULE 5: WHEN IT COMES TO CHIVALRY IN THE WORKPLACE, ASK IF YOU'RE NOT ABLE TO TELL

Men should approach acts of chivalry in the workplace with a simple rule: *definitely* ask if you can't tell (what's appropriate). Ask if she needs help, but never assume she does. Be attuned to a woman's reaction when you offer up an act of chivalry. For instance, I once had a coworker who insisted on holding my bags constantly, even after I would tell him I didn't need help. He wouldn't just require that he handle large bags (which honestly could have been at least useful) but would insist on carrying even the smallest handbag, making me feel like he thought I was inept because of my frail lady bones. That's not chivalry; it's patronizy (yes, I made that word up). If a woman says no to an act of chivalry in the workplace, believe her. On the flip side, I once worked with a producer who wouldn't offer to help me with anything. He would just watch me struggle and it was just as annoying. Now I know this sounds like men are damned if they do, damned if they don't, but generally as a rule, one should never operate in extremes. It's really hard to offend someone by offering help. In fact, it's the lack of attention to the answer that usually causes problems. As my friend's highly mature 9-year-old daughter told me when I asked her if men should open doors for their female boss, "I have nothing against polite people."

And what goes an even longer way and literally cannot backfire is offering to do traditionally female jobs for women in the workplace, like taking notes or doing administrative tasks. Even if you weren't in a position to take the food order or keep the minutes of a meeting, giving a woman a nod for doing it signals an appreciation for her time and work and a recognition that those are laborious tasks, too, even if often performed by women without acknowledgment. Opening the door for your female boss is nice, but booking the conference room so she doesn't have to is even better.

And there are some acts of chivalry that have a place in the dating world but no place at work. My friend Regina is an executive at a prominent media company and laments the way she is greeted differently from her male peers by collaborators. While men usually get a handshake, she often gets a hug. At one video shoot she was conducting, she reached out to the subject they were interviewing with a handshake and he ignored her hand while extending his arms to embrace her. "I'm sorry, I just can't shake a woman's hand," he quipped. This is where chivalry can go too far. Women don't want to be treated differently; they want to be treated equally. Don't hug the women you work with unless you are hugging the men you work with. But how does one know which acts of chivalry should stay in the dating world and not migrate to the work world? This brings me to the next rule.

RULE 6: DON'T DO ANYTHING FOR A WOMAN THAT YOU WOULDN'T ALSO DO FOR A MAN

Would you hold the door open for a man? Absolutely. Would you hug him and say you just can't shake men's hands? Absolutely not. If you wouldn't do it for a man, then you probably shouldn't do it to a woman. That's the only gut check you need. Pretend like people don't have genders. Don't assume they can do less or more based on any part of their identity for that matter. People think that taking identity into consideration means treating people differently, but what it really means is treating everyone equally.

*The mark of a real man is being able to tolerate a
chest infection for three months before laying off the
smokes or asking for medicine.*

—ROBERT WEBB

11   If Patriarchy Is So Great, Why Is It Making You Die?

When I went to the most feminist country in the world to try to save men from the hellscape of gender equality, I was shocked to find out many were not interested. Iceland has received much attention for its number one ranking in the World Economic Forum's Global Gender Gap Index, a measure developed by policy makers to calculate the level of equality between women and men. The country has been at the top of the list for more than a decade. And it turns out that female empowerment seems to make women *and men* pretty happy—the country ranks as the fourth happiest in the world. Perhaps Icelandic people's carefree attitude has something to do with the high-quality universal free health care. Or perhaps it is the state-sponsored childcare, the generous parental leave for both fathers and mothers and the phenomenal social safety net. Whatever it is, the equal-gender political representation in government seemed to be creating some pretty neat laws that kept people of all genders feeling pretty peachy.

Every man I engaged with didn't view gender equality as charity; he viewed it as a necessity. "To have a decent society we need everyone to do their share," Gísli Marteinn, a young father and local news media personality in Iceland, told me. He had been described as the

"Jon Stewart of Iceland" and more than lived up to the hype. He hosted one of the most watched political shows in the country, where he enforced a gender-parity quota for both his production team and his guests. I met him at a restaurant he had opened up with his wife and friends in a neighborhood of Reykjavik that he claimed had the highest equal-pay ratio. He said Björk lived next door, which I joked must help increase that neighborhood's standing. "No one feels like we've got it in Iceland. Every year something comes up and we look closely in the mirror and say, 'Wow, we still have far to go,'" Gisli said. What irked him wasn't all the rights women were getting but rather how much men's political and economic advantage in society was still not eradicated yet. "I hate it when Icelandic men use it as an argument that we don't need to discuss that."

Most of the attention is on how great Iceland is for women, but far underreported is how great it is for men, too. The country may have been crowned the best place on earth to be a woman, but could it also be the best place to be a man? Based on the men I talked to and the research I conducted, a feminist regime doesn't lead to widespread male misery. In fact, one of the most interesting statistics I couldn't get out of my head is that Icelandic men enjoy the highest life expectancy in Europe. It also has the smallest gender gaps in life expectancy in Europe, which means that men live almost as long as women do. If the number of years spent on earth is one of the strongest predictors and indicators of the well-being of a population, Icelandic men were doing pretty well.

Although happiness and well-being are strong predictors of health, there are numerous other health factors, and the more research I did, the clearer the relationship between overall gender equality norms and male health became. There are a whole host of other health problems men experience that are linked to toxic masculinity and lessened if there was more gender equality. Given the way that we often talk about gender equality (if women gain, men lose), can uplifting women also benefit men?

It's not just Iceland. Other countries with stronger gender equality are countries where men tend to fare better. Don't believe me, believe the data. According to the research done by Norwegian sociologist and men's studies expert Øystein Gullvåg Holter, there is a direct correlation between the state of gender equality in a country and male well-being. Men (and women!) in more gender-equal countries in Europe (Iceland included) are less likely to get divorced, be depressed or die from a violent death. Correlation does not equal causation, but it is nonetheless interesting and worth noting that male well-being does not suffer in a country that is focused on ensuring women's well-being. In fact, living in a feminist nation can enhance the lives of men, too. Just like minimizing income inequality in a country benefits the country as a whole, so does limiting gender inequality. In the same way that rich people don't lose out (and, in fact, actually benefit) in a country where income inequality is low, the same goes for men in countries with lower gender inequality. Gullvåg Holter remarks that although a lot of attention is paid to the way income inequality reduction has positive ripple effects on the country as a whole, very little academic attention has been paid to how gender equality also has those positive collective impacts. These benefits are myriad, but for now let's stay laser-focused on how feminism can help men live longer.

It's hilarious that gender equality helps men live longer, because one of the most frequent men's rights activists' arguments to derail a feminist's argument is to point to the fact that men die sooner than women and that because of this, the focus on women is unwarranted. Although it's true that women tend to outlive men in almost every country in the world, the solution these advocates envision—a world without feminism—is the opposite of the solution. Feminism is the antidote to shorter male life expectancy, not the cause of it. Saying feminism makes men die earlier is like saying firefighters cause fire or that pain relievers causes headaches. Men's rights activists fear that any examination of idealized masculinity is an attack on men when scrutinizing it might be one of the most effective ways to help them.

Instead of invalidating feminism, the problem of early male deaths could be (at least partially) solved with more feminism, not less. Although men's rights activists revere the patriarchy and do anything they can to cling to the status quo, several of the reasons why men don't live as long as women can be traced back to the patriarchy—that thing that's supposed to make them so much better off. Mind pretzel, right? Let's dig in.

PATRIARCHY PROMISES MEN FREEDOM
IN EXCHANGE FOR CHAINS

First, let's get the facts straight: in almost every society across the world, women live longer than men, and the majority of centenarians across almost every country are female. The only exception is in certain developing countries where females can be so undervalued that they are more likely to be killed at birth or neglected through being deprived of appropriate food and care. It's the reason there are fewer girls than boys in countries like India, Bangladesh and Pakistan and the life expectancies between men and women are warped.

But in the vast majority of modern societies, the stereotype that women last longer doesn't just apply to sex, it applies to life. On average, women will live about six years longer than men and a lot of it is explained by biology. In fact, across the animal kingdom, the female species tends to outlive the male, including primates and other warm-blooded animals. Female macaques, for instance, outlive their male friends by about eight years. Some of it is hormonal (estrogen might have a protective effect on limiting the likelihood of developing heart disease, for instance), or could be largely in part due to the fact that women have two X chromosomes while men only have one. This offers women chromosomal superiority and a significant health advantage over men. That's because if one of a woman's X chromosomes has a mutation or an irregularity, the other one simply kicks in. Because men only have a single X chromosome, they're stuck with all its deficiencies. That's why disorders and diseases that stem from X chromosome abnormalities, like hemophilia and color blindness, rarely affect women. Chromosomal differences may also partly explain why the vast majority of autistic people are male (although women present different symptoms than boys and we aren't as good at diagnosing it). These chromosome differences also partly explain why most stillbirths and premature deaths happen to boys. In fact, male infants are less likely to survive than their female counterparts because they tend to be more fragile and vulnerable to disease and death. Left under the same circumstances, female babies have a higher chance of survival, full stop. Data on famines, epidemics and slavery conditions shows women have always been more likely to survive under grueling circumstances (and stick around for longer even when they are not healthy). The researchers from the University of Southern Denmark put it very simply: "baby girls were able to survive harsh conditions better than baby boys."

Although there's an assumption that being female is associated with being more frail, nurseries tell a whole different story. The fragile gender is not the female one. In fact, as Susan Pinker notes in *The Sexual Paradox,* "From day one, male embryos, although more numerous, are more susceptible to the effects of maternal stress. When the going gets rough, female embryos are simply more likely to make it. They're better girded to survive the uncertain first hours after conception, and they're less likely to be affected by obstetric disasters, disabilities of all kinds, and early death. Even pollution hits males harder."

Pinker brings up a striking study performed of Hawaiian children raised in poverty-stricken conditions in the 1950s that was conducted by psychologists Emmy Werner and Ruth Smith that found large disparities between the genders. Girls had far higher IQs and half of the boys ended up experiencing learning problems in school. While one in five girls died in infancy, more than half the boys did. Susan Pinker concludes "from a biological perspective, being female simply offers a protective umbrella from cradle to grave." Although testosterone is often associated with giving men an advantage later in life because it's associated with muscle development and stamina, it's associated with many of the factors that put men at higher health risk, like cancer, heart disease and HIV. Because it lowers the body's immune response, male embryos are more fragile, and that explains why premature girls are more likely to survive and thrive than their male counterparts.

But the other part of the gender life expectancy gap is what scientists literally call man-made diseases.[1] These are illnesses or medical conditions that have been created by us as a result of the way we've chosen to organize our world. These circumstances fall outside of the realm of biological determinism and are completely cultural: smoking, alcohol, high-risk behavior and more work accidents. When you look at the list of behaviors that the World Health Organization lists as responsible for this discrepancy, it's hard not to see the stronghold of the patriarchy. Their report sums up the differences in expectancy as explained by:

> [G]reater levels of occupational exposure to physical and chemical hazards, behaviours associated with male norms of risk-taking and adventure, health behaviour paradigms related to masculinity and the fact that men are less likely to visit a doctor when they are ill and, when they see a doctor, are less likely to report on the symptoms of disease or illness.

So according to WHO, there are three big (highly modifiable) reasons men don't live as long: men's relationships with work, risk and doctors. Let's quickly examine each of these in order.

1. MEN AND WORK

We won't spend too much time on this because there's an entire chapter in this book dedicated to challenging men's relationship with work. To put it simply, men are much more likely to die on the job than women, but due to shifts in our economy, this is changing pretty dramatically, especially here in the United States. The vast majority of deaths on the job (about 93 percent depending on the year you examine) are male and men *do* still tend to dominate riskier industries, working in such fields as high-tech agriculture or as electrical power-line installers or truck drivers. The top most dangerous jobs are (so far) all in male-dominated industries. Certain men are more vulnerable than others. Immigrants and men of color, for instance, are even more at risk and have higher numbers of injury or death than white men. However, the most dangerous jobs are not fast-growing jobs; if anything, it's quite the opposite. As more and more men move out of heavy manual labor jobs, work-related deaths will be reduced. These economic changes are actually the number one reason the gap between the life expectancy of men and women has been slightly reduced in the last few years.

2. MEN AND RISK

The first time I realized that the glorification of men who take risks without protection had gone too far is when my friends made me sit through an episode of the MTV show *Jackass*. The extremely popular and controversial show, which ran for several seasons in the early 2000s, featured ten men doing life-threatening stunts, like being thrown eighty feet into the air inside a port-o-potty full of feces, snorting wasabi, and walking on a tightrope over alligators with raw chicken stuffed in their underwear. Although it was one of the most popular and long-standing shows on television, every single cast member ended up in rehab, surgery and a ton more rehab.

One of my favorite and more recent examples of the way we worship men who take risks is Tucker Carlson calling Donald Trump staring into the solar eclipse without protective glasses "perhaps the most impressive thing any president's ever done," because there's nothing more presidential than deliberately attempting to burn your retinas on national television.

Getting bruised or physically hurt more often doesn't just happen to grown men; we observe this phenomenon early, in the gender gap in injuries between boys and girls. Boys have twice as many fatalities from bicycle accidents, and researchers in child development have noted that a difference occurs as early as 9, where boys seem to take more risks than girls. And this effect seems to be global. UNICEF found that in OECD countries boys were 70 percent more likely to die in an accident than girls. Despite boys' experiencing a higher level of injury, boys (and girls) as young as 6 years old believe that boys are at a lower risk of injury than girls even when engaging in the same activities, suggesting that children adopt the idea that risk-taking is suitable and free of consequences for boys (not girls) very early on. However, it's hard to claim that risk-taking can be purely explained by biology, since teenage boys' likelihood to engage in risk depends on how much they subscribe to . . . you guessed it, norms surrounding masculinity! One study that observed teenage boys' willingness to break the rules of the road as pedestrians found that the more they associated with traditional masculinity roles, the more likely they were to engage in unlawful behavior. "Masculine stereotype conformity turns out to be a better predictor of risk-taking than biological sex," the head researcher, Marie-Axelle Granié, wrote. "Being a boy or a girl does not predict the self-reported level of risk-taking; recognizing oneself as masculine, i.e., manifesting behaviors and personality traits that society attributes to the male sex, rather predicts risky pedestrian behaviors." So in other words, being a man doesn't make you take more risks; being a man who thinks men take more risks is what's associated with higher risk-taking.

As I read this troubling data connecting risk with masculinity performance, all I could think about was drowning. A quick look at the data shows that drowning is an almost uniquely male endeavor, and the statistics are indeed staggering. According to the CDC, young men are three times more likely to drown than young women, and 80 percent of fatalities from drowning are male. The CDC attributes this mainly to two factors that fit right into the tenets of idealized masculinity: overconfidence and excessive drinking. "It was concluded that several factors contribute to their relatively high drowning rates," the authors of the report wrote. "Including a possible interaction between overestimation of abilities and heavy alcohol use." One study found that more men reported knowing how to swim despite women being more likely to have taken swimming lessons. In addition, the men in the study were more likely to describe their abilities as "excellent," even those who had never taken swimming lessons.

I became aware of this when I started training to become a lifeguard as a teenager. When I stopped my instructor in the middle of our session after he said in passing that men are more likely to drown, I asked him why. He answered as if it was obvious or inevitable that men just engaged in more high-risk behavior. If the job of a lifeguard was 90 percent prevention as my instructors had repeated ad nauseam, why weren't we properly addressing this high death rate, especially if it's due to something as alterable as chosen behavior?

But drowning is not just gendered; it's also heavily affected by race. Another striking moment in my lifeguard training was when my instructor mentioned that black children are far more at risk. Indeed, in the United States, black children are three times more likely to drown than white children, and the rates are higher for Hispanic children as well. If we only look at children aged 11–12, black kids are ten times more likely to drown than their white counterparts. Again I interrupted him and asked why this was. He attributed this to higher body mass density, which felt like a classic uncomfortable white person answer. It was. Canada, where I grew up and took my lifeguard training, has its own history of enslaving black people and institutionalized oppression against its native people, which impacts education and swimming ability. Less access to swimming lessons means heightened risk for accidents. In America, the problem is even more pronounced and historically rooted. The exclusion of people of color from swimming pools was codified into law until the 1960s, and the segregation of black people in public swimming pools continued well beyond the Jim Crow era. So when it comes to aquatic-related deaths of men and boys of color, there's an additional and heightened risk, but this risk was different: it wasn't chosen behavior—it was structurally induced. Drowning is just one reminder of the way structural inequality intersects with masculinity, making some men even more vulnerable than others.

WHITE MEN TAKE MORE RISKS BECAUSE THEY CAN; MEN OF COLOR TAKE MORE RISKS BECAUSE THEY HAVE TO

The myth that being a man naturally compels you to take risks is disproven by any research that includes diverse subject pools.

Although white men are often used as the norm in scientific studies (and in society at large), it turns out that when it comes to risk behavior, they are the exception rather than the rule. Research has uncovered that while we paint all men as taking lots of risks, the effect is much stronger among white men than nonwhite men. While men tend to assess less risk than women for the same situation, white people also assess far less risk than people of color, which means that white men are actually skewing these statistics disproportionately, inflating their entire gender's relationship to risk. The researchers call this hubristic tendency for risk the white male effect. It was first coined by James Flynn, Paul Slovic and C. K. Mertz in 1994, who wrote:

> [T]hese race and gender differences in risk perception in the United States were primarily due to 30 percent of the white male population who judge risks to be extremely low. The spec-

ificity of this finding suggests an explanation in terms of sociopolitical factors rather than biological factors . . . what we often have branded as the "male effect" of propensity for risk would be more accurate if it was called the "white male effect."

The reason why white men take more risks can be summed up in three words: because they can. Flynn, Slovic and Mertz hypothesized that white men take more risks because they have less to lose. In addition to whiteness and maleness, those who tolerate the most amount of risk also tend to have a strong identification with individualistic and conservative beliefs and demonstrate greater faith in institutions. Trusting institutions to protect you is a luxury that women, people of color and other marginalized folks don't always have. After all, should women trust politicians to make laws that are in their best interest when many have chosen to defund their health programs and clinics because of their personal moral proclivities about birth control? Should African-Americans trust police officers when so many are responsible for killing innocent and unarmed members of their community and the criminal justice system when it has wrongly accused and locked up their loved ones? When the world is not an equal-level playing field, neither is our relation to risk. Flynn and his colleagues wrote in their paper titled "Gender, Race, and Perceptions of Environmental Health Risks":

> Perhaps white males see less risk in the world because they create, manage, control, and benefit from so much of it. Perhaps women and non-white men see the world as more dangerous because in multiple ways they are more vulnerable, because they benefit less from many of its technologies and institutions, and because they have less power and control.

In addition, the data shows that men overall aren't necessarily more comfortable with more risk; they just perceive it less. One of the failures of the academic studies on risk is that they fail to capture how subjective it is. According to Cordelia Fine, the author of *Testosterone Rex: Unmaking the Myths of Our Gendered Minds,* we've been reading the data all wrong. Fine argues that men aren't necessarily more daring—they just perceive fewer consequences. After all, risk is a subjective assessment and it varies across genders. Since white men tend to interpret risk differently, it creates a difference in the behavior, but Fine argues it's not because they are more brave. After all, not all behaviors are created equal. She points out that the same risky behavior, such as drinking or unprotected sex, can have greater objective risk and more dangerous consequences for women than for men, so in a way, women, by engaging in these activities, show more courage in the face of higher objective risk. Finally, women are also judged more harshly when their risks don't work out. We don't say "girls will be girls" when a grown woman screws up. No one says that when a young woman accidentally gets pregnant, and yet we say it about boys who get a girl pregnant. As masculinity scholar Jackson Katz often notes, we always say "she got pregnant" instead of "he impregnated her," or "she was raped" instead of "he raped her." Especially if she is not white. In fact, data shows black girls face harsher discipline as early as preschool. Indigenous girls are more than three times more likely to be suspended than white girls and black girls are 5.5 times more likely to be suspended. Researchers at Georgetown called this phenomenon the "adultification" of girls of color, where they are perceived to be older, more independent and less deserving of as much protection. This unconscious and conscious bias impacts boys, too. The Department of Education finds that black children are nearly four times more likely to be suspended than their white peers. One in five black boys will get suspended while they're in school while only 5 percent of white boys will. No wonder white boys perceive risk differently than boys of color when the consequences they face are so vastly different.

In other words, we often hear people say women are more risk-averse, when perhaps it would be accurate to call them risk-appropriate. That's what Dan M. Kahan, professor of law at Yale Law School (and noted white man), concluded after he conducted his own research. His data shows that white men, especially those who score high on individualism and a belief in hierarchy (as opposed to egalitarianism), are the most risk ignorant. To figure this out, Kahan decided to test something that's objectively perceived as a pretty big risk: the impending threat that climate change poses to our livelihood. When he tested this large-stake policy question, he found no big variance based on gender or race, except for white men who scored high on hierarchy and individualism, who, you guessed it, were a lot more comfortable with the risk of a warming planet. So it's the intersection of whiteness, maleness and a penchant for individualism that creates what we often mislabel as stereotypical "male" behavior when it comes to our perception of who is more risk-taking, but that's largely because most risky things pose less of a threat to white male subjects. Kahan proved this theory by purposely testing male subjects, asking them to weigh the risk of policies that would make white men more susceptible than other populations: he asked subjects how much they would be willing to risk the prosperity of the economy by increasing taxes on corporations. Interestingly, in that scenario where white men have more to lose, women were much less risk-averse than men! Kahan concluded: "[I]t confirms that men are more risk tolerant than women *only* if some unexamined premise about what counts as a 'risk' excludes from assessment the sorts of things that scare the pants off of white men (or at least hierarchical, individualistic ones)." So white men are a lot less comfortable with risk than women and people of color when the tables are turned and they are suddenly the ones who have more on the line.

RISK IS ASSOCIATED WITH STATUS AND RITUALIZED MASCULINITY ACROSS ALL GROUPS

But regardless of whether a man *wants* or *has* to take a risk, he's still expected to have one attitude: fearlessness in the face of it. And when men don't measure up or when they need a hand, they're given a punch, or maybe a smoke or a drink instead.

It's no wonder that American men have always smoked more than women (although the trend is starting to reverse in younger generations, where young women and men are smoking in roughly equal numbers). Prior to WWI, women were culturally sanctioned for smoking, especially in public, and Marlboro famously appealed to men, associating cigarettes with the classic lone cowboy image. Smoking signified freedom, independence, ruggedness, a proof of being a tough man. Given this focus on cigarettes symbolizing ultimate autonomy, it's unsurprising one of their first advertisements to women used feminist coded language and framed it as "a torch of freedom," messaging overtly to the modern woman that she could access her own independence through smoking.

Race also played into their marketing strategy. Starting in the 1960s, Newport explicitly targeted black and brown communities with menthol cigarettes. It's worth noting that the FDA deems menthols more dangerous because they are harder to quit and increase the depth of inhalation because the menthol effect hides the harshness of tobacco. Newport paid black athletes for endorsements, advertised mentholated products in magazines such as *Ebony* and *Essence,* and even went so far as to offer money to black institutions, schools and civil rights organizations. Due to this overt and sustained racialized advertising approach, African-Americans are twice as likely to smoke mentholated cigarettes as white people. In fact, nearly nine out of ten black smokers prefer mentholated cigarettes to this day. Make no mistake: this is a manufactured preference. Although the FDA has banned other flavor additives on the grounds that they can increase addiction in younger smokers, menthol wasn't included in the ban, despite its undeniable harm to the black community.

It's not just smoking that has roots in idealized notions of masculinity; drinking has also been presented to men as a ritual and sign of maleness. And there's no clearer example that drinking is corroding male health than Russia: the capital of vodka and *not coincidentally* the capital of early male death. Men die so prematurely from drinking in Russia that it has the largest gender expectancy gaps in the world. The World Health Organization has certainly noticed and warns that patriarchal cultures encourage behavior that puts men's lives at risk, and heavy drinking is high on their list.

We often associate Russians with vodka, but the link between alcohol and male mortality is one that health care professionals in Russia are all too familiar with. In fact, the excessive consumption of alcohol by men is so bad that men's life expectancy has actually started declining, a rare phenomenon for an industrialized country. According to the World Health Organization International Agency for Research on Cancer, one in four men in Russia won't make it past their fifty-fifth birthday, and they found that the majority of those deaths are alcohol related: liver disease, alcohol poisoning and getting into fights while drunk are at the top of that list. Binge drinking makes men twice as likely to become victims of violence.

Russia is well known for its vodka consumption, but what gets less attention is just how rooted it is in the formation of Russian men's identity.

Although drinking and alcohol-related deaths have been common in Russia since at least the nineteenth century, it was only after the industrial revolution that drinking went from being a communal activity to an exclusively male one. Taverns started popping up near factories and drinking became a way for men to identify as a group. Researchers from Middle Tennessee State University who studied the history of alcoholism in Russia profusely note that "rank-and-file laboring men closely identified with the consumption of alcohol, but this is not to say that women did not drink. Rather, men's drinking was an essential element of worker identity [and] became a way to delineate themselves from 'others' like women and non-workers."

Drinking became such a masculine ritualized performance that working-class Russian men couldn't even drink wine or beer, as those beverages were seen as too effeminate. In other words, vodka became the only option for men. Sobriety also became associated with femininity, as men who didn't drink or didn't drink enough would be called *mokraia kuritsa* ("wet hens"), which is especially relevant because of the super not-sexist Russian proverb "A chicken is not a bird, and a woman is not a person." We even see a pattern of male consumption follow their changing position in society. For instance, government intervention eventually and steadily brought consumption down, but the creation of the Soviet Union made it spike again because the head of the household was no longer the father figure; it was the state. For many men, this pivot in their role was dramatic, and many dealt with this by reinstating their masculinity through the act of heavy drinking. Because men's role inside the home was being replaced by the state, fatherhood become less central. This led men to reassert their masculine dominance in other ways, and drinking was one of them. So when we raise men to have to prove their manhood by taking risks, they can resort to hazardous means to fulfil those expectations.

3. MEN AND DOCTORS: IT'S COMPLICATED

In addition to being encouraged to take more risks with less protection, prototypical "masculine men" are also expected not to seek help when that whole being-a-manly-man thing backfires. And research shows that the more a man subscribes to toxic tenets of stereotypical masculinity, the less likely he is to seek protection in the form of preventative care such as regular checkups or routine prostate exams.

And the effect is not small. Research from Rutgers University shows that men who glamorize rigid unhelpful beliefs about masculinity are 50 percent less likely to seek preventative care. The researchers say their findings "strongly suggest that deep-seated masculinity beliefs are one core cause of men's poor health, in as much as they reduce compliance with recommended preventative health services."

Our ingrained belief that men shouldn't ask for help shapes our entire world. We see its effects in one of the worst epidemics on earth, HIV/AIDS. Experts at the World Health Organization argue the crisis is worsened by the often-ignored power of norms surrounding masculinity for men. Although more women are affected, Michel Sidibé, the executive director of UNAIDS, says in a 2017 report that "there is a blind spot for men—men are not using services to prevent HIV or to test for HIV and are not accessing treatment on the scale that women are." Men who have sex with other men are twenty-four times more likely to contract the disease and yet men are less likely to get tested, visit clinics or get treatment. This is especially lethal in Sub-Saharan Africa, where the epidemic takes too many innocent human lives every year. In South Africa, for instance, 70 percent of the men who end up dying from HIV/AIDS never even sought treatment. In many regions, HIV status is still associated with being an effeminate man, which in a society riddled with toxic masculinity is the worst thing a man can be. Sidibé says that norms surrounding toxic masculinity are largely responsible. "The concept of harmful masculinity and male stereotypes create conditions that make having safer sex, taking an HIV test, accessing and adhering to treatment—or even having conversations about sexuality—a challenge for men," he explained. "But men need to take responsibility. This bravado is costing lives."

This is not to understate the plight of women with HIV/AIDS. In fact, the disease impacts far more women in the developing world, where young women can be more than twice as likely to contract the disease, depending on the region. And yet straight men are the number-one source of transmission of HIV/AIDS for women across the world. Targeting men's reluctance to practice prevention or get treatment could be one of the most cost-effective strategies to help women. The AIDS epidemic in women is worsened by the fact that men aren't getting the right treatment, so when we include them, that investment goes back to women. The women who get AIDS through sexual contact, except for those who exclusively have sex with women, are primarily being infected by the men in their lives. To ignore the way to control the epidemic in men is neglecting the whole spectrum of solutions to the problem. A man who is being treated for HIV has a much smaller chance of transmitting the disease to a woman than a man who isn't. And of course, a man who doesn't get tested or treated is a triple threat: to himself, to his partner and to his community. Ensuring that men feel comfortable seeking treatment and care has benefits to societies at large, including women. Ignoring men's gendered constraints in the fight against HIV/AIDS puts women (and the men they love) at risk.

Sexual orientation and poverty also complicate how men handle HIV/AIDS. Here in the United States, for instance, a staggering 50 percent of black queer men and one-quarter of gay Latino men will be diagnosed with HIV at some point in their life. This isn't because gay men of color engage in riskier behavior, but rather because they don't have access to testing and therefore don't know they're infected. The shame associated with the disease is real and uniquely tied to a threat to performative masculinity. Nothing made that clearer than when Magic Johnson contracted HIV. As Phillip Brian Harper recounts in *Are We Not Men?: Masculine Anxiety and the Problem of African-American Identity,* after the public disclosure of his positive status in 1991, Johnson went on an impressive (and sadly rewarded) masculinity-reaffirming tour. In a late-night show appearance with Arsenio Hall, his utterance of the words "I'm far from being homosexual" were lamentably welcomed with applause. "At the same time," writes Harper, "the fact that Johnson perceived a need to continue asserting his masculinity—specifically by publicizing his heterosexual exploits—even after he had supposedly set the record 'straight' on national television indicates that masculinity, as generally conceived, is a condition whose very validity in any individual instance consists in its being experienced as under constant threat." So even when a man isn't gay he has to deal with the stigma and internalized homophobia that accompanies the diagnosis and treatment. If we were to give men more freedom to be or love who they wanted, could it make a dent in one of the deadliest epidemics of our time?

Whatever pressure discourages men to ask for help for physical pain is exponentially worse when it comes to psychological pain. And again, the more you cling to unrealistic definitions of masculinity, the less likely you are to seek the support you need. Patriarchy demands that men conform, and according to the data, obeying its definition of manhood doesn't always lead to positive outcomes. According to research published by the *Journal of Counseling Psychology*, whether a man subscribes to macho ideals about what it means to be a man has direct impacts on his health. Lead researcher Y. Joel Wong, of Indiana University Bloomington, did a meta-analysis of seventy-eight research samples that included almost twenty thousand male participants and measured their association with eleven masculinity characteristics. The researchers chose eleven norms traditionally associated with ideal masculinity and found that men who subscribed to them showed more overall reluctance to seek medical help and had overall lower health outcomes:

1. Desire to win

2. Need for emotional control

3. Risk-taking

4. Violence

5. Dominance

6. Playboy (sexual promiscuity)

7. Self-reliance

8. Primacy of work (importance placed on one's job)

9. Power over women

10. Disdain for homosexuality

11. Pursuit of status

The most dramatic effects on health came from male subjects' association with "self-reliance, pursuit of playboy behavior and power over women." This led researchers to conclude that "sexism is not merely a social injustice, but may also have a detrimental effect on the mental health of those who embrace such attitudes." Researchers also found that the association with these attitudes lowered men's well-being and, worse, made them less likely to seek mental health help. So masculinity norms make men doubly vulnerable, by first enticing them to conform to ideals that make them unhappy and then making them reluctant to seek help when they need it. Interestingly, though, not all identification with all masculinity traits had negative impacts on men. Primacy of work and desire to win, for instance, were not associated with lower well-being, suggesting that work and seeking success provide men with positive identity-creating ideals that don't encourage them to suppress their needs.

At this point you may feel deflated by this data. But there's a silver lining! There's a simple way to counter these misleading masculinity ideals and their negative impact on health: kindness.

Empathy toward oneself appears to lessen the effects of harmful masculinity on men. Although more than two in three college men who experience mental health issues never seek help, when researchers looked at a sample of 284 undergraduate males, they found that self-compassion and kindness toward one self helped buffer the link between the adherence to masculine ideals (like self-control and self-reliance) and the stigma around seeking help. In other words, empathy appears to have a protective effect on men.

But compassion is still viewed as a transgression of the male code. It was best explained to me by my friend John Haltiwanger. "I still know a lot of men who think depression is basically a choice or a sign of weakness. I think too many men view seeking help as surrender, which is literally killing us," he told me. "You don't have to be in a deep depression to go to therapy. You can be perfectly content with life and still benefit, but in my experience most men don't grasp that concept. Do physically fit people stop going to the gym? No. It takes constant work. So does mental health. I wish more men understood that."

But it's hard to know you need help when you've disconnected from yourself. Subscribing to idealized masculinity also makes a man less likely to be able to understand his own emotions. In fact, researchers have found that identifying with macho and traditional masculinity was correlated with more pronounced alexithymia, an inability to properly describe emotions, across different demographic groups of men. The paradox is that across the board, men are less likely to seek therapy, but they benefit just as much as women from therapy, and some research shows they may even benefit more. It's not that men objectively experience less stress; women and men have different interpretations of whether they are coping with it correctly. For instance, one particularly interesting study that looked at African-American men and women showed that the same behavior can be interpreted very differently. While men believed they were coping with stress by "resting," the women described how they were dealing with stress as "avoidance." In the same study, African-American men described an emotional, social and physical toll of stress in their lives. But the good news is that researchers in the UK found that "alexithymia fully mediated the effect of intimacy on men's attitudes towards psychological help-seeking," which in plain English means that increasing help-seeking for men could be the key to unlocking a greater sense of emotional well-being for them.

HEALTH CARE PROVIDERS—THEY'RE ONLY LIKE SOME OF US

Of course, health care providers have been raised in this same culture—so it's not just male patients who have internalized toxic masculinity but their doctors, too. They aren't created in a vacuum; they're born and raised in the same culture as we all are. Men aren't the only ones who feel like men need to be self-reliant; health care providers (many of whom are, you guessed it, men!) have absorbed that message, too. This makes men less likely to get tested for HIV/AIDS but also less likely to be targeted by providers. The authors of the previously mentioned WHO report saw this with health care workers: "Health programs often view men mainly as oppressors—self-centered, disinterested, or violent—instead of as complex subjects whose behaviors are influenced by gender and sexual norms." It's one big, vicious cycle, where men's individual actions confirm the beliefs of health care workers and then health care workers continue to treat them in a gendered way that doesn't respond to their full set of needs.

And the relationship between masculinity and one's experience of the health care system is complicated further by race. Given the dearth of doctors of color (only about 5 percent are black), the health care system is often treacherous when you're not white, and this problem isn't even getting better with time. According to data from the Association of American Medical Colleges, there were fewer black men enrolled in medical school in 2014 than there were in 1978, while there's been an increase in every other demographic, including black women and Hispanics and Asians of all genders. This is most likely the result of a well-studied hostility toward affirmative-action programs.

Research by Liliana M. Garces and David Mickey-Pabello, who examined the impact of affirmative-action bans in six states, showed a 17 percent decrease in medical students of color receiving matriculations. The absence of men of color as health care providers is worrying because black men have the lowest life expectancy of any demographic group in America. The fact that they are far less likely to be treated by someone who looks like them compounds the problem. Research actually proves there's a tangible black male doctor effect: black men were more responsive and more likely to agree to preventative treatments when they were treated by doctors who were black. The effect was so significant it even surprised researchers tasked with studying it. For instance, the results showed that black men were 50 percent more likely to agree to preventative diabetes screening when it came recommended by a black doctor rather than a white or Asian doctor. The researchers conclude that increasing the number of black doctors alone could reduce the oversized racial gap for death from cardiovascular disease by 19 percent, which is enormous. Black doctors literally save lives and could help restore trust in a health care system that African-Americans have every right to be suspicious of. Although very few studies look at the intersection of masculinity, blackness and health care services, one study showed that black men were more likely to trust information regarding their health that came from their family members than from doctors or nurses. This distrust of the health care system is rational, as there is mounting evidence that doctors respond to and treat patients differently based on their race. One study that came out of the University of Virginia showed *half* of white medical students believe false racialized myths like that black people's bodies are stronger, black people's skin is thicker, their nerve endings are less sensitive than whites' and black people's blood coagulates more quickly (none of which are true). No wonder communities of color don't want anything to do with a health care system that so overtly and dangerously discriminates against them. Increasing the number of black doctors would fundamentally shift the size of the racial life expectancy gap in the United States, across gender.

And then even when communities of color want to trust the health care system, they're much less likely to have access to it because of the way the system works. If you are Hispanic and nonelderly, you are more than three times more likely to be uninsured. Sure, the Affordable Care Act helped slightly narrow the uninsured racial gap, but it's still abysmal. Black Americans are still more likely than white Americans to skip doctor visits because of financial reasons. So the cultural pressures in the black community to stay away from health care are compounded by a lack of access to those services in the first place.

So if men's rights activists are truly committed to solving the problem of shorter male life expectancy, they would be far more effective if they invested all the energy they currently spend on blaming feminism into dismantling institutionalized racism, which is literally killing men of color at far greater rates than any other group. If only these so-called male interest groups were as committed to ending racism as they were to blaming women, perhaps they'd be more successful at actually helping the demographic they purport to be advocating on behalf of.

Another way for men's rights activists to spend their time could be to contest the male code because so long as it's the law of the land, men who don't conform to it suffer. Even when men resist the forces instructing them to partake in risky behavior or eschew protection, the mere transgression of prototypical masculinity norms sets them back, health-wise. For instance, when researchers controlled for unhealthy behaviors such as smoking or drinking, they still found that the men who earned less than their wives for an extended period of time experienced poorer health outcomes, shorter life expectancies and more risk of cardiovascular problems like diabetes, heart disease, high cholesterol, hypertension and stroke. This led researchers to conclude that violating the toxic code of masculinity can be such a point of stress for men that it negatively impacts their overall health. Given how taxing going against the grain of mainstream male culture can be in a world where it is considered the norm, a lot of men self-correct to protect themselves.

In addition to paying a price when they don't conform to idealized masculinity, men can pay a price when they do conform. For far too many men in America who are suffering from mental health issues, it's easier to get a gun than get a therapist. Although more Americans die from guns than from car crashes and AIDS, the CDC cannot call gun violence a health epidemic because of a 1996 law that bars the organization from doing anything that would "advocate or promote gun control." How tied guns are to the male code became clear to me when I was speaking to Tomi Lahren and her friends John and Laura in Dallas. In the middle of our conversation about modern masculinity, John said, unprompted, "God didn't make man equal. Colt did. Any gun-manufacturing companies have made men equal." When I asked for more explanation, he indicated that because guns allowed men to attack and defend themselves against other men, it meant that any difference in status between them could be erased.

While for this white conservative young man, gun ownership represents an equalizer for men, a quick look at reality points to the contrary. Gun ownership is not available to all men in America. In fact, when they were first codified, gun laws only extended to white men, as they feared slaves would revolt if they had the right to possess weapons. However, after they joined the Union Army, black Civil War soldiers returned home with weapons, they were seized by the Black Codes and groups like the Ku Klux Klan. The Second Amendment, guaranteeing the right to bear arms, was consistently denied to people of color. Martin Luther King Jr., for instance, was famously denied a concealed-carry permit in the 1950s after his home was bombed. While white men have a history of casually walking into Starbucks with open-carry guns, black men have a history of casually being arrested in Starbucks without guns and for no reason. Half of what white men can brag about doing openly, black men are considered to be thugs for.

But this conservative position on guns is not original. Among gun rights supporters, the dominating narrative is that men own guns to protect their family. Research shows this is deeply rooted in their identity as men. After all, if they can no longer be the provider, guns ensure they can still be the protector.

Gun manufacturers's marketing has been effective. The vast majority of gun owners are men, especially if they're married. In fact, married male Southerners are more likely to own a gun than any other group. The link between guns and the search for new masculinity has often remained unexamined, but even the "good guys" (as the NRA refers to them) with permits to conceal and carry often seem to indulge in fantasies of alpha masculinity to justify owning a gun. One study conducted on gun owners across the country by Angela Stroud (a gun owner herself) at the University of Texas at Austin found that men who conceal and carry are often "motivated by a desire to protect their wives and children, to compensate for lost strength as they age, and to defend themselves against people and places they perceive as dangerous, especially those involving racial/ethnic minority men." When I spoke to her about her research, she revealed that gun ownership has become one of the very few tools still available to the men who cling to a model of masculinity that is rapidly shifting. With fewer opportunities to provide and protect, guns remain a way for men to feel like they are successfully accomplishing these male responsibilities.

"Defense is the one place where men can maintain this sense of domination over, without it being considered a problem," she explained. But of course, if your identity is defined by protecting your partner and children, what happens when you can't do that? "If your relationship or your sense of self is defined in any way with control over your partner, what happens when you lose control?" Stroud pointed out. "Being the gentle defender of women is the good-guy version of the same sort of ideology that positions women as less than and subservient to men." That's why Stroud makes the argument that we need to rethink what a "good guy" looks like. "Most men are good and most men do not perpetuate violence, but when they have that ideology in their head ready to use when needed you can go from being a good guy to being a bad guy very quickly."

But despite the fact that men say they use guns to defend themselves or their family, the "male protector" model that the NRA has propagated for decades doesn't reflect what men are *actually* doing with guns. The majority of gun deaths aren't a result of men killing intruders; they're a result of men killing themselves. Boys are given toy guns by parents who watch them pretend shoot at other boys, unaware that some of their sons will grow up to use a real gun to kill themselves. Stroud explains that while black males are disproportionately harmed by gun violence, two-thirds of deaths by guns in America are death by suicide and a majority of those are white males. As a demographic, they are more likely to engage in the impulsive type of suicide that takes place with more lethal means and under the influence of alcohol or drugs. It's the most difficult one to prevent because it doesn't have identifiable warning signs that could help curb its incidence.

Although adolescent girls are three to nine times more likely to *attempt* suicide, the suicide rate for adolescent boys is two to four times higher because males tend to use more violent means when choosing to end their life, the most violent of which is, of course, a firearm. Worryingly, the rate of male suicide in the United States has increased since 2000. According to the CDC, the number of men who take their own lives in their fifties has increased by

50 percent between 1999 and 2010. Although there's a potent and ongoing debate about gun homicides, the fact that most gun deaths in America are by suicide doesn't often come up. Oddly, the policy conversations around guns hardly ever focus on how guns are most often used to self-inflict violence, especially given that suicide is on the rise. The suicide rate in America in 2015 was the highest that it's been in the last three decades. And this problem isn't unique to the United States. In every single country in the world (except China), men are more likely to die by suicide than women.

And the abnormal mass availability of guns in the United States doesn't simply impact men; it disproportionately impacts boys. Of all the youth gun deaths between 2012 and 2014, a staggering 84 percent were boys, many of whom had used guns to kill themselves. In fact, the suicide rate by firearm for children has hit an unprecedented high, with the American Academy of Pediatrics showing an increase of 60 percent in child suicide between 2007 and 2014. This is alarming, especially when we consider that young Native Americans have a suicide rate that is double the national rate and that the situation is even more dire for boys whose gender identity doesn't conform with normative conceptions of masculinity. The suicide rate for LGBTQ boys is utterly staggering. For instance, half of transgender boys surveyed by the American Academy of Psychiatrists reported attempting suicide. One study showed that bisexual or gay young men were up to seven times more likely to die from suicide. Although different groups of boys are more vulnerable than others, there seems to be something about growing up male that makes one more likely to choose to die.

WHY ARE BOYS AND MEN KILLING THEMSELVES?

Since men are expected to be strong and self-reliant, even a perception that they cannot fulfill that role can make them averse to seeking help—many experts believe that these masculine ideals are responsible for the male suicide epidemic. Daniel Coleman, a researcher who has spent the last decade studying male suicide, argues that the link between masculinity social scripts and suicide patterns is undeniable. He has found that a need for power, success and self-reliance sets up men for failure because it generates a vicious cycle of pain. Feelings of inadequacy are fueled by unrealistic ideals about masculinity and then those very same beliefs discourage them from asking for help. The more a man identifies with traditional masculinity beliefs, the more vulnerable he is. In fact, Coleman's research concludes that idealizing "high traditional masculinity" is a "risk factor," especially for men who weren't able to fulfill their masculine ideal because of illness, disability or the loss of a job. In other words, having a more flexible way of viewing themselves could protect men from the shocks of everyday life.

Sociologist Émile Durkheim's theory of suicide stems primarily from a disconnection from institutions such as marriage, employment and social networks. The data about modern men largely supports this. For instance, the rate of suicide is highest for men without a college degree. It is also higher for single men and men who have experienced a separation or divorce. Unemployment or income anxiety is also a huge factor. Suicides are also higher in rural areas, and the suicide gap between teenagers in urban and rural areas has been expanding. Working in certain male-dominated fields like law enforcement and the military is also correlated with a higher suicide rate for men, and many of them use firearms. Access to a means for suicide in someone's employment is also an important determining factor of vulnerability. Because we often conflate male independence and self-reliance with male isolation, the men who need the most help often look like the men who don't. That's because the characteristics that are associated with the highest risk of suicide for men also happen to be the ones that we put on a pedestal.

I couldn't help but notice that Wyoming, the state of the lone cowboy—a lasting icon of ideal masculinity: a man who is stoic and unattached—was also the state with the most alarming amount of male suicides. A chilling 80 percent of people who die from suicide in Wyoming are men. Middle-aged white men who live in western states like Wyoming are three times more likely to die from suicide than the national average. When it comes to the number of suicide deaths by gun, no other state has dethroned Wyoming in the last fifteen years. Many factors could explain the prevalence of suicide— the reduction in employment opportunities is one of them—but perhaps the most significant is how common and expected it is for men to have guns in their home. A majority of houses in rural areas contain a gun, and Wyoming has one of the highest rates of gun ownership in the country.

I'm certainly not the first to draw attention to the link between men's gun ownership and their vulnerability to suicide. When researchers from Johns Hopkins Bloomberg School of Public Health dug into the data, they found that men in rural areas were more likely to commit suicide, but when they isolated the data to only look at non-gun suicides, the contrast between men in urban areas and rural men disappeared. "It is often said that people would kill themselves anyway, even if they didn't have access to guns," the lead researcher, Paul Sasha Nestadt, a postdoctoral fellow in the Bloomberg School's Psychiatric Epidemiology Training Program, said when the study was published. "[But] there is an entire body of research that tells us that is simply not true." Although the data is clear, it's still controversial to draw attention to the pattern we see here. Perhaps if guns and power weren't so interlinked for men, it would be easier to label the alarming number of guns in men's hands as one of the most urgent health crises in a generation.

While guns have an impact on the incidence of suicide, research shows that economic and social changes also hugely impact male suicide rates. While for women, the presence of mental health issues and illness is the primary determinant of suicide, men's vulnerability to suicide seems affected more by external factors. For instance, over the course of modern history, suicide has peaked during financial crises like the Great Depression, when suicide rates skyrocketed. In the 1990s, when Hong Kong experienced a financial crisis, male suicide deaths of men aged 30–59 almost doubled. In 2007, as various recessions took over Europe, male suicide rates also took a major hit.

But interestingly, data shows that gender equality may in fact be an unsuspecting antidote to male suicide, because women's empowerment may protect men from economic shocks. It makes sense when you think about it. If women are educated and can work, it lessens the financial responsibility that rests on the shoulders of men. The less gender equality you have, the more you have a traditional society where men are expected to shoulder unequal responsibility. Research by academic Øystein Gullvåg Holter has studied this effect. The data he collected shows that societies with lower levels of gender equality are the ones with the highest rates of male suicide and that the gender gap in suicide is smaller in nations with higher gender equality. One study by Aaron Reeves and David Stuckler found that in countries with high levels of gender equality, like Sweden and Austria, "the relationship between rising unemployment rates and suicide in men disappeared altogether." They concluded that the economic and political empowerment of women could create an actual buffer to mediate and lower the risk of suicidal consequences of economic downturns for men. It makes sense that in a society where the provider role is shared by both men and women, less pressure is put on men to sustain economic shocks.

It turns out that when women do well, it helps men. Who would have thought?[2]

Race fundamentally changes masculinity. We need to think about masculinity as a deeply racial issue.

—NICO JUAREZ

AMUSE-BOUCHE:
Nico's Story

Nicolas is only 22 years old, but he's one of the smartest people I've ever met. Growing up with a white Cajun French mother and a Tzotzil-descendant Mexican father in Louisiana, Nicolas Juarez found it impossible to disconnect his experience of masculinity from his indigenous identity. "Identity categories are not additive processes," he explained to me at the beginning of our conversation. "People tend to think about intersectionality as adding up all their oppressions and their privileges to know where they are. In reality, when you add masculinity into Nativeness, you aren't simply adding a privilege to an oppressed category; you are radically changing both categories."

Nico grew up with kids in middle school who teased him about how he hopped the border when he says the truth is that "we didn't cross the border; the border crossed us." Despite having full knowledge of his ancestors' experience with brutal white colonialism and the anti-immigration rhetoric that followed, he often felt like he needed to co-sign his own racist bullying just to get by. Growing up he certainly knew he had male privilege, but there was always an asterisk next to it. He knew that being a man came with a long list of benefits, but he also didn't seem to see men who looked like him achieve any of them. When he became a visiting scholar at New

York University (I told you he was smart), he discovered why. In his research he found that according to DOJ data, despite Native women facing the highest amount of violence, Native men are just as likely to have experienced intimate violence as white women in the last year. He also found that the rate of control of reproductive choices was twice the rate than white women experienced. The most common way Native men say they experience reproductive violence is being forced to have children they do not want, most often with non-Native women. That heavily complicates the narrative of reproductive and domestic violence being a woman's issue, especially since in the case of some kinds of violence against Native men, these acts are more likely to be perpetuated by women who are white. "If we think of masculinity as position, then what does it mean for Native masculinity to face more violence than white femininity?" Nico told me. "It suggests that for Native men, gender is not a category they are welcome in. Gender is a site of violence."

Nico also pointed out that Native Americans have died at the hands of police more than any other group. Although there are far fewer indigenous Americans than African-Americans or Latinos living in the United States, they face even greater rates of violence from the police. And research shows that Native Americans' stories rarely make it to the news cycle. Nico talked about the radically different way that black or brown men are treated compared to white men when they are arrested.

He recounted the 2017 killing of Jason Pero, a 14-year-old Native boy who was home sick with the flu and left his house holding a butcher knife and was fatally shot by police. "Why is his running perceived as an illogical response to a weapon being drawn on you?" Nico said. "The understanding is that he must therefore be criminal. He's a criminal who deserves to die." Nico contrasted that with the way white men are arrested for far greater crimes than running away. "White men who shoot up theaters are taken alive," he said. "What does it mean for white men to commit these violences and not be marked as people who deserve to die? But indigenous boys who walk home sick deserve to die. There is something about masculinity once it becomes racialized that justifies that violence."

The justification of violence against Native men is nothing new. Nico traces it back to the very first colonial writing in American literature. "One of the first things that Christopher Columbus wrote about is the nudity of Native people and what that must have suggested about them." This exoticization of Native people served as a form of dehumanization that justified their mass murder.

This portrayal of the indigenous man as the savage doesn't just frame how Native men are perceived; it affects how they view themselves. If you're perceived as sub-human, animalistic and uncontrolled, it creates an exaggerated sense of responsibility to control emotions and display stoicism. "Our social order encourages this warrior narrative," he said. "Your job is to die, to be the first one to take the bullet, to put yourself in danger so that other people don't get harmed. You get this romanticized image of the Native man who is standing strong and sovereign, ready to take on the colonizer. This means you should be mentally and physically strong because you need to be a person fighting in the ongoing battle of colonialism."

This intense pressure on indigenous men to be both an emotional and physical warrior is one of the reasons Nico views gender as a site of harm for women but also for men. "Gender itself is a violence," he said. "We all suffer from gender; the only difference is that men are rewarded for that violence."

Idealized definitions of masculinity may be oppressive for men, but Nico says they are still alluring for indigenous men. He noted that men overall get rewarded either financially, socially or politically. In fact, being a man is traditionally associated with higher status, higher economic power and more political influence than women possess. But what often gets lost is that these rewards are not spread equally among all men. Marginalized men may engage in the same kind of masculinity codes but not accrue the privileges that non-Native men get from their engagement. "The idea for men is that if I perform misogynistic violence, I'll be rewarded socially, economically, even if that's the cost of my emotional well-being," he explained. "Masculinity can become a site of oppression if you are Native, but it also becomes an incentive. That you, as a Native man, want to access the things that masculinity tells you are yours, you might perform misogynistic violence because it's the thing that gets you the privileges of masculinity. But it doesn't seem to do that very well. So masculinity becomes this lure, without the social reward." The way Nico described it, performing idealized masculinity seemed like a trap that marginalized men would fall into because of its promise to offer them the mobility they were so desperate to find.

At the end of our conversation, Nico echoed one of the most important points I hope I've been successful in making in this book: that the doctrine of gender dictated by patriarchy doesn't just hurt women; it hurts men, too. To express this, Nico quoted Fred Moten in *The Undercommons: Fugitive Planning and Black Study,* where he wrote in the context of racial justice that white people needed to see how racism hurts them, too. "I don't need your help," he writes. "I just need you to recognize that this shit is killing you, too, however much more softly." Nico explained how this applied to gender just as much as it did to race. "To say we'll fix the problem together is not the same as saying you're wounded and I'm not, because the reality is that there needs to be a recognition that it's killing you, too. Patriarchy is killing men, too."

*To create loving men, we must love males. Loving maleness is
different from praising and rewarding males for living up to sexist-
defined notions of male identity. Caring about men because of what
they do for us is not the same as loving males for simply being.*

—bell hooks

12   The Making of Men

When I arrived in Zambia, I was struck by the beauty of the landscape, the generosity of the people and the largest selection of pea-
nut butter I'd ever seen in my life. Edgar had become our driver after
he helped us cross the border into Zimbabwe one night so we could
bask in the mist and grandiosity of Victoria Falls, the largest waterfall in the world. The original name for the magical curtain of water
was Mosi-oa-Tunya, which means "The Smoke That Thunders" in
the Kololo dialect. The Kololo tribe had occupied the land around the
falls during the 1800s prior to the British colonists who, true to their
brand, renamed the falls after a white lady, Queen Victoria. The ma-
jestic endless curtain of water sits on the Zambezi River, creating
mist for as far as the eye can see. In fact, the neighboring areas receive constant rain all day every day all year round because the spray
from the waterfall is incessant. Often I would be walking through
town and look up to stare at what I thought were clouds only to realize it was mist from the falls.

When Edgar turned to me with his big straw hat and canary-
yellow polo shirt to ask me what I was doing here, I wasn't sure how to
answer. My producing partner, Ashley, was there as a volunteer film-
maker to shoot and edit promotional videos for The Girl Impact, a

nonprofit organization located in Cape Town, Livingstone and Kilimanjaro. The nonprofit was born out of African Impact, one of the most well-regarded and trusted volunteering organizations in the world, to address the specific need for gender equality programs. The Girl Impact creates partnerships between local grassroots organizations and volunteers to help communities who are most in need. A few weeks before leaving, Ashley asked me if I wanted to come with her, using the exact same tone as someone offering you an extra ticket to go to a Knicks game. I was right at the part of writing this book where I felt like I knew less about men than when I started. So I decided to go on the longest flight you can take from New York and see if avoiding all my problems could help me resolve them. Three flights, thirty-six hours and way too much Ambien later, I finally arrived in Livingstone, a large town in southwestern Zambia. Jet-lagged, puffy and hungry, I had no idea I was about to get to know some of the coolest men I'd ever get the chance to meet.

Like every other country in Sub-Saharan Africa, Zambia has a dark colonial history that has had lasting impacts. Zambia's encounter with European imperialists began with the Portuguese in the seventeenth century. That's before a British missionary named David Livingstone arrived in 1855 and in the most British colonialist kind of way named the city after himself. The city's economy was powered by a strong influx of tourism because it contained Victoria Falls, one of the Seven Natural Wonders of the World. Zambia also has the largest man-made lake by volume in the world, Lake Kariba. It's so vast and wide that it's known for tricking tourists into thinking they are staring at the ocean.

Zambia is a rich and vibrant country, but for many of its people life can be a challenge. It ranks 125th out of 189 countries in gender equality. HIV/AIDS is the leading cause of death for adults aged 15 to 59. Zambia has one of the highest rates of child marriage in the world—one-third of girls are married before they turn 18. More than half the population lives in poverty. And almost half of women have been victims of violence.

Just like the United States, Zambia struggles with toxic expressions of masculinity, and as in many other countries with a traumatizing history of European invasion and rule, this is largely a product of colonialism. The British didn't just rename everything after white people; they also imposed an entire new social order that fundamentally transformed relationships between women and men. Colonial forces upended women's roles in their respective tribes and unilaterally pushed them into submissive and dependent roles inside the home, using churches and mining companies to promote the model for the "good housewife." The Western concept of a male breadwinner and a female housewife became a symbol of prestige, a marker of the coveted membership in the African elite. Zambian women were completely excluded from paid employment even in what white imperialists considered female jobs such as domestic servants, because they believed black women were too promiscuous to work in the white man's home. Like any effective institutionalized system of oppression, it was internalized and perpetuated through norms and interpersonal relationships. Since the superior familial model became one where the man was the breadwinner, some Zambian men came to resist their own wife's employment because it became associated with a man's failure to provide for his family. These new imposed economic gender role systems were all-encompassing. The overall attitudes toward women shifted and they became excluded from decision-making and from political involvement. Laws were written without them.

Although every tribe was impacted by colonialism differently, one of the harshest and lasting consequences is the exclusion of women from landowning rights. While women perform most of the agricultural labor on Zambia's land and produce most of the food that's used to feed its children (as is the case in most of Sub-Saharan Africa), the vast majority of land is owned by men and passed on to men. Of course, landowning rights are complex and the plurality of tribes doesn't make it a simple black-or-white issue, but what's clear is that colonialism certainly didn't empower women. The most lasting and pernicious legacy of colonialism for all genders was extreme poverty, which helps cement and preserve structures of gender inequality. For instance, given that six out of ten people in Zambia live under the poverty line, for many families getting a payment for someone to marry their daughter is not just custom; it becomes a source of income. Gender inequality becomes hard to solve when it's both a product and a consequence of extreme poverty.

Given this colonial history, I felt conflicted traveling to Zambia, even as a researcher. While earning my undergraduate degree in international development, I got a master class in why white people have a very long and well-documented history of being terrible.

When white European colonizers weren't creating borders out of thin air, slaughtering indigenous populations and stripping the African continent of all its most valuable resources, they were practicing modern-day colonialism through predatory loans, treaties and terrible trade agreements. I finished college being so sickened that I chose to leave the field entirely and pursue a master's in gender studies, because it felt like my people had already done so much damage that even well-intentioned involvement would always end up doing more harm than good. After all, Zambia's social, political and economic inequalities, particularly those between men and women, had been engineered by its colonial powers. Patriarchy wasn't born in Zambia; it had been imported—you know, along with smallpox, plague, gonorrhea, syphilis and all the other deadly diseases brought along by the colonizers.

But after doing my due diligence on The Girl Impact and learning about their commitment to training and employing locals and creating independent sustainable programs that wouldn't rely on volunteers, I felt like going on this trip could be the best way to put my development degree to work: conduct my research respectfully and share some of my insights with the organization.

One afternoon, I decided to take a break from conducting interviews with locals to offer up one of my most valuable talents and taught an aerobics class for a group of women from the Girl Impact program who had requested it. When the organizers heard I had a knack for aerobics, they asked me to give a class because the women had been requesting one for weeks. I was delighted they were familiar with Shania Twain's greatest hits and so blown away by their dance moves that I didn't even really end up leading the class—they did. Afterwards, we ate my new favorite postworkout snack, off-brand Cheetos with orange soda, and talked a bit about womanhood and naturally the conversation inadvertently pivoted to men. It's worth noting that because these women had self-selected into the Girl Impact program, they were certainly more cognizant of or at least open to discussing matters relating to gender. Out of the six women who came, half of them had been abandoned by their husbands. One man told his wife he was going to go out and find a job. He never came back. She was forced to raise their children on her own. No partner. No income. No assistance. She had not received any education as a young girl, so she had no job to fall back on to make ends meet. Priscah, a strong-willed, energetic and young entrepreneur, told us about going into a deep state of depression after her husband disappeared, leaving her alone with their three boys. She said she stopped hoping for him to come back two years after he left. When I asked her if she would take him back if he suddenly reappeared, she looked out into the distance and gave it a thought. She then looked back at me, warm tears rolling down her cheeks, and shook her head no.

I thought about the unforgiving cruelty of the man you need the most also being the person who betrayed you the most. I fought back tears listening to these women's stories, angry at these men I would never meet but knew I would hate forever. I'd asked myself what was wrong with men before, but I found myself more desperate for an answer than ever. I knew many women back home who had suffered similar hardships, had been abandoned by cowards, but watching these women have to do so much with so little was a different kind of viciousness. It felt like these women had been left to die. They possessed a kind of superhuman resilience that even I couldn't fully grasp the power of. When I broached the topic of domestic violence, I could see a stark generational divide. Although the young women in the group condemned domestic violence and said it was never acceptable, the older women looked away or remained silent. And I get it, from their perspective: Who was I to tell them what was right or wrong? I'm not married. I don't know their life. I myself stayed for months in an abusive relationship. The web of abuse is complicated. You can understand the problem, be an expert in the problem and still become another statistic that you read about.

The next day I was asked to co-lead a gender equality workshop for a group of young boys with one of the local program coordinators, Audrey. Although speaking with these incredible women the day before had been eye-opening, the boys were the reason I had really come all this way. The people who ran the Girl Impact program had realized early on that you can't educate a girl without educating a boy, so they had recently developed an arm of the organization to focus on targeting boys in the community. It was new, but it was an ambitious program aimed at offering different outlets for boys and encouraging them to use their influence in their communities to uplift girls. I agreed with this approach. You can "empower" girls all you want, but if no one is speaking to the boys and men about gender equality, too, the work can be fruitless or even counterproductive. I thought about microfinance programs, a kind of development program that became popular in the early 2000s that I had studied in school. It became one of the most respected and highly revered models for development. The first of its kind was called Grameen Bank and it was founded by the pioneer for the program, Professor

Muhammad Yunus. He won a Nobel Peace Prize for it in 2006. The concept was simple: loan people in struggling economies small amounts of money so that they can develop their own sustainable businesses. Many of the loans happened to go to women because they often didn't have access to loans in the first place, and they were also the most likely to pay loans back on time. Although micro-financing became a very popular grassroots development tactic that made real differences in increasing women's economic opportunities and their control over resources, researchers also noticed that in areas where many women were receiving microloans, there also tended to be spikes in men's violence against women. While these programs were effective at helping women challenge what it means to be a woman, they weren't properly addressing the obvious side effect of how that would challenge what it means to be a man, too. Similar to the way that American men who aren't the primary breadwinners are more likely to engage in domestic violence as I discussed earlier in this book, "manhood-restoring activities" aren't unique to one country or one part of the world. In fact, how common they are and how severe the consequences can be should give us enough of a reason to focus resources and energy to try to address it. Sure, women were being "empowered" both psychologically and economically through microloan programs, but without the proper education of their husbands, that newfound freedom had become a literal threat to them. The solution is not to keep women oppressed so it doesn't threaten men; it's to clear women's barriers to success while working on men's ability to understand how female empowerment benefits society (and them!) as a whole. In many communities, freeing women from gendered constraints might be as important as freeing men from them, too. I still remember learning about targeting men in policy and development work while earning my master's degree. For one assignment, I recall being tasked with arguing about whether gender equality programs should invest resources in men, too. I couldn't believe this was even up for debate. The answer felt self-evident. If we are changing the roles and responsibilities of women, it is crucial to plan for how this changes those for men. Perhaps the fact that we were even asking this question was the reason we were still light-years behind the goals industrialized countries had set for programs aimed to aid women economically, politically and socially in developing countries. Whether it's in Zambia or anywhere else, when our approach to gender equality is exclusively focused on women, we cannot effectively solve anyone's problems.

As we drove through the winding rugged roads leading us to the flag football field where we would be doing the workshop with the boys, I feared no one would show up. "It just rained, so the boys might not be able to cross the river," one of the program organizers said, staring outside, skeptical. What if I came all this way just to find out that the boys weren't interested?

Since the program was still at its inception and only a few boys had shown up in the first few weeks, I went in with zero expectations, but I ended up being pleasantly bowled over. Only one boy showed up but we recruited three others who had come to the field to play football. "Who needs football when you have gender equality workshops?" said no 8-year-old boy ever. Although they were reluctant and a bit silent at first, within a few minutes into our conversation about gender, I was fascinated by what the boys were teaching me. They had never been to America and didn't have phones or televisions at home. They lived halfway across the world, yet they had all been taught a version of the same myths that boys have been taught in North America. They all had heard a version of "boys don't cook," "boys don't sweep" (clean). These boys were barely 7 or 8 years old, and yet they were already fluent in the male code they knew they were expected to follow and obey. I was halfway across the world and yet I was hearing the same gender stereotypes that I had heard from the mouths of the boys in North America. *Boys don't wear makeup; boys don't wear leggings; boys do the work; women do the cooking.*

What was the point of this? Why did we teach this to boys?

Audrey and I had a set of activities planned, and the first one was role-playing. Inspired by the Always commercial that reclaimed the expression "run [or hit or throw] like a girl" from something that's demeaning to something that's empowering, we had the boys perform different actions like "run like a girl" or "throw like a girl" to see how they would react to that language. They acted out every action exactly the way American boys would do it: representing femininity as both inferior and humiliating. When we asked them to explain their choices for the behaviors that they reenacted, we could see the gendered myths they had dutifully absorbed. When I asked them how they acted out "talk like a girl" they said, "The voice for a girl is small and the voice for a boy is big." They also believed "men have more energy than girls." But the most revealing part of the activity came when we asked them to "play football like a girl," and that was the only time there was no discernable difference between those actions and the way they had acted out "play football like a boy." Although it could be due to a number of factors, I couldn't help but notice that right next to our field, a girls' flag football league organized by The Girl Impact just happened to be practicing. Interestingly, when the boys were instructed to play football like a girl there was no difference between those actions and the way they acted out a boy playing football. Although I couldn't assign any correlation or causation to it, it made me marvel at how strongly our environments can dictate our gendered realities and truths. Because the girls were casually kicking ass right next to us, it wasn't just unfair to depict them as lesser; it was inaccurate. It wasn't lost on me that I was working with a small sample size of only four boys, but it still struck me to see all of them not even blink twice on this particular activity. It wasn't scientific, but it sure was fascinating.

Shocked the boys were still listening to me, I kept moving on with another exercise, an interactive one about masculinity, using a drawing of a man with bubbles that associated to his head, his mouth and his heart. I pointed to his head and asked them, "What does a man think about?" Their answers ranged from "trying new things" to "stealing," "driving" and of course, the inevitable "women." When I pointed to the man's mouth and asked, "What does a man say?" the first thing one of the boys said was, "Have *too* much pride," which was followed up with, "They put down their friends." When I asked them what the voice of a man sounds like, they said, "Too big." I was genuinely surprised so much of what they brought up felt like negative behavior. It was clear that these boys had already developed a critical perspective on the way that men acted around them. It was revealing that none of the things they said a man says they viewed as particularly positive. Since I was working through an interpreter for large portions of the exercise, I also don't think they ever really understood what answers were expected of them, which made their assessment even more honest and raw.

Another notable moment was when I pointed to the man's heart and I asked them what a man feels and their first answer was "sad." Although they had all repeated to me that boys aren't supposed to cry, the very first emotion they could think of was the one they had been instructed to avoid. Perhaps the mere act of talking about emotions helped them tap into them. When I asked for an example of when a man feels sad, the boys said "When a man admires a woman and proposes to her, but she says no." Hearing them speak openly about men feeling sadness when being rejected gave me hope.

I kept expecting the boys to doze off, get bored or fidgety or just dump me to go play on the field, but they remained engaged and demonstrated a playful attitude despite some of the questions being tough to answer for a lot of adults, let alone a bunch of kids. We played another game where we asked the boys to perform a set of tasks traditionally performed by women such as cooking, sweeping or taking care of a baby. Again, I could see them do the exact same dance as with the first exercise. They looked at me with a sense of embarrassment as their faces shouted *I can't believe you're making us do this!*, but once the first one got up and started enacting the task somewhat, rolling his eyes as his friends giggled a bit, the next one would get up a little more enthusiastically.

During both activities I could see the boys trying to read one another, which made sense given that men take cues from other men about how to act; in fact, we all do. Just like feminist Ryan Gosling memes invite men in America and Canada to be warmer to feminist ideas, these boys were quietly scanning one another's reactions, trying to tease out exactly how the others felt about doing something that boys don't usually do. I could sense that what was guiding the boys' behavior was less their own willingness to engage in the gender-bending activities and more how acceptable they felt it was to the group. Their faces seemed neutral, but their eyes were screaming *Is this okay?* and *I'll do this but only if you are?* It revealed just how simultaneously arbitrary yet powerful gender norms can be.

The leverage that gender as a system has over us is only as substantial as our willingness to honor it. Its omnipresence is completely diffused through a group's decision to ignore it. In that moment, the boys were able to set their own rules free of judgment and enjoy the freedom that came with it. Once one boy let loose, it gave permission for everyone else to do it, too. It set the tone for the entire activity and for how freely the others engaged in it. It was always a bit hard to find the first volunteer, but once the arms started going up, the pace increased, the awkwardness dissipated and it was hard to get them to stop. It seemed like once one of the boys would break the first hard ice patch of gender, it created a path for everyone else to forge forward a little less carefully and a little bit more freely.

Within a matter of seconds, I got a glimpse of the instantaneous release that comes with being given permission to transgress the code of rigid masculinity. I saw the boys transform before my eyes, going from them shuffling their feet when they were asked to perform the traditional feminine tasks to literally fighting over who went next. They went from being uncomfortable to full-on giddy.

The embarrassment in their eyes slowly turned into sheer excitement. In that moment I realized how meaningfully and quickly men could be different if we gave boys a license to be themselves. It was literally like they were breaking free of a shell they didn't realize they had been carrying. Although we see this shift as a huge lift that requires a lot of time, education and policy, the workshop showed that altering gendered expectations can be well received. I'm not saying it's always easy. We had created the parameters of a social experiment where we encouraged their transgression of social norms and gave positive reinforcement when the boys executed our instructions. Society doesn't have the parameters of a fun game, and it's still not a safe space where those kinds of risks can be taken. If we were only able to shape more environments like this, maybe boys could develop their true selves. I wondered what it would look like to give everyone a little bit more space to play with gender and more space to exist outside of it.

As I looked in the boys' eyes all I saw was potential, which is, after all, the way we all start out. Every single man I had heard about the day before and hated so much had started out this way, too. I wanted to believe the boys I'd met that day would turn out to be kind and loving to one another and to women, but it seemed like in order to be good men, they would need to fight an uphill battle. It felt like they were born having to fight a kind of soul-crushing invisible hand pushing them in the wrong direction. What took boys off the beaten path of innocence?

After the workshop was over, I went looking for answers by speaking to men about their passage into manhood. I went around town asking a question that made no man particularly comfortable: "When did you know you were a man?" I was struck by the variety of the responses I received from men about what it means to be a man. Although most people speak Bantu, which originates from the Bemba ethnic group, there are seventy different tribes or ethnicities and dozens of different dialects and languages, so narrowing down the experience of manhood in Zambia is complicated. But similarly to when I would ask this question of American men, I wasn't struck by the differences; I was struck by the similarities.

Every single man I spoke to had a different point of entry into manhood, but most of them had experienced some kind of ritual right around or after puberty. It varied based on their parents' tribe, where they were from and what kind of community they grew up in, but what astounded me was that all of them had to do with one thing: pain. Almost all of the rituals that were meant to turn boys into men required hurting others or hurting themselves. One middle-aged man I spoke to had experienced an initiation ceremony, fairly common with certain communities in the Bemba tribe in Zambia, where a boy is brought into a remote part of the woods with a few men from the community. The boy is left to survive there for several days (sometimes weeks, depending on the tribe), often alone. On the last day he is circumcised. This can be done without warning or any anesthesia when the boy is as old as 18, fully aware and conscious during the entire procedure. This man had gone through it. When I asked if his father had been through the same ceremony, he shook his head no. He looked off into the distance and replied stoically, "He had to kill a lion."

Of course, manhood rituals are not unique to Zambia; in fact, as Esther Perel had explained to me during our social experiment in Washington Square Park, they are common throughout the world. Even in industrialized countries, men take part in very specific rituals. For example, in the United States, where the age of drinking is 21, young men are often encouraged to mark that day by heavily intoxicating themselves. Before a man gets married, he is often expected to partake in a celebration with other men where naked women dance and perform for them. Although these rituals may seem mundane to those who do them, it's just because they're ingrained in our culture that they feel so normal.

I got a sense of how important self-reliance was to manhood in Zambia when I sat down with a well-respected elder and environmental activist well known in Livingstone, Uncle Benny, as he was called around town. He was 73 years old and had grown up in a small village in Zambia called Mansa. I was introduced to him by his son, 21-year-old Solomon, who was also born and raised in Zambia and worked as one of the program coordinators for the Girl Impact program. Although Uncle Benny was a smart leader in the community, he also had a je ne sais quoi, a sort of swagger that you immediately couldn't help but fall under the spell of. When I asked him about the process of becoming a man, he said that it's what some would describe as "abuse." He said he found those rituals necessary, although he confided he would never make his sons endure them today. "If you saw me carrying logs of firewood or carrying an animal from the bush, they would call it abuse, but for me it's not abuse," he said. "We did a lot of rough things, and I thought my grandfather was very, very cruel at the time, but it's only now that I'm grown-up that I see he was teaching me to be self-reliant." It was clear that Uncle Benny could be grateful for what he had been put through without necessarily wanting his own children to go through it.

"I enjoyed mine because it was a different time. [You] can't do that now." Although the rituals varied from one generation to the other, the values remained the same. When I asked him what he wanted to instill in his son Solomon, he said the means were different, but the ends were the same. "He learned that it's important to be self-reliant and not depend so much on his parents all the time. . . . That's why he's able to [live] outside of my house." When I asked Uncle Benny if he was as determined to transmit self-reliance to his daughters as his sons, he paused. "I think it's more for the men than girls," he responded. "The girls . . ." he said. "Families keep them for a longer time, let them learn this and that and do class and that kind of thing and so on." There was less of a pressure to teach girls independence than boys. The urgency to teach the boys to be self-sufficient wasn't surprising, given the dire consequences that were reserved for men who weren't able to be. Although there's nothing wrong with teaching someone to be self-reliant, there can be negative consequences when it's imposed rather than encouraged. I found that out when I asked Uncle Benny what happened when a man wasn't able to provide. According to him, there was simply no room for error. Not being able to provide was a personal tragedy. "Then you become a failure in one way or another. You are failing to provide. You must provide whether you like it or not. Unless your wife works, or you have children that can provide, otherwise you have to work really hard to provide. That's what we are meant to be," he said. "As men, of course." In that moment I wondered what kind of pressure providing placed on men and whether it encouraged them to leave when they felt like they couldn't fulfill that role or couldn't live up to the self-reliance ideals imposed on them. It didn't make men's abandonment of their families less enraging, but perhaps it could help explain it.

Although speaking with Uncle Benny illuminated how hard it is to fulfill certain ideals of masculinity, speaking with his son also revealed how quickly norms about masculinity can change. One of the ways it showed up was when we talked about gender roles. You could tell that for Uncle Benny, cooking and sweeping were not tasks he could see himself doing. "My tradition is about girls doing a certain job. That is what our tradition says. That's what we do and we love it that way." At the same time, he wasn't alarmed by his son shifting gender roles in the home; in fact, it was the opposite. He seemed fairly cool with it. "Today it is a little bit different," he said. "Now Solomon can pick up a pot and cook. The girls can also do a couple of things because life now is a bit different." When I asked him if he minded that Solomon did something traditionally reserved for women, he was quite indifferent. "Yeah, he cooks what he wants. He does. He eats quite a bit." Uncle Benny laughed. He had no problem with his son obeying a different set of rules.

But the differences between father and son were as stark as the similarities. For instance, unprompted, both of them brought up the importance of pursuing equality in their romantic relationships with women. "She has a lot of control in the house for the good reasons," Uncle Benny said in reference to his wife, Selena. "We are equal partners. I have been very lucky. . . . She is very straightforward. If there is something wrong, she'll always tell you. Even if it's in the middle of the night, she wakes you up and says, 'I didn't like that you did it that way.' I know at the bottom of my heart what she says is correct." Uncle Benny didn't brag about respecting his wife, nor did he credit himself for recognizing her influence in their marriage. He simply proudly spoke about revering his wife and respecting her judgment and her trusting his. When I asked him what the secret was to a long-lasting marriage, he credited it to an equal partnership. "We've been together for forty years. I think we're just blessed."

Although both Solomon and Uncle Benny seemed to know how to bend the rules of masculinity, Solomon seemed to take more pleasure in it. Although he never explicitly criticized traditional masculinity, you could hear some rebellion in his voice. When I asked him what it meant to be a man, he started listing things as if they were military orders to be taken seriously. "Cut your hair short," he said. "Be the breadwinner; be in control of things," he continued. "Don't wear pink." As he said that, I noticed the hat he was wearing was salmon-colored.[1] "Sometimes I wear pink because pink is a statement," he said. "The little I can do, I will do. I'll wear pink. I don't care." When I asked him if he could ever consider being a stay-at-home dad, he was reluctant, but he said he could consider it if it had to happen. "I love cooking and I love staying at home," he said, smiling. But then he got more serious and explained that an equal partnership would be his preferred arrangement. "I wouldn't love to just stay at home and do the cooking. I love to work, so I would rather share," he said. "One day it's me; one day it's you."

One of my favorite things about Solomon is that he seemed to carry zero shame in breaking the rules of the male code, especially when it was in front of his male friends. In fact, he viewed intimacy with other men as key to their relationship. He described crying with one of his friends a few weeks prior. "Those are the moments that bring you together," he said, wide-eyed and almost in awe. "'Dude . . . we cried together.' We were quite close already, but that's like in the files now." He talked about crying in front of his friend as a badge of honor and an important crystallizing step for their friendship. "Crying is awesome," he said. "It's healthy."

After my interview with Uncle Benny, I went to hang out with Solomon and his friends, and they were probably the loveliest group of college-aged men I'd ever hung out with. They embodied a different kind of masculinity that was open and comfortable with difference. They embraced individuality even if it contradicted the beliefs of their parents and their parents' parents. They were part of a global generation of young men who took pride in being nonconforming and brave enough to use their voices to shape a different world.

Through my conversations with different men and boys, I realized that we didn't just allow the squeezing of emotion out of men; we institutionalized it. Toxic masculinity was most powerful when it was invisible, and it was most subtle when it was ritualized. Although it's tempting to think it's coming from a bad place, most often the opposite is true. The people telling these young boys not to cry and not to depend on others weren't trying to hurt them; they were trying to protect them. Even though I wanted to changed it, I started to understand the motivation behind it.

I thought back to the end of the workshop with the boys. I led a ritual that had been on my bucket list for a long time: a fake funeral for gender roles. I asked the boys to choose a stereotype about men they wanted to get rid of, and we held a fake funeral for it with a ceremony, flowers and everything. I made a casket out of cardboard and one by one the boys tore up the stereotype and put it inside the casket. I thought about what a collective funeral for unhelpful definitions of masculinity would look like. I think we'd be shocked by how many men would show up and, given the choice, how much they would throw away.

After my trip to Zambia, I felt elated and excited to be part of a group of like-minded people who didn't need to be convinced about the importance of affecting boys to empower a lasting and radical kind of social change that could benefit everybody. Although I'm certainly not an expert on Zambia and the observational research I conducted was on a very small scale, it was gratifying to come across the work of people who had much more knowledge than me that backed up what I'd observed. Even in the months after I returned, I came across a growing number of experts who are now pointing to the importance of including men in development and policy initiatives, with some going so far as pushing for a new gender equality index that would capture men's experiences in addition to women's all over the world. Although I have many issues with it, a new index was recently created by researchers at the University of Essex and the University of Missouri in Columbia. Their new figure, the Basic Index of Gender Inequality, takes into consideration early male deaths due to lower life expectancy, workplace accidents and hazards, as well as obligatory enrollment into the military, which tends to disproportionately impact men globally, in an index that measures well-being according to gender. Although the measure is far from perfect (case in point: it ranks Saudi Arabia as more equal for women than men, which is absurd) and the motivation of the researchers is not entirely clear, it's pushing us to view how the patriarchy may not hurt equally, but it hurts everybody. The same culture that tolerates violence against women because it assumes they are weaker also promotes violence by (and against) men because it assumes they're naturally violent. The patriarchal beliefs that pressure men to take risky jobs with little protection are the same ones that underpin the pressure for women to be protected and kept inside the home against their will. The root of the belief, although it justifies different treatment for women and men, is the same. Measuring gender equality by only showing the way it has costs for women is inaccurate because it doesn't capture the scope of harm for the entire population. The problem with the Basic Index of Gender Inequality is that it continues to pit women's issues against men as if they weren't related. Recognizing women's pain doesn't preclude us from recognizing men's. Ranking our pain is unproductive because it gets us away from the fact that our afflictions are all connected.

As I looked over the interviews I had conducted, I was struck by the universality of toxic masculinity. The pressures placed on the shoulders of Zambian men and boys were certainly different from the obstacles faced by men I had interviewed in the United States, Canada or Scandinavia, but the underlying factors were strikingly similar: it seemed like no boy was born free. No matter where I turned, masculinity wasn't something that was intuitive or intrinsic; it was carefully learned, delicately transmitted and deliberately propagandized. Idealized masculinity wasn't just a problem in America. I saw it everywhere. It translates into every language and is communicated through cultures. It's the oxygen we breathe. Although there is no uniform experience of manhood (or womanhood, for that matter), the shared commonalities and struggles confirmed my suspicion that the most effective way to solve some of the world's greatest suffering is to address the male pain, because left unaddressed it was turning into the greatest threat to this planet. The factory we put boys through in order to turn them into men is global, and the urgency of exposing and disrupting it could very well be the paramount test of our time. Given the current state of the world, the only question left is: Are we ready to embark on this journey we have been called to?

> *All that is necessary for the triumph*
> *of evil is that good men do nothing.*

—EDMUND BURKE

13   **Compassion As the Antidote to Hate**

Sammy Rangel joined his first gang when he was 11 years old. He survived a race riot at a maximum-security prison and to this day holds the record as the most violent inmate in the state of Wisconsin. Suffice it to say Sammy is not who you'd expect to be leading one of the most prominent peace and reconciliation organizations in the United States. The organization Life After Hate, which he cofounded with several ex–white supremacists, has helped rehabilitate some of the most dangerous perpetrators of extremist hate across America and across the world.

Sammy spent most of his life trying to cope with his own pain. One of his earliest memories is his uncle raping him immediately after raping his older sister. He was three years old. Sammy wasn't fed very often. His mother deprived him of sleep, making him sleep on the floor at the bottom of her bed, preventing him from going to the bathroom. He says that when he would inevitably end up relieving himself, she would take his soiled underwear and forcibly thrust it in his mouth. If he would start to gag or throw up, she would beat him. In an attempt to escape the harrowing trauma, Sammy abandoned his family. "I was only 11 when I ran away, and I made a vow that I would never allow myself to be hurt that way again," he said. "You go through these crazy steps, any length to cover up any signs of weakness, any signs of fear, you put the best parts of yourself away."

Sammy described joining a gang the same way someone would describe falling in love. Although it was connected with pain and trauma, he said that being part of the gang felt like the acceptance and care he had been so desperate to find but had never received. For the very first time in his life, he felt like someone was looking out for him. Members of his gang would ensure his survival, come and check up on him, even sometimes in the middle of the night, to make sure he was safe. "I finally had people that seemed to care," Sammy said. Because he depended on them for safety, he quickly began to feel indebted to them. Like any abusive relationship, it's designed to trap its victim into a state of codependency. Destructiveness became the easiest way to cover up his trauma. "The violence is prevalent because it's the main language we know how to speak out pain through," Sammy said. "The only outlet you have is to speak to violence. You spend your whole life sending a message: *you can't harm me.* It was to hide my brokenness, it was to hide my vulnerabilities. No one knew that my behaviors were symptoms."

Although Sammy has firsthand experience about what can lead a man to fall into the cycle of organized violent crime, he also has a deep understanding of how a man can get out of it. For him, it had come from the most unexpected place: the entirely platonic and unconditional love of another man. "When you create defenses, you're prepared for certain kinds of attacks," he said. "But the attack you're not waiting for is the one that comes from empathy and compassion." That dose of empathy came when Sammy was at his lowest point, from a man named George, a prison case worker. At this point, Sammy was in a triple-max prison, in the basement of the segregation unit, in solitary confinement, where the only physical human contact he could recall was guards handcuffing, disciplining or force-feeding him. His cell was kept behind three different kinds of hard steel walls, with a bright flickering neon light that was turned on twenty-four hours a day. Given Sammy's atrocious living conditions, he was convinced nothing could shock him anymore. But George managed to stun Sammy by doing this one simple thing: knocking. Before entering each of the three steel layers of his cell, he, to Sammy's surprise, asked if he could come in first. "That subtle feature started to change my life," Sammy said.

Being met with George's compassion was so unsettling at first that Sammy accused him of brainwashing him. Sammy told me that he started feeling something that had become foreign to him: guilt. While he knew George disapproved of his actions, he did something unique that no one else in Sammy's life had done: he dismissed what Sammy did, not who Sammy was. "No matter what you do, no matter what you've done, I won't stop loving you," George told Sammy while he was still incarcerated. "If it wasn't for George," Sammy's voice cracked, "I can wholeheartedly say I wouldn't be here today."

Sammy's journey crystalized how preventable men's individual and systemic acts of violence can be. "Based on my experience, men are primarily responsible for well above 95 percent of the violence that happens in the U.S.," Sammy said. But instead of chalking it up as a biological inevitability for men, Sammy described it as a form of addiction. "I grew up in gangs, and the mentality, the lack of empathy, the hatred, the focus of energy and time, a lot of it is similar with addiction." Sammy said that gang members don't even need drugs to get high. "They can become addicted to a lifestyle. It doesn't require substance, because you're triggering certain moods and reactions in the body that are highly addictive." Joining a gang is an individual act, but when you start looking closely, there are collective similarities.

But it's worth asking, if we saw men's violent behavior as a predictable and treatable chronic condition, could we be better at tackling it? That's what Adam Baird, a research fellow at the Centre for Trust, Peace, and Social Relations at Coventry University, concluded when he conducted research and interviews with past gang members of several gangs in Latin America and the Caribbean. In his work, he notes that 90 percent of global deaths don't occur in war zones, which means that even making a small dent in the number of men who join extremist and organized gangs could fundamentally reduce the amount of violence across the world. Baird argues that a person's likelihood of joining organized violence is intrinsically tied to a desire to perform ideal forms of masculinities. He calls gangs an "aspirational site" for many young, poor and marginalized men because it becomes the way they can achieve and perform the economic power and independence they are denied by poverty. When a culture assigns masculine value to violence, it becomes a proxy through which men who become estranged from normative paths to employment and status in their families or communities earn power. That's why Baird describes gangs as a literal "tool to contest emasculation."

The logic that underpins men's participation in gangs can often help us understand why they join terrorist groups, and yet when policy makers take the weight of masculinity scripts seriously, it's seen as outlandish. For instance, when the Trump administration announced an investment of $600,000 into research to "explore gender identities of boys and men in Kenya and how terrorist organizations were exploiting the pressures on Kenyan men 'to be tough, heterosexual, aggressive, unemotional, and achieving' to recruit them for radicalization," conservative commentator David Webb called for a government shutdown over it. Elizabeth Harrington, a writer with the Washington Free Beacon, criticized the program for making mention of gender but not "radical ideology," as if toxic masculinity wasn't one, too.

There's an ease, an almost irresistible comfort, in erroneously assigning certain barbaric characteristics to entire ethnic groups and religions as a result of repeated tragedies or terrorist acts. It's still incredibly common for politicians and public figures to wrongly blame all Muslims for individual acts of terror. President Trump's unconstitutional travel ban barring travel from five Muslim-majority countries is just one example. His then national security advisor, Lt. Gen. Michael Flynn, even once explicitly described Islam as "a vicious cancer inside the body of 1.7 billion people" that "needed to be excised," when the vast majority of Muslims are peaceful and never commit acts of terror. But it's worth asking: if we started calling toxic masculinity a religion, would we start paying attention to it? If we started seeing idealized masculinity as a radical ideology rather than inevitable, would we approach it differently?

Throughout this book I've argued that isolation can lead to personal hardship and poor physical and mental health for men, but what often goes unnoticed is that this also makes men more vulnerable to predators who capitalize on that poor emotional integration to recruit them for violence. The rise of groups like the alt-right, the Proud Boys, neo-Nazi groups and even ISIS takes advantage of the vulnerability that outdated masculinity beliefs impart on the modern man. Rarely discussed is how radicalization explicitly relies on men's unique emotional isolation for recruitment. The more I researched, the closer I came to the conclusion I already knew, that "toxic masculinity" is not just a phrase that feminists use—it's a war tactic.

When we hear foreign policy experts talk about ISIS, it's common to hear them obfuscate an obvious fact: that these groups are largely led by and made up of only one gender—men. If suddenly the vast majority of terrorists were female, you bet we'd be discussing their gender. There would be entire taskforces dedicated to targeting vulnerable women and rigorous research into trying to understand why. But for some reason when it comes to the link between men and terrorism, gender is completely dismissed. Of course, almost every single magazine has run its own tantalizing "women of ISIS" cover story when the truth is that the vast majority of terrorists have one thing in common: they're primarily men. Although politicians focus on finding (often faulty) consistency in the religion or the ethnicity of terrorists, very few pay attention to the glaring commonality of their identity as men. Politicians single out countries, ban specific religions and declare arbitrary danger zones, when in fact they could probably more effectively clamp down on terrorism if they just banned men. This would be a ridiculous solution! But if we are so determined to solve a systemic and severe problem like terrorism that countries are spending millions on its prevention, it's curious that so little attention is paid to the way that men are more vulnerable to recruitment. Despite politicians and pundits debating whether Islam makes you more violent, the gender of terrorists is rarely raised, discussed or politicized while their ethnicity or religion is fair game. It's curious that political leaders and pundits are quicker to blame an entire religion for a problem (especially since it's factually incorrect) than recognize that statistically, gender is a bigger determinant of terrorism than one's religion. Why is it so easy to ignore one of the most glaring, consistent problems in our society?

One of the first groups of people who would be destabilized if we started to challenge faulty definitions of masculinity would be ISIS, because they rely so heavily on outdated models of what it means to be a man to lure vulnerable men into their ranks. In fact, the more experts I spoke to, the clearer it became that the biggest tool for recruitment is tapping into male feelings. "Emotional predation is used to recruit individuals [. . .] it's all about getting the person to feel like they are a part of a community," Alejandro J. Beutel, a researcher for Countering Violent Extremism at the University of Maryland's National Consortium for the Study of Terrorism and Responses to Terrorism, told me. As one of the only experts who studies the intersection of terrorism and gender, he warns how technological advances have not only exacerbated propaganda but also have made recruitment easier, making it much more emotional and personal. "Propaganda is to get people curious," he said, "but when they start talking to recruiters, they stay for the sense of community." When I asked Beutel what was the most common trait that could predict whether someone falls prey to extremist violence recruitment, he said two words: "emotional pliability."

A lot of these men who end up in organized groups aren't inherently bad to begin with, but they are easily influenced, through emotional tactics that promise access to high-status masculinity, to commit horrible acts of violence. Beutel told me that this is precisely why rehabilitation for terrorist recruits often starts with redefining their masculinity before anything else. "We can't ignore the fact that toxic masculinity is used as a pain point for malicious actors seeking the recruitment of people for violence," he said. To demonstrate how pivotal gender identity is in not only recruiting but maintaining ISIS members, he pointed to the work of Usman Raja, an ex–cage fighter who now leads a deradicalization program for ISIS recruits in the UK. Beutel explained that Raja is known for beginning every session with a new group of ISIS recruits the exact same way: by breaking down their assumptions about what it means to be a man. Once Raja challenges the expression of manhood through violence and destruction, the healing process for these men can begin.

While Neo-Nazis and ISIS groups have pretty dissimilar goals, the tools they use to recruit men to commit mass acts of violence are strikingly similar. "When you look at a group like ISIS or a white supremacist group, notions of masculinity are central to the propaganda that's out there," Beutel told me. During our conversation, he talked about one common thread: all these groups portray men as protectors of their communities, and justify violence through that messaging. Violence can easily be explained away if you're doing it for the common good. "Beheadings are a presentation of an emasculation of the state," he explained. Beutel cited the graphic murder of American journalist James Foley by ISIS. His captors made him say, in essence, "The US state government could not protect me," before laying him down and slaughtering him. "The power dynamics that are trying to be communicated is emasculation and dehumanization," Beutel said. "The fear of an entire body politic is projected on that victim." The link Beutel draws between masculine gender socialization and terrorism recruitment is supported by research performed by law professor Fionnuala Ní Aoláin. In an essay for the anthology *Using Human Rights to Counter Terrorism,* titled "The complexity and challenges of addressing the conditions conducive to terrorism," she writes that ISIS will use "hyper-masculine images to portray its fighters" to lure them. She also notes that ISIS promises "access to sexual gratification, marriage and guaranteed income as a reward for the glory of fighting." She describes it as an explicit strategy to "attract marginalized men whose capacity to access any similar social capital or status in their own communities will be extremely limited." Christiana Spens, a PhD candidate in international relations at the University of St. Andrews, also finds that public beheadings conducted by ISIS were one of the first direct, purposeful and gross acts the group used to define their reign of terror on a world stage. She argues that it's hard not to interpret these as public performances of hypermasculinity against the United States. Spens describes the war of images between ISIS and the United States as a form of masculine peacocking, the images of beheadings as a direct response to grueling dehumanizing and bloody images of Iraq's Saddam Hussein's or Libya's Muammar Gaddafi's capture in Western papers. Even Osama bin Laden framed Al Qaeda's war on the West as a fight against "the weakness, feebleness and cowardliness of the US soldiers." In a 1998 interview with Al Jazeera, the mastermind behind the 9/11 terrorist attack said that Western leaders "have been deprived of their manhood. And they think that the people are women." So it's not just individual men who reassert their masculine identity through acts of violence; the scale can be much wider.

When idealized masculinity scripts go unchallenged, emasculation doesn't just become a tool of the state against foreign enemies, it can become a weapon the state uses against its own people. One example of this took place during the unsuccessful 2009 Green Revolution in Iran, where an anti-government protester, Majid Tavakoli, was kidnapped—the photo of him wearing a woman's full-body-covering veil, the chador—was published by news agencies. Although the government insisted that he had used the women's dress to go undercover and avoid arrest, figureheads of the revolution argued that the photo had been doctored by pro-government forces in an attempt to emasculate him, to stagnate the movement he was leading. One Iranian blogger described it as a way "to humiliate [Tavakoli, using] an old practice by the government to prove to the public that the opposition leaders are 'less than men,' lacking courage and bravery." Iranian men reacted to the event within hours, flooding the internet with pictures of themselves sporting women's veils to counter the attempt at his degradation.

Even within the United State's borders, toxic masculinity becomes the prism through which national security strategies are evaluated and analyzed. Conservative figures like Sarah Palin played the part of the opposing party while Obama was in power, implying that he wasn't man enough to combat terrorism because of stereotypical feminine characteristics like "mom jeans." *New York Times* columnist David Brooks pegged the former president's policies on his lack of masculinity. "Obama, whether deservedly or not, does have a—I'll say it crudely—manhood problem in the Middle East," he said on *Meet the Press* in 2014. "Is he tough enough to stand up to somebody like Assad or somebody like Putin?" Putin, who of course, proved his masculinity by staging a shirtless-in-Siberia photo shoot where he does very manly things like ride a horse and kill fish. During his campaign for the presidency, Donald Trump implied that Obama's lack of masculine showmanship meant he was himself a terrorist. "We're led by a man who either is not tough, not smart or has something else in mind," he said on *Fox and Friends*. Trump later went so far as to call President Obama the founder of ISIS, taking his toxic masculinity to a whole new level by combining it with a healthy dose of racism, the same he trafficked in when he accused the first black president of not being born in the United States. And who can forget President Trump's attempt at emasculating North Korean leader Kim Jong-un by saying his nuclear button was "much bigger" than his, adding "And my button works!" to make his metaphor with impotence crystal clear and the most on-the-nose as possible.

The same masculinity scripts are exploited by neo-Nazi groups. Beutel notes that there is a common narrative with white supremacist groups, with recurring messages like "White men built this nation." He mentions the "muscular men holding hammers, looking up in the horizon" and the "serial gaze of this archetypal male there who is strong, robust, a hard worker and a constructed ideal." He explains that "these are the guys who are held up as ideal of strong white males, these Chads—attractive white men—they are the ideals that even white women are supposed to be attracted to." Neo-Nazi propaganda is also very often premised on the control of white women's bodies, a toxic trope of hegemonic masculinity. "The insecurities and fears of white men are projected on white women's bodies, and the antagonists typically make people of color shown as rapists, sexual beasts, so the protectors of women's bodies are archetypal white males," Beutel said. "It's embedded in a lot of our political discourse, the tropes that will often be used, then be dog-whistle politics." Of course, in the last few years, dog whistles have turned into full-on dog marching bands, with Donald Trump referring to Mexicans who are "rapists" of American (i.e., white) women. Beutel described it as a direct and deliberate way to exploit and "play on those fears."

One group that's been part of this swift expansion in emerging radical men's rights groups is the Proud Boys. The group, which only admits men, was founded during the 2016 election by Gavin McInnes (who claims he has now abandoned the group). McInnes is a far-right activist who has called me a FILF (feminist I'd like to f***) in a video he created for his YouTube channel. We once were on a Fox

News panel together where he called women who go on spring break "human garbage whose parents don't love them." I wasn't very surprised when I heard that he had started a group that is boastfully anti-female and pro-white, primarily made up of white men whose religion appears to be toxic masculinity. To be admitted, male recruits reportedly have to wear an official uniform of Fred Perry polo shirts (previously associated with skinheads) and declare, "I am a Western chauvinist who refuses to apologize for creating the modern world." The second part of the initiation reportedly involves being repeatedly physically punched by the other members and beating up militant anti-fascist leftists who label themselves as "antifa." A sister chapter, called the Fraternal Order of Alt-Knights (FOAK), has been called the "tactical defense arm" of the group, to support and intensify the group's physical confrontations at rallies. The group was founded by Kyle Chapman, who was arrested and charged with felony possession of a leaded cane at a peaceful progressive rally opposing Trump. Shortly after that incident, at a "Make Men Great Again" event, he bragged about spanking his son "because he fears me, he respects me." He has also said that white people "are the least racist and most generous ethnicity on the planet" and "the worst sufferers of racism in the world."

Although many alt-right groups are proliferating online, it hasn't stopped them from transforming their online organizing into real-life hate. They have organized numerous rallies. At its first "White Lives Matter" rally in Shelbyville, Tennessee, attendees shouted slogans like "Your daughter is being f——d by n——s!" Others turned violent. One neo-Nazi rally in Charlottesville, Virginia, where a crowd primarily made up of young white men screamed in unison "Jews will not replace us," killed a young woman and injured dozens. It's even inspired acts of domestic terrorism across the border. A young man who shot up a mosque in Québec, killing six Muslims and injuring nineteen, consumed a steady diet of far-right American websites and pundits like conspiracy theorist Alex Jones and conservative radio host Ben Shapiro. In the month before the attack, he had made online searches about Donald Trump no less than eight hundred times. Technology has made the organization and sophistication of these extremist groups more effective. In 2017, which so happens to be the year after the election of Donald Trump, was the deadliest year for white extremist violence in decades. According to the Anti-Defamation League's Center on Extremism, white nationalists killed twice as many people in 2017 as they did the previous year.

There is no quick fix to ending terrorism and organized violence, but disregarding the way that false definitions of manhood are used to prey on marginalized men who end up joining those groups is ignoring one of the potentially most cost-effective paths to a rigorous and global terrorism reduction strategy. Willfully ignoring these links is rendering obscure a solution that could shed light on one of the greatest problems of our time. While it may seem logical to deem any man who joins an extremist group bad to begin with, what if we assumed that they were vulnerable to begin with instead? Could assuming the best in men help us prevent the worst in them?

Anything that isn't masculine is feminine, and . . . it's not something that black men do.

—D'ARCEE CHARINGTON NEAL

AMUSE-BOUCHE:
D'Arcee's Story

D'Arcee knows he doesn't meet the mainstream ideals of masculinity, and frankly, he doesn't care. As a black gay man who uses a wheelchair because of his cerebral palsy, he's spent most of his life being reminded that he is different. He knew early on that he wasn't like other men in his family. He describes his grandfather as hard to know. "People in the 1940s were not nice to black people, so my grandfather had a hard shell," he says. Growing up in the Jim Crow era encoded in his grandfather a rational reluctance to show any weakness. In fact, when black men showed vulnerability it had been used against them systematically. Although more genteel, D'Arcee's father learned everything about what it meant to be a man from his own dad and passed on those lessons. "My dad has a rigid idea of masculinity [where] anything that isn't masculine is feminine, and that it's not something that black men do." D'Arcee explained that although his grandfather was an incredible cook and enjoyed it immensely, he refused to do it in front of the men in the family. "I don't do this; it's women's work," he would say to D'Arcee when he was growing up. Similarly, his father failed to develop passions in fear that it was perceived as a feminine pursuit. "My dad is a really good artist, but he chose to ignore that path because he thought it was not becoming of a black man." D'Arcee told me he was presented with no choice but to be tough as nails:

> We're not slaves anymore, but the repercussions are still there. The only way to get through is to be strong and resilient and pass it onto our children. I was taught over and over again: "don't let these people break you."

When he came out to his family, it was perceived as a major affront to this ideal of black masculinity. "Of course being gay is an erosion of that. Being gay was a direct transgression of everything I had learned about being a man," he said. He was desperately looking for acceptance, but all he received was rejection. "I hear about people who say they had a support network and friends and family, and I didn't have that."

D'Arcee recalled one incident where he had come home from college for the holidays and one friend had been drinking and couldn't drive, so he decided to spend the night. When D'Arcee's father returned, he was boiling with rage. He threw out the friend in the dead of night, shouting at D'Arcee, "If you think we're getting soft because we're getting older, we're not. You know I think being gay is disgusting. You have a mental illness and refuse to get help. The bottom line is, I don't appreciate faggots in my house."

D'Arcee was shaken from that experience but assumed this was just what he should expect as a gay man, because that's all he knew. When he left home to go to college and made friends with other gay black men, he realized how different life could be. "I had never met black gay people whose families were fine with them being gay until college. I got their version of acceptance. I credit them."

But again, the intersection of his multiple identities complicated things. Although his friends were always supportive, they weren't always understanding of what it meant to have a disability. He recalled going to clubs where his friends just pulled him onto the dance floor, not realizing it wasn't accessible and that his presence would make other people in the club feel awkward. He recalled one night when "a drag queen came over and said, 'Who the fuck let a cripple in here?'" and he felt really ashamed. "My friends started yelling at the drag queen. They had no idea that people had been doing this to me all night. I appreciated them trying to include me, but they don't really understand it's very awkward. You can't force people to accept this."

The sense of belonging D'Arcee had been craving when it came to his sexual identity didn't apply to his disability. "The gay community act like people with disabilities don't even exist. You don't see people with disabilities dating in public and you don't see them in the club." He explained that something as mundane as dating for his able-bodied friends is a real struggle for him. It's already rare to see public displays of affection between gay men, but add disability to the mix and it's like affection barely exists. D'Arcee recalled the first time he engaged romantically with someone in public after a date with a man in London as they were riding home in the tube. His date asked if he could kiss him, and although D'Arcee hesitated, they started kissing. It felt both liberating and stressful. "I've seen plenty of straight people kissing, but I have never seen a person with a disability kissing in public and it felt so self-conscious." He recalled feeling like the subject of so much staring. "One woman whispered, 'That's so nice.'" D'Arcee rolled his eyes.

D'Arcee blames this lack of visibility for gay men with disabilities on the fact that gay male culture can be "image obsessed." He feels like his "wheelchair is an immediate and permanent reminder of so-called 'imperfect' bodies." Because there is such a high value on appearance, any kind of deviation from that model is seen negatively. "People don't want to be associated with that," D'Arcee explained.

Using a wheelchair is also a direct transgression of what we expect from men. "Men are supposed to be providers, and if you have a disability it's often perceived that you can't work. There's a ridiculous idea that says, 'How you gonna be a breadwinner and also not be able to walk?'" D'Arcee said. Although he is employed, 80 percent of people with disabilities aren't. It's also still legal to pay people with disabilities less than the minimum wage. Just as much as there is an outdated version of masculinity in society, there is an archaic understanding of disability as well. D'Arcee sees them as inextricably connected. "I hadn't thought about it until talking to you, but I feel like being masculine and the idea of masculinity has a big effect on how society treats people with disabilities," he said. "When I was sixteen years old, my dad told me when he thought I was dating girls, 'Your life is going to be rough because girls will think that half of you is broken.'" Because men are still expected to protect women, men with disabilities are seen as inherently lacking.

Although D'Arcee's father won't really talk about his homosexuality, he still talks as if he blames it on his disability:

> A lot of the issues intersect when it comes to my dad, who views being homosexual as a negative side effect of my disability. It's a constant battle and my dad had told me, "You're gay because women rejected you" as a side effect of my disability. He told me that numerous times. "I don't think you are gay, but you think you are because women rejected you." My father is a computer programmer, so everything is logic based. My parents know that I'm attracted to men with nice legs, and he basically told me that I only liked them because mine don't work properly. My dad was trying to logically explain how his son could be a fag, and yet here I was saying, "I get what you're doing," but I told my parents if God could give me cerebral palsy, why is being gay any different?

If you have come to help me, you are wasting your time. But if you have come because your liberation is bound up with mine, then let us walk together.

—LILA WATSON

Conclusion: The Case for Mindful Masculinity

When I emailed Michael Kimmel about toxic masculinity with the subject line: "do u think we need a new term?" I received a response right away. "I think so," he immediately wrote back. I was worried about the term "toxic masculinity," anxious it wasn't capturing the root of the problem I was so eager to tackle. Michael was, too. He shared a compelling exercise that he's performed with thousands of men all over the world that always gets almost the exact same response no matter where he would do it. When he asks male participants to describe a "good man," they would answer "integrity, honor, being responsible, being a good provider, protector, doing the right thing, putting others first, sacrifice, caring, standing up for the little guy." It's beautiful, right?

But something striking would happen when he would ask them to describe a "real man." This is when the men would start talking over each other and even shouting: "never cry, be strong, don't show your feelings, play through pain, suck it up, win at all costs, be aggressive, get rich, get laid." In other words, the pressures the men would face to prove they're a "real man" would conflict with their capacity to be a *good man*. So masculinity wasn't toxic, it was the monster masquerading as masculinity that was. In other words, masculinity is not the problem, it's the solution.

The conversation we need to have about men is not distinct or separate from the one we've had and will continue to have about women. In fact, the gendered expectations holding girls back are born out of the same system that creates limitations for boys. Those oppressions aren't only connected; they're born out of the same ideology. This requires a fundamental shift in the framing of our conversations about gender, where we don't assume whether someone is the victim or perpetuator based on their gender. Although issues affecting men and women have been framed as a "gender war," with losers and winners, a more mindful conversation about gender only has winners. Women have been approaching their gender consciously for some time, and men can do it that way, too, by practicing mindful masculinity.

I know this radical shift away from conformist notions of masculinity will be scary to many, as it will be construed as an attempt to overthrow the entire system. But I want to be specific: freeing ourselves of gender rules doesn't mean we have to remove it entirely from our lives, but rather that we take and leave the parts that make sense, and that we all are afforded the personal freedom to make those decisions personally and privately.

This isn't an attack on gender; it is an improvement on it.

This isn't an attack on personal freedom; it's an extension of it.

Conservatives who are interested in individual responsibility should feel excited about the prospect of this conversation, not frightened by it. I'm not trying to tell men who to be; I want them to become free to become who they truly are.

We must reject the framing of the so-called gender war, because it's misleading us into believing we are more different than we are alike. It has made us believe that if women win, then men lose, and vice versa. This framing doesn't just dictate conversations in the media; it's also embedded in the way we approach community organizing and even policy making. Initiatives or new laws are framed as either focused on women or focused on men, rarely acknowledging the way they can impact and benefit each other, because we're all part of the same interdependent gender ecosystem. The gender wars myth has warped the conversation and led us to believe women's and men's problems are not connected and that spending time or resources on one doesn't help the other when, in reality, it's challenging the big overarching system that harms all genders that allows us *all* to thrive.

Although pitting women against men may have been a useful way of organizing the gender debate in the past because we often saw women as the only benefactors, the most radical change that I believe we will be seeing unfold in the next decade is a move away from the clearest factions of the gender conversation being women and men to the emergence of two new categories: those who believe in the imposition of a constraining gender system and those who don't. In other words, the most prominent opinion divide will no longer be between women and men; it will be between those who are interested in radical freedom from the traditional framing of gender and those who would like to preserve it. The new gender war will no longer be defined by one's gender identity; it will be split between those who recognize that gender is made up and those who do not.

To convince skeptics that we need a radical change in the way that we raise our boys, the framing of the conversation will be vital. For far too long, we've focused on the risks of a fundamental shift in the way we raise boys when what we need to do is talk about the consequences of *not* doing it. When we talk about the way gendered stereotypes or sex discrimination discourages women from pursuing careers in STEM, we'll often hear people point to the fact that the first person to cure cancer could be a girl who is being discouraged from pursuing science because she is getting the message that it's just for boys. We need to have that same curiosity about the missing men and boys and their stifled destinies and their unfulfilled purpose. The opportunity cost of not overthrowing the current system in which we raise our sons is all the positive missing male contributions in fields from nursing to caretaking to education. There are boys who will never become the men they were meant to be. There is too much unfulfilled potential for us not to take on this challenge of the gender reset for boys.

Not interrogating how our current masculinity ideals stifle boys and men is not only feckless; it's also irresponsible. It's like smelling a gas leak and trying to fix it by looking the other way. Given how many men's and women's psychological and physical safety and lives are at stake, our inaction is criminal. If questioning the falsehoods women absorbed about themselves has led to so much social progress, imagine what reassessing the ones we hold about men could do. We don't know enough about what a world without toxic notions of masculinity could look like to be pessimistic about it.

I know the pushback to the gender reset will be fierce, especially since it concerns fundamentally changing our relationship to men and their gender. Whenever anyone attempts an iota of reflection about the way we raise boys, a classic attack is leveled. People advocating to reform toxic portrayals of masculinity are painted as trying to feminize men. First, let's recognize that this classic deflection preys on our own internalized prejudice that men acting feminine or embracing femininity is a bad thing and that there is something inherently unnatural about men acting like women when we demand that women act like men all the time. But most important, we need to recognize that women aren't trying to make men "more feminine"; the *world* is becoming more feminine.

A more accurate way to put it is that the skills and characteristics that we traditionally associated with women have become more valuable. The world is changing, so it would foolish not to also change the way we raise boys as a result.

One of the ways this plays out is when we look at how emotional intelligence (EQ) is increasingly seen as a valuable skill in our modern world for all genders. EQ, defined as the ability to understand, manage and express emotions, is not just necessary to guarantee men's success in their relationships and friendships; it's also increasingly seen as a crucial predictor of their performance in the workplace and their overall happiness. The concept was coined by psychologist and bestselling author Daniel Goleman, who has found that EQ is almost twice as important as IQ because it is correlated with a child's later success more than any other measure, regardless of gender. He often cites one study that found that cognitive control, which is the ability to self-regulate, predicted financial success and overall health better than IQ or family environment. Goleman, who was the first to advocate the concept of emotional intelligence, says we need to teach our children emotional hygiene just as much as we teach them about physical hygiene. While we tell children to brush their teeth every day and warn them about the dangers of not doing so, we don't spend nearly as much time teaching them how to create healthy emotional habits and what could await them if they don't (especially if those children are boys). Goleman insists that EQ isn't something that some people have; it's a muscle that all of us can develop if we work at it. Healthy emotional intelligence doesn't mean a more expansive expression of emotions; it means a smarter expression of emotions. It means we let boys have feelings so that those feelings don't end up governing them. It's not about having more emotions; it's about knowing how to control them so that they don't control you. Instead of resisting the growing importance of emotional intelligence to protect men from "feminization," let's recognize that emotional intelligence is useful for us all and that denying one gender the full expression of their emotional capabilities is negligent, at best. EQ coming to replace IQ as the best measure of one's self-actualization is just one of the changes we need to properly prepare boys for so that they can be successful and fulfilled in the modern world.

We need a gender reset, and this is where mindful masculinity comes in as a necessary tool to achieve it. Mindfulness is defined as a state of being aware and conscious of one's internal dialogue and behaviors. It's often associated with the act of meditation, but mindfulness is really about getting in touch with the intentions behind your actions. To put it simply, the result is that we become aware of the reason why we do the things we do. Intentional masculinity is the cure for toxic masculinity. It's by attending to masculinity that we can heal it. Mindful masculinity is how we can cleanse it from all the lies it's been associated with. It encourages men to look inward to remain connected to all those things that make them a good man instead of the unhelpful trash they've inadvertently absorbed and are inadvertently carrying around about what it means to be a "real man." Being mindful about our gender means we awaken ourselves to the habits and behaviors we've automatically come to identify with and choose which ones serve us and which ones don't. It's about becoming an observer of those behaviors rather than being lost in them. At its core, it's about getting masculinity off cruise control. Instead of seeing certain male behaviors as innate, inflexible and inevitable, we will come to see them as learned, changeable and avoidable. Mindful masculinity is all about taking back control. In order to truly be autonomous, we need to let go of the feelings we identify with.

Although practicing mindful masculinity is about men getting in touch with what makes them feel aligned with what makes them feel good about being a man, it's also about facing pain and taking radical responsibility for it. In the process of becoming more conscious of what drives us, we may encounter pain and even trauma, and that can be one of the most difficult challenges, especially if you've been trained to avoid it. But the urgency of mindfully approaching what has harmed you can be summed up by spiritual leader and author Richard Rohr, who says that whatever pain you don't transform, you will transmit. Indeed, what you don't become conscious of ends up controlling you. The journey of conscious masculinity means being brave enough to examine pain as well as love and get knowledge and control over your life. It's the ultimate form of protecting others, because there's no greater way to show love for others than by taking responsibility for yourself.

Practicing mindful masculinity requires courage, a central virtue that men cite as connected when you ask them what makes them proud to be a man. If we go back to Michael Kimmel's enlightening exercise with men from the very beginning of this chapter, it's clear that the characteristics associated with a "good man" come from a place of strength and that characteristics associated with a "real man" come from a place of fear. "Standing up for the little guy" requires bravery. "Integrity" necessitates audacity. But *be aggressive* and *never cry* don't originate from a place of courage; their birthplace is shame. Mindful masculinity allows men to ensure that their choices align with the virtues that make them honored to be a man and practice the virtues connected with the things they know to be true. It's by consciously approaching masculinity that they can see the barriers that being a "real man" poses to being a good man.

The most important thing about mindful masculinity is that it's not about shunning masculinity; it's about claiming it back. It was best summed up by a comment Jason Shaw McDonald left me on Facebook. "One of the most beautiful revelations I've had of late, is that there is nothing more masculine than having control over your emotions and mental health," he said. "That's not to say to not be sad, or angry, or scared, rather, to acknowledge those emotions, have the right tools to deal with them when they arise, and to face situations with measured discipline and restraint." He told me he had struggled to come to grips with healthy masculinity for a long time, but that he had finally understood that so much of his energy had been misdirected. "Instead of trying to control the world around us, we need to do a better job of controlling the storm inside us."

Mindfully approaching gender is not just crucial for men; it's a practice that all of us can find healing in. For many of us—not just men—gender is a lot like our closet: there's some stuff back there just collecting dust and no longer assisting us that's taking up a whole lot of space. I'm not going to tell men, or anyone else for that matter, what they need to get rid of; I'm just asking all of us to think deeply about what we're holding on to and consciously let go if it's not aligning with the person we want to be. Think of it as decluttering, but for your gendered habits. Is holding on to the idea that women are more emotional or that boys don't need intimacy working for you? No? Then start decluttering your gender and throw away all the crap you've acquired over the years.

I'll wait.

Notes

INTRODUCTION

1. https://www.ncbi.nlm.nih.gov/pmc/articles/PMC2902177/.
2. https://www.ncbi.nlm.nih.gov/pubmed/14695019/.
3. https://www.ncbi.nlm.nih.gov/pmc/articles/PMC2902177/#R14.
4. https://promundoglobal.org/2018/01/26/new-analysis-toxic-masculini
   ties-sexual-abuse/.
5. https://toronto.citynews.ca/2016/03/22/men-less-likely-to-wear-seatbelts
   -more-likely-to-die-in-crashes-opp/.
6. http://www.unodc.org/gsh/en/index.html.
7. https://www.ncbi.nlm.nih.gov/pmc/articles/PMC5734535/.
8. https://www.ncbi.nlm.nih.gov/pubmed/17599274/.

2. MANHOOD IS NEVER FULLY EARNED AND NEEDS TO BE RENEWED OVER AND OVER AGAIN

1. By the way, men's razors being both cheaper and sharper than women's
   razors is patriarchy in a nutshell.

6. MALE SHAME: WHAT IS IT LIKE TO FEEL LIKE YOU NEED TO PROVE SOMETHING YOU NEVER QUITE FEEL LIKE YOU HAVE?

1. https://zdoc.site/homeless-men-exploring-the-experience-of-shame
   .html.

11. IF PATRIARCHY IS SO GREAT, WHY IS IT MAKING YOU DIE?

1. I hate terms that assume a male gender like "manpower" or "mankind," but this is the one case where not using a gender-neutral term is entirely accurate.

2. I did. Many women do. Lots of women do.

12. THE MAKING OF MEN

1. Which, let's be honest, is just a color invented to avoid calling men's clothing pink.

Bibliography

INTRODUCTION

Good, Glenn E., P. Paul Heppner, Kurt A. Debord, and Ann R. Fischer. "Understanding Men's Psychological Distress: Contributions of Problem-Solving Appraisal and Masculine Role Conflict." *Psychology of Men & Masculinity* 5, no. 2 (2004): 168–77. doi:10.1037/1524-9220.5.2.168.

Heller, Sara, Anuj Shah, Jonathan Guryan, Jens Ludwig, Sendhil Mullainathan, and Harold Pollack. "Thinking, Fast and Slow? Some Field Experiments to Reduce Crime and Dropout in Chicago." *The Quarterly Journal of Economics* 132 (February 2017): 1–54. doi:10.3386/w21178.

Hoxby, Caroline. "Peer Effects in the Classroom: Learning from Gender and Race Variation." 2000. doi:10.3386/w7867.

Jakupcak, Matthew. "Masculine Gender Role Stress and Men's Fear of Emotions as Predictors of Self-Reported Aggression and Violence." *Violence and Victims* 18, no. 5 (2003): 533–41. doi:10.1891/088667003780928116.

Kerrigan, Deanna, Katherine Andrinopoulos, Raina Johnson, Patrice Parham, Tracey Thomas, and Jonathan M. Ellen. "Staying Strong: Gender Ideologies among African-American Adolescents and the Implications for HIV/STI Prevention." *Journal of Sex Research* 44, no. 2 (2007): 172–80. doi:10.1080/00224490701263785.

Leary, Mark R., Robin M. Kowalski, Laura Smith, and Stephen Phillips. "Teasing, Rejection, and Violence: Case Studies of the School Shootings." *Aggressive Behavior* 29, no. 3 (2003): 202–14. doi:10.1002/ab.10061.

Lynch, Louise, Maggie Long, and Anne Moorhead. "Young Men, Help-Seeking, and Mental Health Services: Exploring Barriers and Solutions."

American Journal of Men's Health 12, no. 1 (2016): 138–49. doi:10.1177 /1557988315619469.

Parker, Kim, Juliana Menasce Horowitz, Ruth Igielnik, J.Baxter Oliphant, and Anna Brown. "The Demographics of Gun Ownership in the U.S." Pew Research Center's Social & Demographic Trends Project. October 25, 2018. Accessed March 02, 2019. http://www.pewsocialtrends.org/2017 /06/22/the-demographics-of-gun-ownership/.

Pinquart, Martin. "Loneliness in Married, Widowed, Divorced, and Never-Married Older Adults." *Journal of Social and Personal Relationships* 20, no. 1 (2003): 31–53. doi:10.1177/02654075030200001186.

Sánchez, Francisco J., Stefanie T. Greenberg, William Ming Liu, and Eric Vilain. "Effects of Masculine Ideals on Gay Men Survey." PsycTESTS Dataset, 2009. doi:10.1037/t39702-000.

Tager, David, Glenn E. Good, and Sara Brammer. "'Walking over' Em': An Exploration of Relations between Emotion Dysregulation, Masculine Norms, and Intimate Partner Abuse in a Clinical Sample of Men." *Psychology of Men & Masculinity* 11, no. 3 (2010): 233–39. doi:10.1037/ a0017636.

"Unmasking Sexual Harassment: How Toxic Masculinities Drive Men's Abuse in the US, UK, and Mexico and What We Can Do to End It." Promundo. Accessed March 02, 2019. https://promundoglobal.org /resources/unmasking-sexual-harassment/.

1. YOU'RE NOT BORN A MAN

Liddon, Louise, Roger Kingerlee, and John A. Barry. "Gender Differences in Preferences for Psychological Treatment, Coping Strategies, and Triggers to Help-Seeking." *British Journal of Clinical Psychology* 57, 1 (2017): 42–58. https://doi.org/10.1111/bjc.12147.

Rosette, Ashleigh Shelby, Jennifer S. Mueller, and R. David Lebel. "Are Male Leaders Penalized for Seeking Help? The Influence of Gender and Asking Behaviors on Competence Perceptions." *The Leadership Quarterly* 26, 5 (2015): 749–62. https://doi.org/10.1016/j.leaqua.2015.02.001.

West, Candace, and Don H. Zimmerman. "Doing Gender." *Gender & Society* 1, 2 (1987): 125–51. https://doi.org/10.1177/0891243287001002002.

2. MANHOOD IS NEVER FULLY EARNED AND NEEDS TO BE RENEWED OVER AND OVER AGAIN

Bosson, Jennifer K., and Joseph A. Vandello. "Precarious Manhood and Its Links to Action and Aggression." *Current Directions in Psychological Science* 20, 2 (2011): 82–86. https://doi.org/10.1177/0963721411402669.

Cheryan, Sapna, Jessica Schwartz Cameron, Zach Katagiri, and Benoît

Monin. 2015. "Manning Up." *Social Psychology* 46, 4 (2015): 218–27. https://doi.org/10.1027/1864-9335/a000239.

Kniffin, Kevin M., Ozge Sigirci, and Brian Wansink. "Eating Heavily: Men Eat More in the Company of Women." *Evolutionary Psychological Science* 2, 1 (2015): 38–46. https://doi.org/10.1007/s40806-015-0035-3.

Munsch, Christin L., and Robb Willer. "The Role of Gender Identity Threat in Perceptions of Date Rape and Sexual Coercion." *Violence Against Women* 18, 10 (2012): 1125–46. https://doi.org/10.1177/1077801212465151.

Tourjée, Diana. "Why Do Men Kill Trans Women? Gender Theorist Judith Butler Explains." Broadly. VICE. December 16, 2015. https://broadly.vice.com/en_us/article/z4jd7y/why-do-men-kill-trans-women-gender-theorist-judith-butler-explains.

3. MASCULINITY IS UNDER ATTACK

Bowles, Nellie. "Jordan Peterson, Custodian of the Patriarchy." *The New York Times,* May 18, 2018. https://www.nytimes.com/2018/05/18/style/jordan-peterson-12-rules-for-life.html.

Frey, William H. "The US Will Become 'Minority White' in 2045, Census Projects." Brookings.edu. The Brookings Institution. September 10, 2018. https://www.brookings.edu/blog/the-avenue/2018/03/14/the-us-will-become-minority-white-in-2045-census-projects/.

Peterson, Jordan B. *12 Rules for Life: An Antidote to Chaos.* Toronto: Random House Canada, 2018.

Sanneh, Kelefa. "Jordan Peterson's Gospel of Masculinity." *The New Yorker,* May 31, 2018. https://www.newyorker.com/magazine/2018/03/05/jordan-petersons-gospel-of-masculinity.

4. MEN ARE SLAVES TO THEIR BODIES AND THEIR NETHER REGIONS

Adams, Tim. "Testosterone and High Finance Do Not Mix: So Bring on the Women." *The Guardian,* June 18, 2011. https://www.theguardian.com/world/2011/jun/19/neuroeconomics-women-city-financial-crash.

Atzil, Shir, Wei Gao, Isaac Fradkin, and Lisa Feldman Barrett. "Author Correction: Growing a Social Brain." *Nature Human Behaviour* 2, 9 (2018): 624–36. https://doi.org/10.1038/s41562-018-0431-3.

Booth, A., D. A. Granger, A. Mazur, and K. T. Kivlighan. "Testosterone and Social Behavior." *Social Forces* 85, 1 (2006): 167–91. https://doi.org/10.1353/sof.2006.0116.

Coates, John. *The Hour Between Dog and Wolf: How Risk Taking Transforms Us, Body and Mind.* UK: HarperCollins, 2013.

Cohen, Dov, Richard E. Nisbett, Brian F. Bowdle, and Norbert Schwarz. "Insult, Aggression, and the Southern Culture of Honor: An 'Experimental Ethnography.'" *Journal of Personality and Social Psychology* 70, 5 (1996): 945–60. http://dx.doi.org/10.1037/0022-3514.70.5.945.

Dreher, Jean-Claude, Simon Dunne, Agnieszka Pazderska, Thomas Frodl, John J. Nolan, and John P. O'Doherty. "Testosterone Causes Both Prosocial and Antisocial Status-Enhancing Behaviors in Human Males." *Proceedings of the National Academy of Sciences* 113, 41 (2016): 11633–38. https://doi.org/10.1073/pnas.1608085113.

Ehrenkranz, Joel, Eugene Bliss, and Michael H. Sheard. "Plasma Testosterone: Correlation with Aggressive Behavior and Social Dominance in Man." *Psychosomatic Medicine* 36, 6 (1974): 469–75. https://doi.org/10.1097/00006842-197411000-00002.

Eisenegger, Christoph, Johannes Haushofer, and Ernst Fehr. "The Role of Testosterone in Social Interaction." *Trends in Cognitive Sciences* 15, 6 (2011): 263–71. https://doi.org/10.1016/j.tics.2011.04.008.

Goode, Erica. "What Provokes a Rapist to Rape?; Scientists Debate Notion of an Evolutionary Drive." *The New York Times*, January 15, 2000. https://www.nytimes.com/2000/01/15/books/what-provokes-a-rapist-to-rape-scientists-debate-notion-of-an-evolutionary-drive.html.

Hudson, Valerie M., et al. *Sex and World Peace*. New York: Columbia University Press, 2012.

Hyde, Janet Shibley. "The Gender Similarities Hypothesis." *American Psychologist* 60, 6 (2005): 581–92. https://doi.org/10.1037/0003-066x.60.6.581.

Klinesmith, Jennifer, Tim Kasser, and Francis T. McAndrew. "Guns, Testosterone, and Aggression." *Psychological Science* 17, 7 (2006): 568–71. https://doi.org/10.1111/j.1467-9280.2006.01745.x.

Lightdale, Jenifer R., and Deborah A. Prentice. "Rethinking Sex Differences in Aggression: Aggressive Behavior in the Absence of Social Roles." *Personality and Social Psychology Bulletin* 20, 1 (1994): 34–44. https://doi.org/10.1177/0146167294201003.

Magid, Kesson, Robert T. Chatterton, Farid Uddin Ahamed, and Gillian R. Bentley. "Childhood Ecology Influences Salivary Testosterone, Pubertal Age and Stature of Bangladeshi UK Migrant Men." *Nature Ecology & Evolution* 2, 7 (2018): 1146–54. https://doi.org/10.1038/s41559-018-0567-6.

Mazur, Allan, Alan Booth, and James M. Dabbs. "Testosterone and Chess Competition." *Social Psychology Quarterly* 55, 1 (1992): 70–77. https://doi.org/10.2307/2786687.

McKie, Robin. "Male and Female Ability Differences Down to Socialisation, Not Genetics." *The Guardian*, August 14, 2010. https://www.theguardian.com/world/2010/aug/15/girls-boys-think-same-way.

"Men and Women: No Big Difference." American Psychological Association. October 20, 2005. https://www.apa.org/research/action/difference.

Mims, Christopher. "Strange but True: Testosterone Alone Does Not Cause Violence." *Scientific American*, July 5, 2007. https://www.scientificamerican.com/article/strange-but-true-testosterone-alone-doesnt-cause-violence/.

Potts, Annie. "The Man with Two Brains: Hegemonic Masculine Subjectivity and the Discursive Construction of the Unreasonable Penis-Self." *Journal of Gender Studies* 10, 2 (2001): 145–56. https://doi.org/10.1080/09589230120053274.

Potts, Annie. *The Science/Fiction of Sex: Feminist Deconstruction and the Vocabularies of Heterosex.* Florence: Taylor and Francis, 2014.

Skewes, Lea, Cordelia Fine, and Nick Haslam. "Beyond Mars and Venus: The Role of Gender Essentialism in Support for Gender Inequality and Backlash." PLOS ONE 13, 7 (2018). https://doi.org/10.1371/journal.pone.0200921.

Sreenivasan, Shoba, and Linda E. Weinberger. "Surgical Castration and Sexual Recidivism Risk." *Sexual Offending* 33, 1 (2005): 769–77. https://doi.org/10.1007/978-1-4939-2416-5_33.

Thornhill, Randy, and Craig Palmer. *A Natural History of Rape: Biological Bases of Sexual Coercion.* Cambridge, MA: MIT, 2001.

Wibral, Matthias, Thomas Dohmen, Dietrich Klingmüller, Bernd Weber, and Armin Falk. "Testosterone Administration Reduces Lying in Men." PLOS ONE 7, 10 (2012). https://doi.org/10.1371/journal.pone.0046774.

Wong, Jennifer S., and Jason Gravel. "Do Sex Offenders Have Higher Levels of Testosterone? Results from a Meta-Analysis." *Sexual Abuse: A Journal of Research and Treatment* 30, 2 (2016): 147–68. https://doi.org/10.1177/1079063216637857.

Zentner, Marcel, and Klaudia Mitura. "Stepping Out of the Caveman's Shadow." *Psychological Science* 23, 10 (2012): 1176–85. https://doi.org/10.1177/0956797612441004.

5. MEN DON'T NEED INTIMACY

Cox, Ana Marie. "Janet Mock Struggles with Being Called a 'Trans Advocate.'" *The New York Times,* May 24, 2017. https://www.nytimes.com/2017/05/24/magazine/janet-mock-struggles-with-being-called-a-trans-advocate.html.

Heiman, Julia R., J. Scott Long, Shawna N. Smith, William A. Fisher, Michael S. Sand, and Raymond C. Rosen. "Sexual Satisfaction and Relationship Happiness in Midlife and Older Couples in Five Countries."

Archives of Sexual Behavior 40, 4 (2011): 741–53. https://doi.org/10.1007/s10508-010-9703-3.

Mock, Janet. *Redefining Realness: My Path to Womanhood, Identity, Love & So Much More.* New York: Simon & Schuster, 2015.

Reiner, Andrew. 2017. "The Power of Touch, Especially for Men." *The New York Times,* December 5, 2017. https://www.nytimes.com/2017/12/05/well/family/gender-men-touch.html.

Stephens-Davidowitz, Seth. 2017. "Everybody Lies: How Google Search Reveals Our Darkest Secrets." *The Guardian,* July 9, 2017. https://www.theguardian.com/technology/2017/jul/09/everybody-lies-how-google-reveals-darkest-secrets-seth-stephens-davidowitz.

Tang-Martínez, Zuleyma. 2016. "Rethinking Bateman's Principles: Challenging Persistent Myths of Sexually Reluctant Females and Promiscuous Males." *The Journal of Sex Research* 53 (4–5): 532–59. https://doi.org/10.1080/00224499.2016.1150938.

6. MALE SHAME: WHAT IS IT LIKE TO FEEL LIKE YOU NEED TO PROVE SOMETHING YOU NEVER QUITE FEEL LIKE YOU HAVE?

Brown Brené. *Daring Greatly: How the Courage to Be Vulnerable Transforms the Way We Live, Love, Parent, and Lead.* London, England: Penguin Books Ltd., 2015.

Fall, Kevin L. n.d. "Homeless Men : Exploring the Experience of Shame—PDF Free Download." Zdoc.site. ZDOC.SITE. Accessed March 4, 2019. https://zdoc.site/homeless-men-exploring-the-experience-of-shame.html.

"Full Report: The State of Gender Equality for U.S. Adolescents." Plan International USA. 2018. https://www.planusa.org/full-report-the-state-of-gender-equality-for-us-adolescents.

Harnish, Veronica. "I've Been Homeless 3 Times. The Problem Isn't Drugs or Mental Illness—It's Poverty." Vox.com. Vox Media. March 8, 2016. https://www.vox.com/2016/3/8/11173304/homeless-in-america.

Jakupcak, Matthew, Matthew T. Tull, and Lizabeth Roemer. "Masculinity, Shame, and Fear of Emotions as Predictors of Men's Expressions of Anger and Hostility." *Psychology of Men & Masculinity* 6, 4 (2005): 275–84. https://doi.org/10.1037/1524-9220.6.4.275.

Ryan, Kimberly D., Ryan P. Kilmer, Ana Mari Cauce, Haruko Watanabe, and Danny R. Hoyt. "Psychological Consequences of Child Maltreatment in Homeless Adolescents: Untangling the Unique Effects of Maltreatment and Family Environment." *Child Abuse & Neglect* 24, 3 (2000): 333–52. https://doi.org/10.1016/s0145-2134(99)00156-8.

Shier, Micheal L., Marion E. Jones, and John R. Graham. "Social Communities and Homelessness: A Broader Concept Analysis of Social Relationships and Homelessness." *Journal of Human Behavior in the Social Environment* 21, 5 (2011): 455–74. https://doi.org/10.1080/10911359.2011.566449.

Taywaditep, Kittiwut Jod. "Marginalization Among the Marginalized." *Journal of Homosexuality* 42, 1 (2002): 1–28. https://doi.org/10.1300/j082v42n01_01.

"The 2018 Annual Homeless Assessment Report (AHAR) to Congress." 2018. December 2018. https://www.hudexchange.info/resources/documents/2018-AHAR-Part-1.pdf.

Thompkins, Christine Durham, and Robert A. Rando. "Gender Role Conflict and Shame in College Men." *Psychology of Men & Masculinity* 4, 1 (2003): 79–81. https://doi.org/10.1037//1524-9220.4.1.79.

7. THE GREAT SUPPRESSION

Addis, Michael E., and James R. Mahalik. "Men, Masculinity, and the Contexts of Help Seeking." *American Psychologist* 58, 1 (2003): 5–14. https://doi.org/10.1037/0003-066x.58.1.5.

"Asian-American Man Plans Lawsuit to Stop 'Sexual Racism' on Grindr." NBCNews.com. July 13, 2018. https://www.nbcnews.com/feature/nbc-out/asian-american-man-threatens-class-action-discrimination-suit-against-grindr-n890946.

Gottman, John M., James Coan, Sybil Carrere, and Catherine Swanson. "Predicting Marital Happiness and Stability from Newlywed Interactions." *Journal of Marriage and the Family* 60, 1 (1998): 5–22. https://doi.org/10.2307/353438.

Gul, Pelin, and Tom R. Kupfer. "Benevolent Sexism and Mate Preferences: Why Do Women Prefer Benevolent Men Despite Recognizing That They Can Be Undermining?" *Personality and Social Psychology Bulletin* 45, 1 (2018): 146–61. https://doi.org/10.1177/0146167218781000.

Hammond, Matthew D., and Nickola C. Overall. "When Relationships Do Not Live Up to Benevolent Ideals: Women's Benevolent Sexism and Sensitivity to Relationship Problems." *European Journal of Social Psychology* 43, 3 (2013): 212–23. https://doi.org/10.1002/ejsp.1939.

Jansz, Jeroen. "Masculine Identity and Restrictive Emotionality." *Gender and Emotion* (2000): 166–86. https://doi.org/10.1017/cbo9780511628191.009.

OkCupid. "A Woman's Advantage." The OkCupid Blog. March 5, 2015. https://theblog.okcupid.com/a-womans-advantage-82d5074dde2d.

Perales, Francisco, and Janeen Baxter. "Sexual Identity and Relationship Quality in Australia and the United Kingdom." *Family Relations* 67, 1 (2017): 55–69. https://doi.org/10.1111/fare.12293.

Scelfo, Julie. "Men and Depression: New Treatments." *Newsweek*, March 13, 2010. https://www.newsweek.com/men-and-depression-new-treatments -105091.

Stephens-Davidowitz, Seth. *Everybody Lies: Big Data, New Data, and What the Internet Can Tell Us About Who We Really Are.* Bloomsbury, 2018.

Venker, Suzanne. "Chivalry Is Dead Because Women Killed It." Fox News. April 30, 2018. https://www.foxnews.com/opinion/suzanne-venker -chivalry-is-dead-because-women-killed-it.

Venker, Suzanne. "Society Is Creating a New Crop of Alpha Women Who Are Unable to Love." Fox News. February 8, 2017. https://www.foxnews .com/opinion/society-is-creating-a-new-crop-of-alpha-women-who-are -unable-to-love.

Venker, Suzanne. "Most Men Just Want a Woman Who's Nice." Fox News. May 11, 2017. https://www.foxnews.com/opinion/most-men-just-want-a -woman-whos-nice.

Wilcox, W. B., and S. L. Nock. "What's Love Got To Do With It? Equality, Equity, Commitment and Women's Marital Quality." *Social Forces* 84, 3 (2006): 1321–45. https://doi.org/10.1353/sof.2006.0076.

8. BROMANCE

Alcaraz, Kassandra I., Katherine S. Eddens, Jennifer L. Blase, W. Ryan Diver, Alpa V. Patel, Lauren R. Teras, Victoria L. Stevens, Eric J. Jacobs, and Susan M. Gapstur. "Social Isolation and Mortality in US Black and White Men and Women." *American Journal of Epidemiology* 188, 1 (2018): 102–9. https://doi.org/10.1093/aje/kwy231.

Arbes, Vicki, Charlie Coulton, and Catherine Boekel. "Men's Social Connectedness." Hall & Partners, Open Mind. June 2014. https://www .beyondblue.org.au/docs/default-source/research-project-files/bw0276 -mens-social-connectedness-final.pdf.

Cole, Steve W., Margaret E. Kemeny, Shelley E. Taylor, and Barbara R. Visscher. "Elevated Physical Health Risk among Gay Men Who Conceal Their Homosexual Identity." *Health Psychology* 15, 4 (1996): 243–51. https://doi.org/10.1037//0278-6133.15.4.243.

Cole, Steven W., John P. Capitanio, Katie Chun, Jesusa M. G. Arevalo, Jeffrey Ma, and John T. Cacioppo. "Myeloid Differentiation Architecture of Leukocyte Transcriptome Dynamics in Perceived Social Isolation." *Proceedings of the National Academy of Sciences* 112, 49 (2015): 15142–47. https://doi.org/10.1073/pnas.1514249112.

Fowler, James H., and Nicholas A. Christakis. "Dynamic Spread of Happiness in a Large Social Network: Longitudinal Analysis over 20 Years in

the Framingham Heart Study." *BMJ* 337 (December 2008). https://doi
.org/10.1136/bmj.a2338.

Garfield, Robert. *Breaking the Male Code: Unlocking the Power of Friendship.*
New York: Gotham Books, 2015.

Godbeer, Richard. *The Overflowing of Friendship: Love Between Men and the
Creation of the American Republic.* Baltimore: Johns Hopkins University
Press, 2009.

Holt-Lunstad, Julianne, and Timothy Smith. "Social Relationships and
Mortality Risk: A Meta-Analytic Review." *SciVee* (July 2010). https://doi
.org/10.4016/19911.01.

Holt-Lunstad, Julianne, Timothy B. Smith, Mark Baker, Tyler Harris, and
David Stephenson. "Loneliness and Social Isolation as Risk Factors for
Mortality." *Perspectives on Psychological Science* 10, 2 (2015): 227–37.
https://doi.org/10.1177/1745691614568352.

Independent Age. "Isolation: The Emerging Crisis for Older Men." Independent Age. October 13, 2014. https://www.independentage.org/press
-releases/isolation-emerging-crisis-for-older-men.

McPherson, Miller, Lynn Smith-Lovin, and Matthew E. Brashears. "Social
Isolation in America: Changes in Core Discussion Networks over Two
Decades." *American Sociological Review* 71, 6 (2006): 353–75. https://doi
.org/10.1177/000312240807300610.

Mineo, Liz. "Over Nearly 80 Years, Harvard Study Has Been Showing
How to Live a Healthy and Happy Life." *Harvard Gazette,* November 26,
2018. https://news.harvard.edu/gazette/story/2017/04/over-nearly-80
-years-harvard-study-has-been-showing-how-to-live-a-healthy-and-happy
-life/.

Orth-Gomér, K., A. Rosengren, and L. Wilhelmsen. "Lack of Social Support
and Incidence of Coronary Heart Disease in Middle-Aged Swedish Men."
Psychosomatic Medicine 55, 1 (1993): 37–43. https://doi.org/10.1097
/00006842-199301000-00007.

Pinker, Susan. *The Village Effect: How Face-to-Face Contact Can Make Us
Healthier, Happier, and Smarter.* Toronto: Random House Canada, 2014.

Rath, Tom, and Jim Harter. "Your Friends and Your Social Well-Being."
Gallup.com. Business Journal. August 19, 2010. https://news.gallup.com
/businessjournal/127043/friends-social-wellbeing.aspx. Adapted from
Wellbeing: The Five Essential Elements

Robinson, Stefan, Adam White, and Eric Anderson. "Privileging the
Bromance." *Men and Masculinities* (October 2017). https://doi.org/10.1177
/1097184x17730386.

Ruberman, William, Eve Weinblatt, Judith D. Goldberg, and Banvir S.
Chaudhary. "Psychosocial Influences on Mortality after Myocardial

Infarction." *New England Journal of Medicine* 312, 1 (1984): 50–51. https://doi.org/10.1056/nejm198501033120113.

Silk, Joan B., Jacinta C. Beehner, Thore J. Bergman, Catherine Crockford, Anne L. Engh, Liza R. Moscovice, Roman M. Wittig, Robert M. Seyfarth, and Dorothy L. Cheney. "The Benefits of Social Capital: Close Social Bonds among Female Baboons Enhance Offspring Survival." *Proceedings of the Royal Society B: Biological Sciences* 276, 1670 (2009): 3099–3104. https://doi.org/10.1098/rspb.2009.0681.

Silk, Joan B., Jacinta C. Beehner, Thore J. Bergman, Catherine Crockford, Anne L. Engh, Liza R. Moscovice, Roman M. Wittig, Robert M. Seyfarth, and Dorothy L. Cheney. "Strong and Consistent Social Bonds Enhance the Longevity of Female Baboons." *Current Biology* 20, 15 (2010): 1359–61. https://doi.org/10.1016/j.cub.2010.05.067.

Taylor, Shelley E., Laura Cousino Klein, Brian P. Lewis, Tara L. Gruenewald, Regan A.R. Gurung, and John A. Updegraff. "Biobehavioral Responses to Stress in Females: Tend-and-Befriend, Not Fight-or-Flight." *Foundations in Social Neuroscience* 107, 3 (2002): 411–29. https://doi.org/10.7551/mitpress/3077.003.0048.

"The Australian Longitudinal Study of Aging." n.d. Flinders University. Accessed March 4, 2019. http://flinders.edu.au/sabs/fcas/alsa/.

"The Way We Are Now: The State of the UK's Relationships 2015." Relate— The Relationship People. September 1, 2015. https://www.relate.org.uk/policy-campaigns/publications/way-we-are-now-state-uks-relationships-2015.

Wade, Lisa. "American Men's Hidden Crisis: They Need More Friends!" Salon.com. December 7, 2013. https://www.salon.com/2013/12/08/american_mens_hidden_crisis_they_need_more_friends/.

Way, Niobe. *Deep Secrets: Boys, Friendships and the Crisis of Connection.* Cambridge, MA: Harvard University Press, 2013.

9. WAFFLES ARE HIS LOVE LANGUAGE

Adams, Matthew, Carl Walker, and Paul O'Connell. "Invisible or Involved Fathers? A Content Analysis of Representations of Parenting in Young Children's Picturebooks in the UK." *Sex Roles* 65, 3–4 (2011): 259–70. https://doi.org/10.1007/s11199-011-0011-8.

Alexander, Michelle. *The New Jim Crow: Mass Incarceration in the Age of Colorblindness.* New York: New Press, 2012.

Badger, Emily, Claire Cain Miller, Adam Pearce, and Kevin Quealy. "Extensive Data Shows Punishing Reach of Racism for Black Boys." *The New York Times,* March 19, 2018. https://www.nytimes.com/interactive/2018/03/19/upshot/race-class-white-and-black-men.html.

Bartel, Ann, Maya Rossin-Slater, Christopher Ruhm, Jenna Stearns, and Jane Waldfogel. "Paid Family Leave, Fathers' Leave-Taking, and Leave-Sharing in Dual-Earner Households." *Journal of Policy Analysis and Management* 27, 1 (2015): 10–37. https://doi.org/10.3386/w21747.

Caprino, Kathy, and Terry Real. "Gender, Power and Relationships: The Crushing Effects of Patriarchy." Finding Brave (blog). January 25, 2018. https://findingbrave.org/episode-4-gender-power-relationships-crushing-effects-patriarchy-terry-real/.

Carlsson, Christoffer. "Masculinities, Persistence, and Desistance." *Criminology* 51, 3 (2013): 661–93. https://doi.org/10.1111/1745-9125.12016.

Coontz, Stephanie. "Do Millennial Men Want Stay-at-Home Wives?" *The New York Times,* March 31, 2017. https://www.nytimes.com/2017/03/31/opinion/sunday/do-millennial-men-want-stay-at-home-wives.html.

Datchi, Corinne C. "Masculinities, Fatherhood, and Desistance From Crime." *The Journal of Men's Studies* 25, 1 (2016): 44–69. https://doi.org/10.1177/1060826516641100.

Donovan, Sarah A. 2018. "Paid Family Leave in the United States." https://fas.org/sgp/crs/misc/R44835.pdf.

Ehrenreich, Barbara. *The Hearts of Men: American Dreams and the Flight from Commitment.* London: Pluto Press, 1983.

Fate-Dixon, Nika. "Are Some Millennials Rethinking the Gender Revolution? Long-Range Trends in Views of Non-Traditional Roles for Women." Council on Contemporary Families. March 31, 2017. https://contemporaryfamilies.org/7-fate-dixon-millennials-rethinking-gender-revolution/.

Guo, Jeff. "America Has Locked Up so Many Black People It Has Warped Our Sense of Reality." *The Washington Post,* February 26, 2016. https://www.washingtonpost.com/news/wonk/wp/2016/02/26/america-has-locked-up-so-many-black-people-it-has-warped-our-sense-of-reality/.

Haskins, Anna. "Unintended Consequences: Effects of Paternal Incarceration on Child School Readiness and Later Special Education Placement." *Sociological Science* 1 (April 2014): 141–58. https://doi.org/10.15195/v1.a11.

Horne, Rebecca M., Matthew D. Johnson, Nancy L. Galambos, and Harvey J. Krahn. "Time, Money, or Gender? Predictors of the Division of Household Labour Across Life Stages." *Sex Roles* 78, 11-12 (2017): 731–43. https://doi.org/10.1007/s11199-017-0832-1.

Hurd, Noelle M., Marc A. Zimmerman, and Yange Xue. "Negative Adult Influences and the Protective Effects of Role Models: A Study with Urban Adolescents." *Journal of Youth and Adolescence* 38, 6 (2009): 777–89. https://doi.org/10.1007/s10964-008-9296-5.

Jones, Jo, and William D. Mosher. "Fathers' Involvement With Their Children: United States, 2006–2010." *National Health Statistics Report* 71 (2013). https://www.cdc.gov/nchs/data/nhsr/nhsr071.pdf.

Lee, Esther, and Brody Brown. "Jennifer Garner: No One Asks Ben about Work-Family Balance." TODAY.com. October 21, 2014. https://www.today.com/popculture/jennifer-garner-no-one-asks-ben-about-work-family-balance-1D80232707.

Livingston, Gretchen. "Most Dads Say They Don't Spend Enough Time with Kids." Pew Research Center. January 8, 2018. http://www.pewresearch.org/fact-tank/2018/01/08/most-dads-say-they-spend-too-little-time-with-their-children-about-a-quarter-live-apart-from-them/.

Mascaro, Jennifer S., Kelly E. Rentscher, Patrick D. Hackett, Matthias R. Mehl, and James K. Rilling. "Child Gender Influences Paternal Behavior, Language, and Brain Function." *Behavioral Neuroscience* 131, 3 (2017): 262–73. https://doi.org/10.1037/bne0000199.

Matos, Kenneth. "Modern Families: Same- and Different-Sex Couples Negotiating at Home." Families and Work Institute. 2015. http://www.familiesandwork.org/downloads/modern-families.pdf.

McMahon, Susan D., Joshua A. Singh, Lakeasha S. Garner, and Shira Benhorin. "Taking Advantage of Opportunities: Community Involvement, Well-Being, and Urban Youth." *Journal of Adolescent Health* 34, 4 (2004): 262–65. https://doi.org/10.1016/j.jadohealth.2003.06.006.

Miller, Claire Cain. "Men Do More at Home, but Not as Much as They Think." *The New York Times,* November 12, 2015. https://www.nytimes.com/2015/11/12/upshot/men-do-more-at-home-but-not-as-much-as-they-think-they-do.html.

Mirkinson, Jack. "WATCH: All-Male Fox Panel's Amazingly Sexist Chat." TheHuffingtonPost.com. July 30, 2013. https://www.huffingtonpost.com/2013/05/30/fox-female-breadwinners_n_3358926.html.

"Modern Parenthood." Pew Research Center's Social & Demographic Trends Project. March 14, 2013. http://www.pewsocialtrends.org/2013/03/14/modern-parenthood-roles-of-moms-and-dads-converge-as-they-balance-work-and-family/5/.

Parker, Kim, and Renee Stepler. "Men Seen as Financial Providers in U.S., Even as Women's Contributions Grow." Pew Research Center. September 20, 2017. http://www.pewresearch.org/fact-tank/2017/09/20/americans-see-men-as-the-financial-providers-even-as-womens-contributions-grow/.

Pepin, Joanna, and David Cotter. "Trending Towards Traditionalism? Changes in Youths' Gender Ideology." Council on Contemporary

Families. April 3, 2017. https://contemporaryfamilies.org/2-pepin-cotter
-traditionalism/.

Sassler, Sharon. "Brief: Is the Glass Half Empty, or Three-Quarters Full?"
Council on Contemporary Families. July 29, 2014. https://
contemporaryfamilies.org/gender-revolution-rebound-glass-half-empty/.

Silcoff, Mireille. "'The Daddy Quota': How Quebec Got Men to Take
Parental Leave." *The Guardian,* June 15, 2018. https://www.theguardian
.com/world/2018/jun/15/the-daddy-quota-how-quebec-got-men-to-take
-parental-leave.

Society for Human Resource Management. "National Study of Employers."
SHRM. January 31, 2018. https://www.shrm.org/hr-today/trends-and
-forecasting/research-and-surveys/Pages/National-Study-of-Employers
.aspx.

Stemen, Don. "The Prison Paradox." Vera Institute of Justice. July 2017.
https://www.vera.org/publications/for-the-record-prison-paradox
-incarceration-not-safer.

Stuart, Elizabeth. "How Anti-Poverty Programs Marginalize Fathers." *The
Atlantic,* February 25, 2014. https://www.theatlantic.com/politics/archive
/2014/02/how-anti-poverty-programs-marginalize-fathers/283984/.

Thompson, Derek. "The Liberal Millennial Revolution." *The Atlantic,*
February 29, 2016. https://www.theatlantic.com/politics/archive/2016
/02/the-liberal-millennial-revolution/470826/.

Unilever. "Dove Men Care Launches 'Real Strength' Campaign on
Sports' Biggest Stage to Celebrate the Caring Side of Modern Men."
PR Newswire. January 20, 2015. https://www.prnewswire.com/news
-releases/dove-mencare-launches-real-strength-campaign-on-sports
-biggest-stage-to-celebrate-the-caring-side-of-modern-men-300022814
.html.

"Women Shoulder the Responsibility of 'Unpaid Work.'" Office for National Statistics. November 10, 2016. https://www.ons.gov.uk
/employmentandlabourmarket/peopleinwork/earningsandworkinghours
/articles/womenshouldertheresponsibilityofunpaidwork/2016-11-10.

10. THE MANCESSION

Abraham, Katharine, and Melissa Kearney. "Explaining the Decline in the
U.S. Employment-to-Population Ratio: A Review of the Evidence," The
National Bureau of Economic Research (February 2018). https://doi.org
/10.3386/w24333.

Bem, Sandra Lipsitz. "Genital Knowledge and Gender Constancy in
Preschool Children." *Child Development* 60, 3 (1989): 649. https://doi.org
/10.2307/1130730.

Cherney, Isabelle D., Lisa Kelly-Vance, Katrina Gill Glover, Amy Ruane, and Brigette Oliver Ryalls. "The Effects of Stereotyped Toys and Gender on Play Assessment in Children Aged 18–47 Months." *Educational Psychology* 23, 1 (2003): 95–106. https://doi.org/10.1080/01443410303222.

Correll, Shelley J., Stephen Benard, and In Paik. "Getting a Job: Is There a Motherhood Penalty?" *Inequality in the 21st Century* 112, 5 (2007): 1297–1338. https://doi.org/10.1086/511799.

Egalite, Anna J., Brian Kisida, and Marcus A. Winters. "Representation in the Classroom: The Effect of Own-Race Teachers on Student Achievement." *Economics of Education Review* 45 (2015): 44–52. https://doi.org/10.1016/j.econedurev.2015.01.007.

Ely, Robin J, and Debra Meyerson. "Unmasking Manly Men." *Harvard Business Review,* August 1, 2014. https://hbr.org/2008/07/unmasking-manly-men.

"Fewer Mothers Prefer Full-Time Work." Pew Research Center's Social & Demographic Trends Project. July 12, 2007. http://www.pewsocialtrends.org/2007/07/12/fewer-mothers-prefer-full-time-work/.

Franklin, Ben. "The Future Care Workforce." International Longevity Centre UK. October 15, 2018. https://ilcuk.org.uk/the-future-care-workforce/.

Hodges, Melissa J., and Michelle J. Budig. "Who Gets the Daddy Bonus?" *Gender & Society* 24, 6 (2010): 717–45. https://doi.org/10.1177/0891243210386729.

Horowitz, Juliana Menasce. "More in US Say It's Good for Girls to Try Boy-Oriented Toys, Activities than Vice Versa." Pew Research Center. December 19, 2017. http://www.pewresearch.org/fact-tank/2017/12/19/most-americans-see-value-in-steering-children-toward-toys-activities-associated-with-opposite-gender/.

Katz, Lawrence W. "Long-Term Unemployment in the Great Recession." 2010. https://scholar.harvard.edu/lkatz/files/long_term_unemployment_in_the_great_recession.pdf

Lindsay, Constance A., and Cassandra M. D. Hart. "Exposure to Same-Race Teachers and Student Disciplinary Outcomes for Black Students in North Carolina." *Educational Evaluation and Policy Analysis* 39, 3 (2017): 485–510. https://doi.org/10.3102/0162373717693109.

Mill, Jessica, Yixuan Huang, Heidi Hartmann, and Jeff Hayes. "The Impact of Equal Pay on Poverty and the Economy." April 5, 2017. Institute for Women's Policy Research. https://iwpr.org/publications/impact-equal-pay-poverty-economy/.

Miller, Claire Cain. "The Motherhood Penalty vs. the Fatherhood Bonus." *The New York Times*, September 6, 2014. https://www.nytimes.com/2014/09/07/upshot/a-child-helps-your-career-if-youre-a-man.html.

Miller, Claire Cain. "Why Men Don't Want the Jobs Done Mostly by Women." *The New York Times*, January 4, 2017. https://www.nytimes.com/2017/01/04/upshot/why-men-dont-want-the-jobs-done-mostly-by-women.html.

Mui, Ylan Q. "Study: Women with More Children Are More Productive at Work." *The Washington Post*, October 30, 2014. https://www.washingtonpost.com/news/wonk/wp/2014/10/30/study-women-with-more-children-are-more-productive-at-work/.

Ngai, L. Rachel, and Barbara Petrongolo. "Gender Gaps and the Rise of the Service Economy." IZA Discussion Paper No. 8134 (2014). http://ftp.iza.org/dp8134.pdf.

Parker, Kim. "Women Still Bear Heavier Load than Men in Balancing Work, Family." Pew Research Center. March 10, 2015. http://www.pewresearch.org/fact-tank/2015/03/10/women-still-bear-heavier-load-than-men-balancing-work-family/.

Quillian, Lincoln, Devah Pager, Ole Hexel, and Arnfinn H. Midtbøen. "Meta-Analysis of Field Experiments Shows No Change in Racial Discrimination in Hiring over Time." *Proceedings of the National Academy of Sciences* 114, 41 (2017): 10870–75. https://doi.org/10.1073/pnas.1706255114.

Schmitt, John, and Kris Warner. "Ex-Offenders and the Labor Market." *WorkingUSA* 14, 1 (2011): 87–109. https://doi.org/10.1111/j.1743-4580.2011.00322.x.

Smith, Carol L.F. "Using Personal Dolls to Learn Empathy, Unlearn Prejudice." *The International Journal of Diversity in Education* 12, 3 (2013): 23–32. https://doi.org/10.18848/2327-0020/cgp/v12i03/40062.

Sweet, Elizabeth. "Gender-Based Toy Marketing Returns." *The New York Times*, December 21, 2012. https://www.nytimes.com/2012/12/23/opinion/sunday/gender-based-toy-marketing-returns.html.

Thompson, Derek. "Why Are Millions of Prime-Age Men Missing From the Economy?" *The Atlantic*, June 27, 2016. https://www.theatlantic.com/business/archive/2016/06/the-missing-men/488858/.

"Tipped Over the Edge—Gender Inequity in the Restaurant Industry." Restaurant Opportunities Centers United. February 13, 2012. http://rocunited.org/publications/tipped-over-the-edge-gender-inequity-in-the-restaurant-industry/.

Wilson, Valerie, and William M. Rodgers. "Black-White Wage Gaps Expand with Rising Wage Inequality." Economic Policy Institute. September 20, 2016. https://www.epi.org/publication/black-white-wage-gaps-expand-with-rising-wage-inequality/.

Yeung, Sui Ping, and Wang Ivy Wong. "Gender Labels on Gender-Neutral Colors: Do They Affect Children's Color Preferences and Play Performance?" *Sex Roles* 79, 5–6 (2018): 260–72. https://doi.org/10.1007/s11199-017-0875-3.

11. IF PATRIARCHY IS SO GREAT, WHY IS IT MAKING YOU DIE?

"Addressing a Blind Spot in the Response to HIV—Reaching out to Men and Boys." UNAIDS. November 30, 2017. http://www.unaids.org/en/resources/documents/2017/blind_spot.

Agerbo, Esben, David Gunnell, Jens Peter Bonde, Preben Bo Mortensen, and Merete Nordentoft. "Suicide and Occupation: the Impact of Socio-Economic, Demographic and Psychiatric Differences." *Psychological Medicine* 37, 08 (2007): 1131. https://doi.org/10.1017/s0033291707000487.

Alsan, Marcella, Owen Garrick, and Grant Graziani. "Does Diversity Matter for Health? Experimental Evidence from Oakland." NBER Working Paper No. 24787. 2018. https://doi.org/10.3386/w24787.

"Altering the Course: Black Males in Medicine." Association of American Medical Colleges. 2015. https://members.aamc.org/eweb/upload/Altering the Course - Black Males in Medicine AAMC.pdf.

"Americans in Crisis: Access to Guns Increases Death by Suicide." Brady Campaign to Prevent Gun Violence. September 2017. http://www.bradycampaign.org/the-truth-about-suicide-guns.

Andreev, Evgeny, Dmitri Bogoyavlensky, and Andrew Stickley. "Comparing Alcohol Mortality in Tsarist and Contemporary Russia: Is the Current Situation Historically Unique?" *Alcohol and Alcoholism* 48, 2 (2013): 215–21. https://doi.org/10.1093/alcalc/ags132.

Baker, Peter, Shari L. Dworkin, Sengfah Tong, Ian Banks, Tim Shand, and Gavin Yamey. "The Men's Health Gap: Men Must Be Included in the Global Health Equity Agenda." *Bulletin of the World Health Organization* 92, 8 (2014): 618–20. https://doi.org/10.2471/blt.13.132795.

Barker, G., C. Ricardo, M. Nascimento, A. Olukoya, and C. Santos. "Questioning Gender Norms with Men to Improve Health Outcomes: Evidence of Impact." *Global Public Health* 5, 5 (2010): 539–53. https://doi.org/10.1080/17441690902942464.

Barry-Jester, Anna Maria. "Surviving Suicide In Wyoming." FiveThirtyEight. July 13, 2016. https://fivethirtyeight.com/features/suicide-in-wyoming/.

Bates, Betsy, and David Freed. "Aversion to Therapy: Why Won't Men Get Help?" Pacific Standard. June 25, 2012. https://psmag.com/social-justice/why-wont-men-get-help-42910.

Chang, Shu-Sen, David Gunnell, Jonathan A.C. Sterne, Tsung-Hsueh Lu, and Andrew T. Cheng. "Was the Economic Crisis 1997–1998 Responsible for Rising Suicide Rates in East/Southeast Asia? A Time-Trend Analysis for Japan, Hong Kong, South Korea, Taiwan, Singapore and Thailand." *Social Science & Medicine* 68, 7 (2009): 1322–31. https://doi.org/10.1016/j.socscimed.2009.01.010.

Coleman, Daniel, Mark S. Kaplan, and John T. Casey. "The Social Nature of Male Suicide: A New Analytic Model." *International Journal of Men's Health* 10, 3 (2011): 240–52. https://doi.org/10.3149/jmh.1003.240.

"Data Snapshot: School Discipline." Office for Civil Rights. 2014. https://ocrdata.ed.gov/Downloads/CRDC-School-Discipline-Snapshot.pdf.

Ellis, Katrina R., Derek M. Griffith, Julie Ober Allen, Roland J. Thorpe, and Marino A. Bruce. "'If You Do Nothing about Stress, the Next Thing You Know, You're Shattered': Perspectives on African American Men's Stress, Coping and Health from African American Men and Key Women in Their Lives." *Social Science & Medicine* 139 (August 2015): 107–14. https://doi.org/10.1016/j.socscimed.2015.06.036.

Escobedo, Luis G., and John P. Peddicord. "Smoking Prevalence in US Birth Cohorts: the Influence of Gender and Education." *American Journal of Public Health* 86, 2 (1996): 231–36. https://doi.org/10.2105/ajph.86.2.231.

Fine, Cordelia. *Testosterone Rex: Unmaking the Myths of Our Gendered Minds.* London: Icon, 2017.

Finucane, Melissa L., Paul Slovic, C. K. Mertz, James Flynn, and Theresa A. Satterfield. "Gender, Race, and Perceived Risk: The White Male Effect." *Health, Risk & Society* 2, 2 (2000): 159–72. https://doi.org/10.1080/713670162.

Flynn, James, Paul Slovic, and C. K. Mertz. "Gender, Race, and Perception of Environmental Health Risks." *Risk Analysis* 14, 6 (1994): 1101–8. https://doi.org/10.1111/j.1539-6924.1994.tb00082.x.

Fontanella, Cynthia A., Danielle L. Hiance-Steelesmith, Gary S. Phillips, Jeffrey A. Bridge, Natalie Lester, Helen Anne Sweeney, and John V. Campo. "Widening Rural-Urban Disparities in Youth Suicides, United States, 1996–2010." *JAMA Pediatrics* 169, 5 (2015): 466. https://doi.org/10.1001/jamapediatrics.2014.3561.

Gallup, Inc. "Six in 10 Americans Support Stricter Gun Laws." Gallup.com. October 17, 2018. https://news.gallup.com/poll/243797/six-americans-support-stricter-gun-laws.aspx.

Garces, Liliana M., and David Mickey-Pabello. "Racial Diversity in the Medical

Profession: The Impact of Affirmative Action Bans on Underrepresented Student of Color Matriculation in Medical Schools." *The Journal of Higher Education* 86, 2 (2015): 264–94. https://doi.org/10.1080/00221546.2015.11777364.

Giovino, Gary A., Andrea C. Villanti, Paul D. Mowery, Varadan Sevilimedu, Raymond S. Niaura, Donna M. Vallone, and David B. Abrams. "Differential Trends in Cigarette Smoking in the USA: Is Menthol Slowing Progress?" *Tobacco Control* 24, 1 (2013): 28–37. https://doi.org/10.1136/tobaccocontrol-2013-051159.

Graham, David A. "Do African Americans Have a Right to Bear Arms?" *The Atlantic.* June 22, 2017. https://www.theatlantic.com/politics/archive/2017/06/the-continued-erosion-of-the-african-american-right-to-bear-arms/531093/.

Granié, Marie-Axelle. "Effects of Gender, Sex-Stereotype Conformity, Age and Internalization on Risk-Taking among Adolescent Pedestrians." *Safety Science* 47, 9 (2009): 1277–83. https://doi.org/10.1016/j.ssci.2009.03.010.

Griffith, Derek M., Katrina R. Ellis, and Julie Ober Allen. "How Does Health Information Influence African American Men's Health Behavior?" *American Journal of Men's Health* 6, 2 (2012): 156–63. https://doi.org/10.1177/1557988311426910.

Halladay, Alycia K., Somer Bishop, John N. Constantino, Amy M. Daniels, Katheen Koenig, Kate Palmer, Daniel Messinger, et al. "Sex and Gender Differences in Autism Spectrum Disorder: Summarizing Evidence Gaps and Identifying Emerging Areas of Priority." *Molecular Autism* 6, 1 (2015). https://doi.org/10.1186/s13229-015-0019-y.

Harper, Phillip Brian. *Are We Not Men?: Masculine Anxiety and the Problem of African-American Identity.* New York: Oxford University Press, 2010.

Heath, Patrick J., Rachel E. Brenner, David L. Vogel, Daniel G. Lannin, and Haley A. Strass. "Masculinity and Barriers to Seeking Counseling: The Buffering Role of Self-Compassion." *Journal of Counseling Psychology* 64, 1 (2017): 94–103. https://doi.org/10.1037/cou0000185.

Hinote, Brian P., and Gretchen R. Webber. "Drinking toward Manhood." *Men and Masculinities* 15, 3 (2012): 292–310. https://doi.org/10.1177/1097184x12448466.

Hoffman, Kelly M., Sophie Trawalter, Jordan R. Axt, and M. Norman Oliver. "Racial Bias in Pain Assessment and Treatment Recommendations, and False Beliefs about Biological Differences between Blacks and Whites." *Proceedings of the National Academy of Sciences* 113, 16 (2016): 4296–4301. https://doi.org/10.1073/pnas.1516047113.

Howland, J., R. Hingson, T. W. Mangione, N. Bell, and S. Bak. "Why Are Most Drowning Victims Men? Sex Differences in Aquatic Skills and

Behaviors." *Journal of Safety Research* 28, 1 (1997): 66. https://doi.org/10
.1016/s0022-4375(97)90043-8.

Jacobs, Tom. "The Rural Suicide Rate Is Driven by Men With Guns." Pacific
Standard. August 17, 2017. https://psmag.com/social-justice/rural
-suicide-rate-driven-by-men-with-guns.

Kahan, Dan M., Donald Braman, John Gastil, Paul Slovic, and C. K. Mertz.
"Culture and Identity-Protective Cognition: Explaining the White-Male
Effect in Risk Perception." *Journal of Empirical Legal Studies* 4, 3 (2007):
465–505. https://doi.org/10.1111/j.1740-1461.2007.00097.x.

Lappegård Lahn, Åshild. "Gender Equality Gives Men Better Lives." Kilden.
October 15, 2015. http://kjonnsforskning.no/en/2015/10/gender-equality
-gives-men-better-lives.

Levant, Ronald F., Katherine Richmond, Richard G. Majors, Jaime E.
Inclan, Jeannette M. Rossello, Martin Heesacker, George T. Rowan, and
Alfred Sellers. "A Multicultural Investigation of Masculinity Ideology
and Alexithymia." *Psychology of Men & Masculinity* 4, 2 (2003): 91–99.
https://doi.org/10.1037/1524-9220.4.2.91.

Luo, Feijun, Curtis S. Florence, Myriam Quispe-Agnoli, Lijing Ouyang, and
Alexander E. Crosby. "Impact of Business Cycles on US Suicide Rates,
1928–2007." *American Journal of Public Health* 101, 6 (2011): 1139–46.
https://doi.org/10.2105/ajph.2010.300010.

Milner, A., K. Witt, H. Maheen, and A.D. LaMontagne. "Access to Means of
Suicide, Occupation and the Risk of Suicide: A National Study over
12 Years of Coronial Data." *BMC Psychiatry* 17, 1 (2017). https://doi.org/10
.1186/s12888-017-1288-0.

Mitchell, Travis. "The Demographics of Gun Ownership in the U.S." Pew
Research Center's Social & Demographic Trends Project. October 25,
2018. http://www.pewsocialtrends.org/2017/06/22/the-demographics-of
-gun-ownership/.

Morin, Rich. "The Demographics and Politics of Gun-Owning Households." Pew Research Center. July 15, 2014. http://www.pewresearch.org
/fact-tank/2014/07/15/the-demographics-and-politics-of-gun-owning
-households/.

Morrongiello, Barbara A., Corina Midgett, and Kerri-Lynn Stanton. "Gender
Biases in Children's Appraisals of Injury Risk and Other Children's
Risk-Taking Behaviors." *Journal of Experimental Child Psychology* 77,
4 (2000): 317–36. https://doi.org/10.1006/jecp.2000.2595.

Nestadt, Paul S., Patrick Triplett, David R. Fowler, and Ramin Mojtabai.
"Urban–Rural Differences in Suicide in the State of Maryland: The Role
of Firearms." *American Journal of Public Health* 107, 10 (2017): 1548–53.
https://doi.org/10.2105/ajph.2017.303865.

Nostrand, S.M. Van, L.N. Bennett, V.J. Coraglio, R. Guo, and J.K. Muraskas. "Factors Influencing Independent Oral Feeding in Preterm Infants." *Journal of Neonatal-Perinatal Medicine* 8, 1 (2015): 15–21. https://doi.org/10.3233/npm-15814045.

Ostan, R., D. Monti, P. Gueresi, M. Bussolotto, C. Franceschi, and G. Baggio. "Gender, Aging and Longevity in Humans: an Update of an Intriguing/Neglected Scenario Paving the Way to a Gender-Specific Medicine." *Clinical Science* 130, 19 (2016): 1711–25. https://doi.org/10.1042/cs20160004.

Pinker, Susan. *The Sexual Paradox: Men, Women, and the Real Gender Gap.* New York: Scribner, 2009.

Pridemore, William Alex. "Hazardous Drinking and Violent Mortality Among Males: Evidence from a Population-Based Case-Control Study." *Social Problems* 63, 4 (2016): 573–89. https://doi.org/10.1093/socpro/spw018.

Qin, Ping, Esben Agerbo, and Preben Bo Mortensen. "Suicide Risk in Relation to Socioeconomic, Demographic, Psychiatric, and Familial Factors: A National Register-Based Study of All Suicides in Denmark, 1981–1997." *American Journal of Psychiatry* 160, 4 (2003): 765–72. https://doi.org/10.1176/appi.ajp.160.4.765.

Reeves, Aaron, David Stuckler, Martin McKee, David Gunnell, Shu-Sen Chang, and Sanjay Basu. "Increase in State Suicide Rates in the USA during Economic Recession." *The Lancet* 380, 9856 (2012): 1813–14. https://doi.org/10.1016/s0140-6736(12)61910-2.

Reeves, Aaron, Martin McKee, and David Stuckler. "Economic Suicides in the Great Recession in Europe and North America." *British Journal of Psychiatry* 205, 03 (2014): 246–47. https://doi.org/10.1192/bjp.bp.114.144766.

Reeves, Aaron, and David Stuckler. "Suicidality, Economic Shocks, and Egalitarian Gender Norms." *European Sociological Review* 32, 1 (2015): 39–53. https://doi.org/10.1093/esr/jcv084.

Reinhart, RJ. "Six in 10 Americans Support Stricter Gun Laws." Gallup.com. October 17, 2018. https://news.gallup.com/poll/243797/six-americans-support-stricter-gun-laws.aspx.

Rostron, Allen. "The Dickey Amendment on Federal Funding for Research on Gun Violence: A Legal Dissection." *American Journal of Public Health* 108, 7 (2018): 865–67. https://doi.org/10.2105/ajph.2018.304450.

Seabury, Seth A., Sophie Terp, and Leslie I. Boden. "Racial and Ethnic Differences in the Frequency of Workplace Injuries and Prevalence of Work-Related Disability." *Health Affairs* 36, 2 (2017): 266–73. https://doi.org/10.1377/hlthaff.2016.1185.

Shimotsu, Scott, Anne Roehrl, Maribet Mccarty, Katherine Vickery, Laura Guzman-Corrales, Mark Linzer, and Nancy Garrett. "Increased Likelihood of Missed Appointments ('No Shows') for Racial/Ethnic Minorities in a Safety Net Health System." *Journal of Primary Care & Community Health* 7, 1 (2015): 38–40. https://doi.org/10.1177/2150131915599980.

Slovic, Paul. "Risk-Taking in Children: Age and Sex Differences." *Child Development* 37, 1 (1964): 169–76. https://doi.org/10.2307/1126437.

Springer, Kristen, and Dawne Mouzon. "Masculinity and Health Care Seeking Among Midlife Men: Variation by Adult Socioeconomic Status." American Sociological Association Annual Meeting, San Francisco. 2008. http://citation.allacademic.com/meta/p305722_index.html.

Toomey, Russell B., Amy K. Syvertsen, and Maura Shramko. "Transgender Adolescent Suicide Behavior." *Pediatrics* 142, 4 (2018). https://doi.org/10.1542/peds.2017-4218.

Wong, Y. Joel, Moon-ho Ringo Ho, Shu-Yi Wang, and I.S. Keino Miller. "Supplemental Material for Meta-Analyses of the Relationship Between Conformity to Masculine Norms and Mental Health-Related Outcomes." *Journal of Counseling Psychology* 64, 1 (2016): 80–93. https://doi.org/10.1037/cou0000176.supp.

Wunderlich, U., T. Bronisch, H.U. Wittchen, and R. Carter. "Gender Differences in Adolescents and Young Adults with Suicidal Behaviour." *Acta Psychiatrica Scandinavica* 104, 5 (2001): 332–39. https://doi.org/10.1111/j.1600-0447.2001.00432.x.

Wyder, Marianne, Patrick Ward, and Diego De Leo. "Separation as a Suicide Risk Factor." *Journal of Affective Disorders* 116, 3 (2009): 208–13. https://doi.org/10.1016/j.jad.2008.11.007.

Zarulli, Virginia, Julia A. Barthold Jones, Anna Oksuzyan, Rune Lindahl-Jacobsen, Kaare Christensen, and James W. Vaupel. "Women Live Longer than Men Even during Severe Famines and Epidemics." *Proceedings of the National Academy of Sciences* 115, 4 (2018). https://doi.org/10.1073/pnas.1701535115.

12. THE MAKING OF MEN

Stoet, Gijsbert, and David C. Geary. "A Simplified Approach to Measuring National Gender Inequality." *PLOS ONE* 14, 1 (2019). https://doi.org/10.1371/journal.pone.0205349.

13. COMPASSION AS THE ANTIDOTE TO HATE

Baird, Adam. "Becoming the 'Baddest': Masculine Trajectories of Gang Violence in Medellín." Studies in Interreligious Dialogue. Peeters Publishers. July 3, 2017. https://pureportal.coventry.ac.uk/en/publications/becoming-the-baddest-masculine-trajectories-of-gang-violence-in-m.

"Murder and Extremism in the United States in 2017." Anti-Defamation

League. January 17, 2018. https://www.adl.org/resources/reports/murder
-and-extremism-in-the-united-states-in-2017.

Nowak, Manfred, ed. *Using Human Rights to Counter Terrorism.* London: Edward Elgar, 2018.

CONCLUSION: THE CASE FOR MINDFUL MASCULINITY

Moffitt, T. E., L. Arseneault, D. Belsky, N. Dickson, R. J. Hancox, H. Harrington, R. Houts, et al. "A Gradient of Childhood Self-Control Predicts Health, Wealth, and Public Safety." *Proceedings of the National Academy of Sciences* 108, 7 (2011): 2693–98. https://doi.org/10.1073/pnas .1010076108.

Acknowledgments

If it weren't for my loved ones, the book you're holding wouldn't be a pile of pages, it would be a pile of sweat and tears bound together with loose Cheetos crumbs. To all my friends and family who thought I couldn't possibly be more anxious, depressed and dramatic, I accepted your challenge and you are extremely welcome! I undoubtedly will forget to thank someone who helped me immensely throughout this process but hopefully they won't have bothered to buy this book and will never know.

OK here we go.

Eve Attermann, thank you. You are the most extraordinary agent and friend I could have ever asked for and I cannot tell you what it means to have you in my corner. Thank you, for responding to all my panicky texts, calls, emails, subtweets, and coded Instagram stories. Special shout-out to the time you thought you were peacefully coming out of your Soul Cycle class only to find me ugly-crying all over the overpriced spandex shorts for sale in the lobby. I'm sorry for the higher power who felt like that coincidence needed to happen but I'm also thankful it led to you successfully extending my deadline. I feel so lucky the universe put me in the direction of your magic ability to see in people what they can't yet see in themselves.

My fellow Hungarian and dobosh-torte–loving editor, Hannah Braaten, at St. Martin's Press, as well as Nettie Finn and everyone at Macmillan and St. Martin's Press, thank you, for believing in this book when so many other publishers told me not to. Thank you for bringing actual, real-life men to our first meeting and believing in the wacky idea that men can and do in fact buy books! Your support has meant the world to me.

Quinn Heraty. If I could hand over all my decisions to one person it would be you. You're an impeccable lawyer, but you're also so much more than that to me and so many other female journalists who work in an industry that undervalues their contributions and their talent. Thank you, for helping so many women harness their superpowers and make the necessary plans to own them.

My hilarious, caring and brave sister, Emilie Plank. You gave me the idea to write this book over spicy ramen late one night in the East Village and you have found every possible way to support me both emotionally and intellectually throughout this project and every other creative endeavor I've ever attempted. Ever since we started stealing Dad's camcorder to shoot our first talk show about monkeys and farts, you have always been my creative collaborator, co-conspirator and best friend. Thank you, for always believing in the best of humanity and the best of my worst ideas. And speaking of my family, although my mom hasn't read this book yet because she thinks "Google Docs" is where she can get a good fresh piece of salmon, I really hope she likes it, because she has inspired every single thing I've ever done. She raised me to believe that gender equality is not a probability, it's an inevitability. She modeled a kind of resilience and strength that has given me the confidence to believe that I, too, can take my worst experiences and transform pain rather than transmit it. And of course, big ups to my dad, for setting the standard of how a man should look and cook far too high to ever be met by any man I'll ever meet, and my grandmother Erzsébet, for surviving the worst circumstances, to raise the best man I'll ever know. Thank you, for praying for us. We can tell.

Holy freaking cats, Meredith Bennett-Smith. You are the only reason I didn't end up escaping to a remote island and deleting this entire book three months before it was due. You saved this book, even if you took out all my food jokes and I'm still pretty upset about it. Speaking of saviors, Esther Bergdahl, I don't even know what to say! Thank you, for swooping in like a superhero when I needed you most to make sure this book was bulletproof. To me, you will always be the LeBron James of fact-checking.

Ashley Bearden! Thank you, for continuously giving me the silly idea to keep believing in myself. You invited me on life-changing trips, read this entire book off a janky Google Doc and have always seen the best in everything I do. You came up with the new book title, helped me craft new perspectives, walked me through countless existential brainstorms and have always pushed me to see all the ways my vision could exist in the world. The Delta Skymiles app may have us legally filed as a married couple, but that doesn't even begin to capture how important you are to me!

Steven Cape, thank you, for reading the first and definitely worst draft that was ever written and still giving me productive feedback and advice. Matteen Mokalla, thank you, for reading the introduction twice when no one asked you to. Jemila Ashley Brady, thank you, for giving me your seal of approval and being way too good at way too many things. Thank you, Michelle Garcia, for agreeing to read parts of this book when you had just grown a human inside of you. Thank you, Justin Carter and Chelsea Livingston, for your valuable insights. Thanks to Lindsey Taylor Wood, for challenging me to take care of my mental health so that I could take care of this book. And a special thank-you to my therapist, Margo, for reminding me that you don't have to like this book as long as I do.

Catherine Gratton-Gagne, you are my sister and my life partner. Thank you, for always supporting me in every possible way from so many many miles away. Caira Conner, you are the rock every woman deserves. You are an endless source of support, unconditional love and texts that make me accidentally spit out my coffee. I cannot wait for YOUR book (keep your eyes out for it, people). Rachel Sklar and Glynnis MacNicol, thank you, for always cheering me on; your support has been so healing. Thank you, Ruth Anne and Bill Harnish, for opening up your home to me when I was in deep need of serenity. Jonathon Ende! You created a space in your summer home for me to find this book, and you created a space inside your heart where I could find myself. I'm eternally grateful the universe chose us over and over and over again. I can't wait to read YOUR book.

Thank you, Anna Holmes, Anand Giridharadas, Samantha Irby, Stacy London, John Heilmann and Ari Melber, for having so much blind faith in me to back my first book before it was published.

I also want to thank the staff at the East Village Bean and the Wing, for letting me enter your respective establishments every day to work on this book even when I had visibly not showered or used a comb in several days. I also want to thank all my ex-boyfriends. Many of you offered guidance or material for this book (or both!), so thank you.

I will hold space in my heart forever for every single man who agreed to speak to me about the deeply private and personal aspects of their lives. Thomas, Victor, Wade, Glen, Mau, D'Arcee and Nico, you are some of the greatest humans I know and your vision of masculinity is what has inspired me to keep working at this project. I cannot tell you how grateful I am for you doing that, especially when so much hate is reserved for the men who do. Every male subject I interviewed for this book, including all the extraordinary, thoughtful and enlightened men who follow my work on various social media platforms, and especially those who participated in Facebook threads I quote in the book, thank you. Your candor and honesty have made me laugh, cry and rethink this entire conversation. Each and every one of you gives me hope and has taught me that we can in fact all be on the same team. Thank you to everyone, regardless of how you identify, for following my work online. Your support is the reason I was able to write this book.

Also if anyone sees Oprah, please thank her for everything. She'll know what I mean.

ABOUT THE AUTHOR

James Bareham

LIZ PLANK is an award-winning journalist and was the executive producer and host of several critically acclaimed digital series at Vox Media and NBC News. She's a columnist for MSNBC and has been listed as one of *Forbes*'s 30 Under 30, Mediaite's Most Influential in News Media, and *Marie Claire*'s Most Powerful Women, and was named one of the World's Most Influential People in Gender Policy by Apolitical. She's built a loyal following on numerous social media platforms, but her proudest accomplishment by far remains being blocked by the 45th president of the United States.